HALF A CENTURY
of
YORKSHIRE CRICKET

HALF A CENTURY
of
YORKSHIRE CRICKET

by
DERRICK BOOTHROYD

Foreword by Sir Leonard Hutton

Kennedy Brothers Publishing Ltd.
1981

Published by Kennedy Brothers (Publishing) Ltd.
Healey Works, Goulbourne Street, Keighley, West Yorkshire

ISBN: 0 9507909 0 7

Printed by Fretwell & Brian Ltd., Healey Works, Goulbourne Street, Keighley, W. Yorkshire

CONTENTS

ACKNOWLEDGMENTS

Nearly all the illustrations in this book are reproductions of Yorkshire Post copyright pictures and I am greatly indebted to the Editor of The Yorkshire Post, Mr. John Edwards, for permission to use them. I am also indebted to him for permission to use extracts from cricket articles of mine published in The Yorkshire Post.

I am also extremely grateful to Sir Leonard Hutton for reading the manuscript and writing such an apt Foreword, and to Bill Bowes for also reading the MS and allowing me to quote extensively from his own book, "Express Deliveries."

Sir Leonard Hutton, the only Yorkshire cricketer ever to be knighted for his services to the game, pictured with Lady Hutton at a Headingley test match.

FOREWORD by Sir Leonard Hutton

Derrick Boothroyd has written a most fascinating book about cricket—in particular about the Yorkshire County Cricket Club, the finest cricket club in the world. I say that because Yorkshire cricket represents for me the very essence of life with all its diversity, its humour and sometimes, as at present, its sadness.

Like Mr. Boothroyd I became fascinated by cricket at an early age. I was eleven when I saw my first county match, Yorkshire v. Notts., at Bradford Park Avenue in 1927. Equipped with the necessary scorecard and lunch, wrapped in the *Pudsey News*, alas no more, I watched George Gunn make 50. This innings was a classic and I can see him now, making the hostile Yorkshire attack, which included Waddington, Robinson and Rhodes, look very friendly.

I came from a cricketing background, from a cricketing village called Fulneck, a Moravian settlement near to Pudsey, and Mr. Boothroyd took me back to those early days and the excitement of watching Yorkshire play at Park Avenue or Headingley. I preferred Park Avenue and this has remained my favourite cricket ground—the spectator is nearer the action. What wonderful days they were! I appreciate Mr. Boothroyd's sentiments for they were mine too.

I was fortunate in having some aptitude for the game and this talent was to take me, over the years, very close to many of the cricketers about whom Mr. Boothroyd writes. Somebody once said to me that cricket is only a game and I had been in the company of my schoolboy heroes for a very short time when I realised that playing for Yorkshire was much more than a game. It was a very serious business. But a sense of humour was always necessary. Fielding at short leg along with Cyril Turner at Lord's to the bowling of George Macaulay, Patsy Hendren snicked the ball catch-high between Cyril and myself. I left the chance to Cyril and Cyril left it to me. We both looked at Macaulay who, with hands on hips, glared back at us and said "I'll get you two put in Madame Tussaud's!"

I was apprehensive about Mac. because he could be very hard on young cricketers. But I found him very funny. He amused me on many occasions by his remarks, on and off the field.

Almost as far back as I can remember I knew Herbert Sutcliffe, about whom Mr. Boothroyd writes very fondly. My father played with Herbert and with Herbert's father, who was also a good cricketer. When I was a schoolboy of no more than thirteen I was taken to meet Herbert at his home. He lived only a stone's throw from me. Herbert had selected a Harrow size cricket bat for me and this bat became my magic wand. With it I made my first half century and also my first century. A year or two later, one cold February day at the indoor cricket school at Headingley, I had my first meeting with Bill Bowes.

George Hirst asked Bill if he would come along and bowl to "this promising lad from Pudsey." Bill looked me up and down and said "It's about time tha had a new bat isn't it?" Those words shattered me. That dark, well-oiled and battered bat which I used to take to bed with me never missed a ball!

Bill hurled them down to me in that Winter Shed, as it was known to us at that time.

The bat stood the onslaught very well and George Hirst, placing his hand on my shoulder, said "Well done." But, looking at my magic wand that evening, I thought "Bill's right. I do need a new bat."

Bill Bowes, along with Hedley Verity, became my great friends in the Yorkshire team. I spent many hours at Bill's home in Menston, talking cricket and watching him do card tricks. With Hedley I learnt how to drive a car and also to play golf. No young cricketer could have been more fortunate than I was to have been so close to these two fine cricketers and gentlemen.

Mr. Boothroyd tells many stories of Yorkshire cricketers. Many are new to me but these stories illustrate so well the men behind the bat and ball who loved cricket and playing for Yorkshire.

Mr. Boothroyd writes a lot about the Roses matches and refers to Arthur Mitchell. In my first Roses match at Old Trafford I was batting with Arthur Mitchell. I don't think I had got off the mark when I played a square cut. I missed the ball by an eighth of an inch and Arthur, from twenty yards away, shouted "That's no bloody good." I thought: "He's not a very nice sort of a chap saying that to a young player in his first match at Old Trafford against the great enemy." The shot I had just played was one of the very few which I possessed at that time. I was rather shaken by this statement from Arthur. What had I to do? My best stroke was no bloody good!

One hot August day at the Oval, during the time when the whole playing area was used, I found it hard on the feet, very hard. Surrey made a huge score and I ran about the field, throwing in as hard as I could, for six long hours. Sitting in the dressing room at 6.40 pm, with my boots and socks off, giving my feet a little cool air, Mitchell looked at me and said in his best Yorkshire dialect "What were wrong wi' thee today? Had ta got six inch nails in thi' booits?" Not a very nice chap I thought, but then I did not know the man from Baildon!

They were hard days but in the background was the most lovable cricketer I have ever known, George Hirst, about whom Mr. Boothroyd also writes with affection. In cricketing circles he was known as George Herbert. I loved to be in his company and I thank God that I was able to spend so many hours with him.

After practising in the Winter Shed during February and March often I would carry his bag from the Headingley cricket ground to the tram terminus. Sitting with him one day on the tram he said to me "Whatever you do don't get like Victor Trumper." In a quiet, surprised voice I asked why. George said Victor Trumper was so superstitious he made his life a misery. I remembered this advice. But how nice it was for George to give it to a fifteen year old boy!

For 50 years Mr. Boothroyd has retained his love of cricket. In this book he tells of the changes that have taken place in the game, as well as giving intimate pictures of cricketers who were houshold names at one time or another. One of them is Emmott Robinson. It was a source of comfort to me to find Emmott umpiring at Trent Bridge on my first appearance against Australia in 1938.

I came to know Emmott well during his period as an umpire. At Headingley during the April nets he would come along and talk to me quite often. On one occasion he was umpiring in the Yorkshire v. Hampshire match at Bournemouth. Yorkshire won the toss and during my innings, when I was at the non-striker's end, I received a coaching lesson from Emmott. It would not have been too bad at the end of an over but this happened in the middle of an over, with the poor bowler having to wait until Emmott had finished his sermon!

Mr. Boothroyd also deals with the controversies which have occurred in the Yorkshire club during recent years and criticises some of the committee's actions. Should you hear that some members of the Yorkshire committee do not understand cricket, and are not good judges of it, the following story illustrates the wisdom of a Yorkshire committee man in 1939.

Shortly after my return from the MCC tour of South Africa in the spring of 1939 I was batting in one of the nets at Headingley. It was late April, just before the season started. At this stage in my career I had made three centuries for England, including 364 at the Oval in 1938.

A member of the Yorkshire committee said to George Hirst, who was in charge, "George, I have been watching this chap batting in this net and I think he ought to be given a trial in the second eleven." He was referring to me! They were good judges in those days!

This book will be enjoyed wherever cricket is played. The reader will be brought close to those who devoted the best years of their lives to the game. The stories are good and true and I shall be very pleased to add this book to my collection.

1 MY FIRST TEST MATCH

With two seasons of watching county cricket already behind me, and having reached the advanced age of nine, I was ready for my first test match in July, 1930. I had carefully studied the brochures on the Australian touring team which had been on sale at the county matches and I was as familiar with them as I was with all the English cricketers—not only those likely to be selected for the test matches but those whose cricketing destiny would certainly not take them to such dizzy heights. Thanks to Wisden's Cricketers' Almanack, Player's cigarette cards and a variety of other sources I was a walking encyclopaedia on the game. I knew the names and initials of practically every first class cricketer in the world and which county or, in the case of the Australians, which state he played for. My knowledge of current cricket was far more comprehensive then than it is today, 50 years later.

The test match in question was the third test between England and Australia starting at Headingley on July 11th and I looked forward to it with a sense of eager expectation which was only equalled in my experience by the now long past joy of looking forward to Santa Claus coming at Christmas. When my father had announced that he would take me I had boasted about it at school and put a ring round the date on the calendar.

"You don't think you'll get restless sitting all day?" my father had asked me—we had usually gone to the county games after lunch and, as he pointed out, there would be a big crowd at the test match and I would not be able to keep dashing out to the refreshment rooms for bottles of pop. I would have to SIT STILL ALL DAY, from 11.30 am to 6.30 pm. Was I sure I could do it? It was such an absurd question that I don't think I deigned to reply to it. If he had asked me to queue up all night at the turnstiles he would not have got 'no' for an answer.

I got a bit of a shock on the eve of the match when my mother announced that my grandmother was coming unexpectedly to visit us and could my father pick her up at the station in Leeds at 5.30 pm. I could not bear the thought of having to leave the ground before the close of play. But I need not have worried. My father was normally a very considerate man and tolerated his mother-in-law with good grace. But England v. Australia came much higher in his order of priorities than she did. "It's absolutely out of the question" he replied firmly. "Stumps are drawn at 6.30 pm." "But you could leave early for once, couldn't you?" pleaded my mother. "Leave early?" expostulated my father. "I wouldn't leave Headingley early tomorrow to meet Queen Mary at the station, never mind your mother."

This reply was not prompted to promote harmony in the household and my mother prepared our sandwiches and hard-boiled eggs that evening with not quite as much good grace as usual. "Your father's cricket mad" she grumbled bitterly as she buttered the bread and put in the ham and tongue. "I don't know what it is about cricket but it has a mesmerising effect on him." She smiled and added "But thank goodness you've got to go with him this year! He insisted on dragging me off to Headingley to see the Australians in

1921 when you were a little baby and Jack Hobbs got appendicitis and Lionel Tennyson couldn't bat, and in 1926 he dragged me off again when you had the measles and that man Macartney got a century before lunch. You don't know how glad I am that you've got to go with him tomorrow!"

My first concern the following morning was the state of the weather and I was examining it closely through the window at 6.30 am, and duly thanked God that it was fine. On this occasion I was not to be my father's sole companion and when we left home at 9.30 am in the Arrol Johnson, with the thermoses protruding out of the top of a very delapidated carrier bag, which was used exclusively for cricket matches and looked as though it had been in regular use since W. G. Grace was a lad, our first job was to pick up Mr. Fox who lived on the outskirts of Leeds. Mr. Fox was a business friend of my father's in the wool trade and for some reason which I know not provided us with a regular supply of pheasants, crayfish and salmon at wholesale prices which greatly enriched our table at the appropriate seasons. My father was a great man for getting things wholesale and he was repaying Mr. Fox for his gastronomical services by taking him to the test match with one of his Yorkshire county tickets—he always had two or three of them for such usage.

But all my recollections are that Mr. Fox did not enjoy his test match at Headingley nearly as much as we enjoyed his pheasants. Indeed, although he was very polite about it, I don't think he enjoyed it much at all. For Mr. Fox, a balding, chubby little man with a very red face and a thick neck which looked several sizes larger than his starched collar, was the sort of cricket spectator who takes a casual interest in the game rather than devoting himself to it with the masochistic concentration displayed by spectators like my father. It became clear during the day that Mr. Fox liked to pop out regularly to the bar—indeed it could be said that he liked his cricket and his beer drinking in about equal proportions. But this was anathema to my father who never stirred from his seat unless nature obliged him to do so—and that had to be restricted to the lunch and tea intervals.

Having collected Mr. Fox we headed straight for Headingley and managed to park the car without difficulty in one of the streets near the members' entrance to the ground. My father never patronised official car parks at cricket matches because he said they were badly organised and got you in a great deal quicker than they could get you out. It was a bright and sunny morning and we entered the ground to see a big crowd already assembled, encircling the whole playing area. My father took one expert look at it and said "Just over 20,000"—an estimate which proved to be very accurate.

We did not have reserved seats—this was a sophistication which was to come with later test matches at Headingley—but we were able to get good seats in the pavilion with our members' tickets, and with our various accoutrements arranged around us—the carrier bag with the sandwiches and thermos flasks, the binoculars, the car rug to keep us warm if needed, and, last but by no means least, the large cushion which my father always took to cricket matches in order to make the hard wooden seats more tolerable—we listened to the buzz of conversation which echoed round the large green oval space in front of us where shortly the thrilling battle was to commence. The test match atmosphere, compounded of tension and eager expectation, was complete.

There were, of course no score cards because they were in the process of being printed and we had to rely on the bush telegraph for information about the teams. The word was passed round from somewhere that W. H. Ponsford, the Australian opening batsman, was ill with gastritis and that another of their leading batsmen, Fairfax, had to have an operation and that neither of them would play. Although it was not cricket in its true sense at all, this information was greeted by the hugely partisan crowd as a very good omen for England, and good omens were needed because in the last test match at Lord's the Australians had won by seven wickets.

This turned out to be an accurate rumour and I was rather sorry because I wanted to see Ponsford, the 30-year-old Victoria batsman, who had contributed 81 in the Lord's test to the huge Australian total of 729 for six declared. But my main concern was that Don Bradman should be playing. Bradman was already being acclaimed as a boy wonder. He had made his debut in English cricket at Worcester with a score of 236 and proceeded to Leicester where he got 185 not out. In the first test at Trent Bridge he had scored 131 and in the second test at Lord's 254. I was sufficiently partisan not to want to see him score another double century at Headingley but I nevertheless greatly wanted to see him bat. I little realised how fully that wish was to be fulfilled in the subsequent six hours of play.

About eleven o'clock the two captains, W. M. Woodfull for Australia and A. P. F. Chapman for England, came onto the field and tossed, and although no-one thought of making any announcement about the result, it was indicated by some subtle gestures not clear to me that Woodfull had called correctly and that presumably Australia would bat first. The buzz of excitement rose again and continued unabated until 11.30 when, as expected, Chapman led the England team onto the field. I sighed with relief at the presence of my heroes, Herbert Sutcliffe and Maurice Leyland, the two Yorkshiremen in the team.

Woodfull and Jackson opened the Australian innings and almost immediately there was drama which brought a roar from the crowd which must have penetrated as far as Leeds Town Hall. Off Maurice Tate's fifth ball of his first over Jackson was caught by Larwood for one. It was a shock for Australia and a thrill for everyone else, and with the score at two for one Don Bradman came in. He was a slight young man of 22, not nearly as burly as Woodfull, and there was nothing in his appearance to signify cricketing genius. Nor was there about the way he played his first ball from Tate. It beat him completely, missed the off stump by a hair's breadth and so surprised the wicket-keeper, George Duckworth of Lancashire, that it went for four byes.

But from the second ball onwards it was a very different story. Bradman began to pull and drive as though he had been at the crease for hours and his score leapt ahead so rapidly that the scoreboard could hardly keep up with him. When Mr. Fox left for his first visit to the bar he was in his 30's and when he returned, irritating a whole row of spectators in doing so, he had got his 50. He made the English bowling look innocuous and soon there was speculation as to whether he would equal C. G. Macartney's great feat at Headingley in 1926 by scoring a hundred before lunch. He did it with about 15 minutes to spare and received an acclamation from the crowd the like of which I had never seen before. I had seen Sutcliffe and Leyland and other players score centuries in county games, sometimes before bigger crowds than 20,000, but I had never seen anything like this.

The players came in for lunch at 1.30 pm with the total at 136 for one, Bradman not out 105. Woodfull, whom one had hardly noticed, was in his 20's. The fact that Bradman was no longer at the crease brought the optimists out of hiding and a man two rows in front of us expressed the opinion that once Woodfull and Kippax had been dismissed there would be no-one else left who could stay with Bradman. His neighbour hopefully recalled that Larwood had on one occasion taken five wickets for 14 runs immediately after lunch.

But after lunch Bradman proceeded remorselessly to treat the English bowlers with the same disdain as he had done earlier and neither Tate nor Larwood nor Geary nor Tyldesley nor even Hammond could do anything to contain him. There were Yorkshire cries from the crowd of "Put Leyland on" and Chapman eventually responded, but to no better effect. Bradman was breaking the bowlers' hearts one by one and it made no difference whether balls were good ones, bad ones or indifferent ones—they were discharged to the boundary with effortless monotony. Woodfull was out eventually, bowled by Hammond for 50 with the total at 194 and Bradman 136. But the next man in, A. F. Kippax, made it clear that he intended to keep the other end going while Bradman raced on to his double century, which he reached shortly before the tea interval, taken at 4.15 pm with the total 305 for two, Bradman not out 220.

Mr. Fox, whose face had been getting redder and redder in the sun, and who had been out twice to the bar sinch lunch, said he had never seen anything like it in his life. He tried to add that Bradman was a phenomenon. But his speech was a little slurred by now and the words would not quite come out.

I was busy reminding my father that the record individual score in a test match was R. E. Foster's 287 at Sydney in the 1903–04 tour. He said he would not like to put any money on the record lasting until close of play that night. And of course he was right. Foster's record was duly broken to tumultuous applause from the knowledgeable Yorkshire crowd and Bradman waved his bat in acknowledgement of this very sportsmanlike gesture.

The English players joined in the applause but not with any great enthusiasm it seemed. The portly figure of Richard (Dick) Tyldesley, the Lancashire slow leg break bowler, whom Bradman had treated with no more respect than if he had been a schoolboy bowling underhand, did not join in the applause at all. Neville Cardus later recorded that when he met Tyldesley after the close of play and asked him his opinion of Bradman he replied brusquely "He's no ruddy use to me."

Kippax was caught by Chapman off Tate for 77 with the score at 423 for three and Stan McCabe came in to take his place. Shortly afterwards there was another burst of applause to mark Bradman's third century, although it was not perhaps quite as enthusiastic and prolonged as those for the first and second centuries, for with all the goodwill and sportsmanship in the world it had become beyond a joke. A test match was supposed to be a battle between equals, and in that sense this was no test match at all. It was the slaughter of one side not by the other side but by one member of the other side, D. G. Bradman.

When blessed relief for the English players came in the shape of close of play at half past six the Australian score was 458 for three and Bradman with 42 boundaries to his name was 309 not out. Mr. Fox (who had scarcely been in his seat since the tea interval) said it had been the most dramatic day's cricket he had ever seen. "You want to remember this, son," he said to me as we gathered up our accoutrements. "You will probably never see an innings like this again as long as you live." He was wrong because I was to see Bradman score another triple century at Headingley in 1934, but that is another story.

When we got home, dusty and somewhat dishevelled, my grandmother had arrived safely, having got a taxi from the station. "Have you had a good day?" she asked. "Hasn't this young man Donny Bradshaw or whatever his name done well?" I have always remembered that as the cricketing understatement of the century.

Next morning we were up and off in good time, again calling for Mr. Fox who didn't

Don Bradman leads the players off the field in the third test at Headingley in 1930 in which he scored 334.

appear to have been given any option about attending the second day's play. Had he known what he was in for I am sure he would have sought one—and turned it down. For when we arrived at Headingley it was to find the ground packed with people, a crowd estimated by my father at well over 30,000. The actual figure was 33,000, just short of the ground record.

There was not a seat to be found anywhere except on the edge of the field and after searching in vain for more comfortable accommodation we had no alternative but to join the throng of people on the grass in front of the pavilion—an area of which had been roped off for the overflow. We found ourselves sitting in uneven rows about ten deep and although it did not depress me in the least—indeed I was rather glad to be nearer the wicket than we had been the previous day—my father and Mr. Fox viewed the prospect of seven hours in such discomfort with dismay. This was particularly the case with Mr. Fox, who observed ruefully that the sun was already quite hot and that being stationed where we were would make access to the refreshment room exceedingly difficult.

While we were waiting for the umpires to come out my father managed with difficulty to read his Yorkshire Post and announced that the paper had devoted a leading article to Bradman's innings, as well as a long report and half a page of pictures. "There are no adjectives applicable to such a performance, possibly the finest innings ever played" he read out to us and those around us who listened with awed attention. "The English bowlers must have said what one of the victims of W. G. Grace once said—'I puts 'em where I like and he puts 'em where he likes'."

I had visions of Bradman beating his own record of 452 as the highest ever score in first class cricket, which he had achieved the previous season for New South Wales v. Queensland at Sydney, but this was not to be. With his score at 334 he touched a ball from Tate outside the off stump and Duckworth, the wicket-keeper, made the catch and followed it with one of the loudest and most historic appeals in cricketing history. The umpire's finger went up and the marathon was over. Along with a few hundred other people on the edge of the boundary in front of the pavilion I leapt to my feet and helped to form an avenue of adulation for Bradman as he walked back to the pavilion. The great man passed within inches of me and as I clapped and cheered I realised it was something I should never forget.

No-one else in the Australian team put up much resistance—the score after all was big enough already—and half an hour before lunch the last wicket fell with the total at 566. There was now for me the thrill of seeing Hobbs and Sutcliffe open for England—and for Mr. Fox the opportunity to escape from his vernal imprisonment to the bar. I had seen Sutcliffe bat many times and he was my number one cricketing hero but Hobbs I had never seen. This great pillar of English cricket for so many years was now 47 and nearing his retirement, and as he walked out with Sutcliffe I consulted my Wisden (which I always took to cricket matches) and saw that this most celebrated of all English opening pairs had on 26 occasions—15 in test matches—put on 100 or more for the first wicket. Hobbs, whose career had started in 1905, had himself taken part in no fewer than 166 three figure opening partnerships in first class cricket, 66 of them with his Surrey colleague Sandham. But the hope that at Headingley that afternoon Hobbs and Sutcliffe would achieve their 16th three figure opening partnership in a test match was not to be. They survived the awkward 25 minutes to lunch without much anxiety and after lunch put the 50 up, but with the score at 53 Hobbs was out to a brilliant diving catch by

Jack Hobbs and Herbert Sutcliffe, England's greatest opening pair, who put on over 100 for the first wicket in 15 tests.

a'Beckett for 29, and 11 runs later Sutcliffe was caught in the slips by Hornibrook for 32, both of them victims of the slow leg break bowling of C. V. Grimmett.

Another of the greatest of all English batsmen, Walter Hammond, came in number 3 and K. S. Duleepsinhji, a nephew of the famous Ranjisinhji, number 4 and there was a splendid partnership between these two contrasting stylists which put on 59 runs before the Indian was bowled by Hornibrook for 35. Riotous cheering now broke out as the chubby figure of Maurice Leyland came down the gangway and walked through the crowd round the boundary edge onto the field. Leyland was my number two hero and as with Sutcliffe, I always closed my eyes during his first three or four balls as I could not bear to watch him in case he was out for a duck. Throughout the first few years of my cricket watching I had the same desperate anxiety and sense of intimate involvement with both of these players when they got into the 90's. I could scarcely bear to watch them in case they might not succeed in getting their century, so desperately important was it to me that they did so.

Leyland was in good form and hit the ball with his usual forcefulness right from the start, bringing cheers of delight from the crowd when he smote Grimmett for two towering sixes—a most unexpected happening in a test match. Meanwhile with Hammond batting confidently at the other end English hopes rose and the Australian total of 566 no longer seemed so formidable. "At least we shall save the follow on" said my father, who could rarely be accused of undue optimism. With the score at 206, however, disaster struck again. Leyland was caught by Kippax off Wall in the gulley for 44 and at the same total Geary was needlessly run out for a duck.

The captain, A. P. F. Chapman, should have been the next man in but he decided to save himself for the following day and sent in Duckworth as the night watchman. He and Hammond batted out time without further loss and close of play came with England 212 for 5, Hammond not out 61. We still needed a further 204 to save the follow on and with only Chapman, Tate, Larwood and Tyldesley to come it was likely to prove a pretty tall order.

Cramped beyond endurance by the long hours on the grass Mr. Fox announced on the way home that he had urgent business to conduct on Monday and perhaps my father would like to lend his ticket to someone else. My father seemed to regard this as a bit of an affront and said surely Mr. Fox was not going to let a little thing like business interfere with his cricket. "I've never let my business interfere with my cricket in my life" he said admonishingly. "And what's more I never shall." It was a precept he was to live up to very assiduously for the next 32 years.

But Mr. Fox in fact need not have feared further vernal imprisonment at Headingley. As so often happens with cricket in England—the last place in the world to play cricket really—great beginnings often lead to dismal endings and this was the case with the third test match in 1930. Just after the gates were opened on the Monday, with thousands clamouring for admission, there was a thunderstorm and a terrific downpour of rain and play was washed out completely until half past five in the afternoon. Hammond and Duckworth then continued the English innings in stygian gloom and after threequarters of an hour play was abandoned for the day because of bad light. Father and I were on our way to the ground when the thunderstorm burst but fortunately we turned back and thus avoided a day of frustration and disappointment waiting for the next umpires' inspection of the wicket.

On the Tuesday, the final day, England were all out for 391, Hammond making 113, and duly followed on 175 behind with three hours still to play. Hobbs was brilliantly run out by Bradman for 13 but Sutcliffe defended grimly, partnered by Hammond, and, on his dismissal, by Duleepsinhji and with bad light once again bringing the day's proceedings to an early close England were 95 for 3, Sutcliffe not out 28 and Leyland not out 1 when stumps were drawn. The weather had saved us from fairly certain defeat and Bradman's amazing innings had been in vain. It was rather a sad end to my first test match but nevertheless it was one I was never to forget.

Another Yorkshire boy I was later to know was in the crowd to see Bradman's record-breaking innings in this match. He was five years older than I was—14 to be precise—but probably my dreams and his were similar. I did not aspire to break Bradman's record; that was too fanciful even for a dream. Playing for Yorkshire was quite an ambitious enough dream for me. Alas I never came within a hundred miles of it! But that other boy in the crowd at Headingley did rather better. Eight years later—when he was 22—I spent a whole day of my summer holiday at Bridlington glued to a wireless set listening to the fifth test match against Australia at the Oval. My erstwhile companion in the Headingley crowd of 1930 performed rather well. His name was Len Hutton and he beat Bradman's record with a score of 364. I shall be mentioning him again later.

2 THE GREATEST EVER

I was to see quite a lot of Don Bradman at Headingley test matches over the next 18 years. I saw him get his 304 in the fourth test in 1934, 103 in the fourth test in 1938 and, after the gap of the war years, his final innings of 173 not out in the fourth test in 1948. Including his two low scores of 16 in the second innings of the 1938 test and 33 in the first innings of the 1948 match, his six test innings at Headingley produced 963 runs, giving him an average of 192. In a career spanning 22 years, including six cricketless years of war, he played in 52 test matches, had 80 innings, scored 6,996 runs and averaged 99.94. In first class cricket generally he scored 28,067 runs with an average of 95.14. In a total of 338 innings he scored 117 centuries. To be less statistical but more incredible it can be said that he got a century virtually every other time he went in.

These figures are so fantastic that I can never understand why there is any question among cricket lovers as to whether Bradman was the greatest player the game has ever produced—or is ever likely to produce. Admittedly he was not a bowler and therefore does not feature among the great cricket all-rounders such as Grace, Hirst, Rhodes and Woolley. But his achievements as a batsman so dwarf the batting achievements of every other cricketer from W. G. Grace to Geoffrey Boycott that to me his supremacy is unassailable. Compared with Bradman's test average of 99.94 the next best Australian is S. G. Barnes with an average of 63.05. The English batsman with the highest test average is Herbert Sutcliffe with 60.73. Hammond averaged 58.45, Hobbs 56.94, Hutton 56.67, Compton 50.06, Hendren 47.63, Leyland 46.06, Cowdrey 44.06, Woolley 36.07 and W. G. Grace 32.29. Of Australians only Greg Chappell (53.20), A. G. Fairfax (51.25) and J. Ryder (51.62) have averages of 50 or over in test matches, for South Africa only A. Melville, A. D. Nourse, G. Pollock and B. A. Richards, and for the West Indians only C. A. Davies, G. A. Headley, I. V. A. Richards, G. S. Sobers, C. L. Wallcott and E. D. Weekes. These figures measure the pre-eminence of Bradman. All the other great cricketers—be they batsmen or bowlers or all-rounders—compare with each other. There is any amount of room for argument as to whether Hobbs was a greater player than Hammond or Woolley greater than Hendren or Rhodes greater than Hirst or Hutton greater than Sutcliffe. Their vital statistics are all very comparable. But Bradman stands out head and shoulders above all the rest. One can say with certainty that there never was a cricketer of his equal and that there never will be.

The people who dispute that Bradman was the greatest player ever, claim that he was not a world beating batsman on a bad wicket. There is some justification for this claim but the plain fact is that Bradman was an Australian used to hard Australian wickets. He had not a fraction of the experience of wet and drying wickets of the top calibre English players and it is therefore hardly surprising that Sutcliffe may have been a better bet to score 50 on a sticky wicket at Bradford. Bradman was a forceful, aggressive batsman whose whole technique was moulded by pitches which behaved "normally." But if he had played his cricket in England instead of Australia I am sure he would have adapted his technique to English conditions without difficulty and outshone even Sutcliffe. He had all the necessary qualities to master the sharply spinning ball—the quickness of foot and eye—and he would not have floundered for long.

That Bradman appreciated the skill and concentration necessary on these sort of wickets is underlined by his selection of Sutcliffe's 135 on a sticky wicket at Melbourne (of all places) on the 1928/29 tour as the finest innings he had ever witnessed. Neville Cardus remarks that Bradman once argued, irrationally in Cardus's opinion, that as sticky wickets were unfair some covering should be used to render them obsolete. "You might as well expect Inman to play on a torn billiard table" he said. Cardus felt, and I am sure most cricket watchers will agree with him, that this would be a retrograde step. "A torn table is not usually to be found in the highest circles of billiards, but a sticky wicket is natural to the environment of cricket" he wrote.

Other critics of Bradman have said that he was not so much a batsman as a run getting machine. I have never seen the validity of this criticism because the main object of cricket is to score runs and if a man can make himself as efficient in doing so as a machine he has surely achieved the ultimate in cricketing perfection. That, fortunately, can never be because a machine can be set never to be out. If no-one had been able to get Bradman out it would have brought the game of cricket to a peremptory halt.

It reminds me of a very funny radio play I listened to years ago called "The Atom Bowler." It was a fantasy about a young village cricketer who produced bowling of such speed and accuracy that he was completely unplayable and took all ten wickets for no runs in several consecutive matches. The MCC called him up to play for England in the next test match against Australia and he did the same thing with them. This produced consternation and bewilderment in the cricketing world and the result was a diplomatic crisis between England and Australia, with war only averted and the game of cricket preserved by the atom bowler being banned from every cricket ground in the world. If Bradman had been much more of a batting genius than he was it might have had the same result!

The purists have criticised Bradman because they say he used his bat more as a machine gun than as a sabre. There was no finesse, no stroking the ball through the covers or delicately glancing it to fine leg. It was just bang, bang, bang, with boundaries in every direction. He could certainly not be described as a classical stylist. He thought nothing of pulling a ball pitched outside the off stump to the long on boundary or even on occasions to the square leg boundary, and when Larwood and Voce were bowling bodyline at him he would frequently move like lightning to leg and force the ball out to the off. But if poetry was hardly the word for Bradman's batting I always found it a fascinating joy to watch.

I think the innings I enjoyed most was his 304 at Headingley in 1934. My father and I (not this time accompanied by Mr. Fox) arrived at the ground bright and early on the Saturday morning along with a record-breaking crowd of 38,000 with high hopes of seeing Australia humbled. England had batted first on the previous day and with Sutcliffe injured and out of the team had failed rather miserably, being skittled out by Grimmett and O'Reilly for 200, C. F. Walters being top scorer with 44. Brown and Ponsford opened for Australia and sailed serenely to 37 without loss. Then the drama came thick and fast. With the clock close to half past six Bill Bowes, the Yorkshire fast bowler, bowled Brown

Don Bradman acknowledges applause for yet another century. He averaged 99.94 every time he went to the wicket in a test match.

for 15 and in his next over had night watchman Oldfield caught by Ames behind the wicket for a duck. Woodfull, the captain, came in to play out time and, glory of glories, Bowes bowled him for a duck too. Three wickets were down for 39 and Australia were really on the run.

I had very mixed feelings when Bradman and Ponsford came out to carry on the Australian innings at 11.30 next morning. My partisan spirit dearly wanted the Australian collapse to continue but I also wanted to see a bit of Bradman again. Not too much. Just enough to remind me of the glory of 1930. I think the Headingley crowd shared my ambivalent attitude. We were encouraged in our optimism that Bradman would not bat the living daylights out of our bowlers this time because on this tour he had proved to be fallible. In his previous five test innings he had scored only 133 runs—an average of 26—and there were many who said that the master had had his day. The Bradman magic was no more.

This as I say was at half past eleven in the morning. At six o'clock that night Bradman and Ponsford were still together. They had batted all day and Bradman was nearing 300 and Ponsford nearing 200. The score was 427 and there seemed no way of stopping the wild saturnalian feast of scoring which had all but broken the hearts of Bowes, Verity, T. B. Mitchell, Hammond, Hopwood and Leyland. Indeed if Ponsford had not trodden on his wicket for 181 while hitting another of the endless stream of boundaries it seems doubtful in retrospect whether they would ever have been parted. The day ended with Australia 494 for 4—Bradman 271 not out.

We assembled again on the Monday—only 3,000 fewer of us than on the Saturday—with long faces and very flattened hopes. But one of the great joys of cricket is its unpredictability, and this morning the English attack, dominated by Bowes had an inspiration which had been completely lacking earlier. Bradman was not at all comfortable and, after being missed by Verity in the slips at 280, was clean bowled by Bowes for 304. Bowes also hit the stumps of McCabe for 27 and Darling for 12 and when Australia were all out for 584 had the splendid figures of 6 for 142, 5 of them clean bowled.

England began their second innings needing 384 to avoid an innings defeat and never looked like getting them. But, as in 1930, a violent thunderstorm with torrential rain came to their rescue and the match was washed out as a draw with England 229 for six. Once again the Don had laboured in vain at Headingley.

The last time I saw Bradman was at the Headingley test in 1948. On this occasion nature had evidently abandoned its anti-Australian bias and a thunderstorm did not come to the assistance of England on the last day. They didn't really seem to need one. England declared on the Tuesday morning at a second innings score of 365 for 8, leaving Australia the impossible target of 404 to win—a higher total than had ever been achieved in a fourth innings in any test match. Bradman joined the stylish left-handed A. R. Morris with the score at 57 for one and these two put on 301 runs for the second wicket before Morris was out for 182. Australia sailed to victory with a quarter of an hour to spare—404 for 3 with Bradman not out 173. It was a fitting climax to an amazing series of innings at Headingley.

It was, of course, evident when Bradman came in to bat in the Australian second innings that this would be his last appearance at Headingley—he was already only a month short of his 40th birthday. The crowd rose to him as a man and he was cheered all the way to the wicket and was so evidently overcome with emotion that it was some time before he

A too familiar sight at Headingley. This downpour on the final day robbed Australia of victory in the fourth test in 1934.

could take his first ball. The generosity of this Yorkshire reception must have touched him deeply for he was not—nor could he be—a man of great emotional reaction. Indeed his critics have described him as being completely without emotion, which is just as ridiculous as saying his batting was machine-like.

That Bradman was sometimes a cool customer is no doubt true. He has said that the secret of his success was concentration—treating every ball that came to him as though it was his first. He was also single-minded, ruthlessly self-disciplined and vastly self-confident. Neville Cardus recalls that in the 1934 test at Headingley, which I have described, he had invited Bradman to dinner at the Queens Hotel in Leeds, where the Australian party were staying, on the Friday night. But earlier that evening had seen the partial rout of Australia by Bill Bowes and 3 wickets were down for 39. Bradman wrote Cardus a note of apology saying that he was going early to bed. Thinking he might not be well, Cardus went to see him in his room. No, he said, he was not ill but things had gone wrong at Headingley and he did not feel like coming down to dinner if Cardus did not mind. "I shall have to score 200 tomorrow at least" he added. Comments Cardus: "I could not resist reminding him that in his previous test at Headingley he had passed the 300 mark. That the law of averages was against him getting anywhere near 200 again. Very gravely he answered 'I don't believe in the law of averages.'" And as I have recorded he actually scored not 200 but 304.

He was said by his critics to be unsociable, stand-offish, wary of the press and generally not very helpful. I cannot give much of an opinion about this because although I saw him score thousands of runs the only time I ever spoke to him was when I passed him one morning going up to the press box at a Headingley test match years after he had retired. I was writing background articles for the Yorkshire Post and wanted to do a feature on the famous ex-players who were writing about the game—all masquerading as journalists and most of them putting their names to commentaries which were written by 'ghosts'—other journalists who sat alongside them and did the work. Bradman was one of the genuine commentators (no 'ghost' for him) and he was coming down the stairs as I went up. I said 'good morning' and he smiled very agreeably and said 'good morning' back. I was no longer a boy but it was still a thrill to talk to Bradman!

I suspect that some of the stories about Bradman's social manners are more a reflection of his natural reserve and aloofness rather than of any intention to hurt. And as with all great stars his detractors often seem to have been activated by envy, which leads to distortion and misrepresentation of things he is alleged to have said or done.

E. W. Swanton in his fascinating book "Sort of a Cricket Person" recounts the story of how Bradman was supposed to have snubbed a former England captain, the Honourable Lionel Tennyson, who did a good turn for Bradman by keeping his side in the field in heavy rain to enable him to reach his thousand runs one season before the end of May—a feat only achieved by six other players—W. G. Grace, Hammond, Hallows, Hayward, W. J. Edrich and G. M. Turner of New Zealand (Bradman, needless to say, did it twice—in 1930 and 1938). Years after Tennyson's retirement, when Bradman was the Australian captain, Tennyson, during a test match at Lord's, went to the Australian dressing room, sent in his name and asked to see Bradman. The reply came back that Bradman was busy and could not see Lord Tennyson at the moment. An Australian journalist happened to hear this and cabled back to Sydney that Bradman had insulted an old English captain.

Swanton says the truth behind the facts was that Tennyson, having lunched far too well, went to the England dressing room and spent some time there. Bradman knew this, was appraised of his state of health and decided he did not want his team to see the great man in this particular situation. With one eye on the field and one ear cocked towards another visitor who was present he sent his message. Comments Swanton "Can one blame him?" adding that he was very widely blamed on the facts as printed and that the really galling thing about it was that when interviewed Bradman could not give the actual explanation.

But whatever his social graces Don Bradman was unquestionably the greatest cricketer of all time and the fact that I can see him now quite clearly in my mind's eye, crashing balls to the boundary as I saw him doing in person 50 years ago, is one of the most satisfying memories of my half century of cricket watching. His like will not be seen again.

3 BOYHOOD HEROES

When I think of the cricketers I have known my mind turns instinctively to the matches and the players of my boyhood in the 1930's. They are so much more clearly etched in my memory than the games and players of recent times. Every cricket lover says this and it is not, of course, surprising that boyhood should be one's most impressionable time in cricket as in most other things. One is in the process of discovery and, like first love, first cricket is no doubt always the sharpest and the sweetest.

I can remember the cricketers I grew up with far more clearly than some of the relatives I grew up with. They were just as much members of my family. In fact, they played a far more important part in my young life than most of my uncles and aunts. I look back on them with an affectionate nostalgia.

I came across in a drawer quite recently some Players' cigarette cards of "Cricketers 1934", a series of 50 which I had collected that year, and I was not at all surprised to find that I remembered practically every one of them with crystal clarity. They included, of course, such players as Hobbs and Sutcliffe and Hammond and Larwood and Verity and Jardine and Wyatt and Robins and Farnes and other test stars of the period, but there were also some of the more run-of-the-mill players whom I could have been expected to have forgotten. But I instantly recognised almost every one of these players and recalled not only his initials and his county but quite a few other details as well. The series included J. Arnold and A. E. Pothecary (Hampshire), A. H. Bakewell and E. H. Clark (Northampton), G. Berry and E. W. Dawson (Leicestershire), M. J. Turnbull and A. H. Dyson (Glamorgan), H. H. Gibbon and C. F. Walters (Worcester), J. H. A. Hulme (Middlesex), F. R. Santall (Warwickshire), L. F. Townsend and D. B. Mitchell (Derbyshire), B. H. Valentine (Kent) and A. W. Wellard (Somerset).

But it is, of course, the stars I remember most vividly—not only those included in the Players' cigarette series but many others as well—G. O. B. (Gubby) Allen, M. J. C. Allom, W. E. Astill, C. J. Barnett, A. W. Carr, A. P. F. Chapman, A. P. Freeman, T. W. J. Goddard, G. Gunn, C. Hallows, E. H. (Patsy) Hendren, C. P. Mead, M. S. Nichols, I. A. R. Peebles, A. Sandham, G. T. S. Stevens, G. E. Tyldesley, W. W. Whysall and F. E. Woolley, to name a few. I did not see a lot of these players but I remember them all very distinctly. I can remember their faces, their figures, their gestures and other facets of them which made them into distinct and individual personalities—A. P. F. Chapman, a very tall, gangling fellow with a fancy multi-coloured cap, a man who was renowned for his big hitting and was always entertaining to watch; Patsy Hendren with the gnarled, puckered, good-humoured face and the broad bat which not all cricketers realise came second only to that of Jack Hobbs in the number of centuries it scored—170 against Hobbs's 197; Frank Woolley, the tall, elegant, willowy, somewhat ethereal Kentish man, whom some regard as the greatest stylist of them all, who came sixth in the list of century makers with 145 and who died only a year or two ago at the advanced age of 91; Andrew

Sandham, the dour, grizzled opener for Surrey who, with Hobbs, came second only to Holmes and Sutcliffe in the number of century opening partnerships—63 against 69.

And so I could go on, ad infinitum, recalling memories of the cricketing gods I worshipped from afar. But for me, of course, the peaks of Mount Olympus were occupied almost exclusively by Yorkshiremen. And the king of the gods was Herbert Sutcliffe. He reigned through all my boyhood as supremely as Zeus ever did.

I cannot remember when I first saw Sutcliffe bat or when I became captivated by his performances and his personality, but it was some time early in 1928 at the age of seven. I know that 1928 was my first season as a Yorkshire cricket supporter because the records tell me that Captain (later Sir) William Worsley became skipper of the team in that year and Worsley was in that position when my cricket watching began. I never saw Yorkshire play under their previous captain, Major Lupton, who retired in 1927, nor did I ever see the wicket-keeper Arthur Dolphin, and the fast medium bowler Abe Waddington, who also retired that year, or that wonderful all-rounder Roy Kilner, who died tragically early in 1928 aged 38 from a fever contracted during a coaching engagement in India.

I had certainly joined Sutcliffe's fan club by January, 1929, because I then wrote him my first letter—to congratulate him on his century on a sticky wicket at Melbourne in the third test match against Australia. As I have recorded in my book, "Nowt So Queer As Folk", that letter took me hours to compose and was not very literate when I had finished it. But I gave it to my father to post, addressed "Mr. H. Sutcliffe, Melbourne Cricket Ground, Australia." I came across it in 1962 when going through my father's effects following his death in that year, and it was marked "D's letter to Herbert Sutcliffe—very funny." It may have been funny to him but it was not to me. It was the most passionately sincere and profoundly earnest letter I had written in my life. I wanted to let Sutcliffe know that he was not only the greatest cricketer in the world, but in my opinion the greatest man in the world. Beside him the famous men in my school books such as Alexander the Great and Julius Caesar were comparative nonentities. And my judgement was not all that unformed because no less an authority than Don Bradman himself has described Sutcliffe's innings on this occasion as "the nearest approach to mastery" he had ever seen!

When the cricketers were back from Australia and summer came round again I went with my father to as many Yorkshire matches as possible and watched my hero batting with, I suspect, the same mesmeric intensity that one observes nowadays on the faces of youngsters at pop concerts. I revelled in his every action and when he got a century my joy was scarcely containable. The only times he disappointed me were when he was unduly defensive and slow in scoring—which he was rather frequently. But I was not amused when a wag in the crowd at Sheffield, I believe it was, one day shouted out to him "Come on, Herbert, get a move on. What does tha think tha art, a bloody war memorial?" Neither, I think, was Sutcliffe very amused. He merely held out his bat to his critic, inviting him to take his place.

So smitten was I with Sutcliffe that after seeing him bat at Headingley, Park Avenue or Bramall Lane I would return home and play fantasy games with myself in which I took the part of the great man. I resembled him in one way only—I had black hair—so I plastered it down with brilliantine and parted it like he did. Then I would put my pyjama trousers on top of my shorts so that I could put my pads on just like he did, a slight bulge of flannel between the straps. I would then put on my batting gloves and

Yorkshire's three greatest batsmen, Geoffrey Boycott, Herbert Sutcliffe and Len Hutton, take a bow together at the Headingley test against Australia in 1977 when Boycott scored his hundredth hundred in first class cricket. Sutcliffe scored 149 centuries and Hutton 129.

march down to what we called the bottom lawn, where throughout the summer we always had a cricket net in position.

I would go to the wicket to take my stance just as elegantly as he did, the feet close together, and ask the umpire for leg and middle or centre with just that touch of imperiousness that he had and proceed to make my block hole unhurriedly and keep the bowler and the field waiting whilst I patted down a few non-existent bumps on the pitch in front of me and looked carefully all round the field, noting exactly where all the fielders were stationed.

Then I would begin my innings and after a few brilliant cover drives, leg glances and late cuts, with an occasional fierce hook (Sutcliffe was a great hooker) I would raise my bat nonchalantly to acknowledge the crowd's applause for my 50 and after a few more flourishes raise it again, a little higher this time, to respond to the acclamation of my century. But even we Sutcliffes had to be out sometime and eventually I would fall victim to a brilliant catch at the wicket, accepting my dismissal in the approved sportsmanlike Sutcliffe manner by leaving the crease before the umpire's finger went up. I would then walk back up the path to the front door, taking my gloves off on the way and go into the pavilion, raising my bat to the enthusiastic plaudits of the crowd.

This boyhood fantasy was played out many times and even when I was a good deal older and batting against real bowling in our net on the bottom lawn, fantasy would replace reality and I would be Herbert Sutcliffe for a few thrilling moments once again.

By the time I started watching him, of course, Sutcliffe's career was half over. The season of 1929 was his 11th as Yorkshire's opening batsman with Percy Holmes and he was already 35 years old. His most triumphant tour of Australia in 1924/5 was well behind him and so were most of the 15 occasions when he and Jack Hobbs put on a hundred or more for England's first wicket in test matches. But there was a lot more to come before the second world war brought an end to his career at the age of 45 in 1939 and most of it was of vintage Sutcliffe quality. His best-ever season in England was in 1931 when he scored over 3,000 runs with 13 centuries and topped the English averages with an average of 96.96. Then in 1932, the year in which he and Holmes broke Brown and Tunnicliffe's long standing record of 554 for the first wicket, Sutcliffe again scored more than 3,000 runs and 14 centuries with an average of 74.13.

I could take pages up quoting Sutcliffe's achievements in statistical terms but they all add up to showing that he was one of the greatest batsmen that England has ever produced. In the averages as quoted by Wisden he scored 50,135 runs in first class cricket with an average of 52.00—a figure beaten only by Hammond (56.10), Hutton (55.51), Sobers (54.87) and, needless to say, Bradman (95.14). Hobbs, who scored 50.65 for every innings he played, Compton 51.85, C. B. Fry 50.22 and Patsy Hendren 50.80 are the only other players who completed their careers averaging over 50. And in test matches Sutcliffe has the highest average of any English player—60.73. Hobbs' test average was 56.96, Hammond's 58.45, Hutton's 56.67, Compton's 50.06 and, surprisingly, Barrington's 58.67. Bradman's test average by comparison was 99.94.

Sutcliffe's two great innings were undoubtedly his 161 which was instrumental in England winning the Ashes against the Australians in the final test at the Oval in 1926 and the 135 at Melbourne in 1929 which I have already mentioned.

The position in the Oval test was that Australia had a lead of 22 in the first innings and when stumps were drawn Hobbs and Sutcliffe had replied for England with 49 for 0.

That night there was a thunderstorm and next morning, with the sun shining, the England opening pair were faced with the grim prospect of batting on a sticky wicket which would probably ease later on in the day. Sutcliffe was 40 minutes before he scored a run—content merely to survive—but he and Hobbs were still batting at lunchtime and had taken the total to 161. Hobbs was bowled by Gregory shortly after completing his century but their job had been well and truly done and the wicket was now beginning to ease. But Sutcliffe continued in what Hobbs was later to describe as "superbly, dominatingly, flawlessly" and was out in the last over of the day, bowled by Mailey for 161.

Hammond said later that Sutcliffe was unsighted by people in the pavilion getting up to leave and he added that it was after losing his wicket in this match that Sutcliffe always refused to play a ball so long as any movement was taking place behind the bowler's arm. "Many will remember his lordly gestures with the bat when such occasions arose" Hammond very accurately commented.

Sutcliffe had a wonderful reception from the crowd as he returned to the pavilion after seven hours at the crease and next day Larwood and Wilfred Rhodes, playing in his last test at the age of 49, skittled the Australians out for 125, to give England the Ashes.

But as I have said it was not only Sutcliffe's dazzling performances which made him the brightest star in my boyhood cricketing firmament. There was so much about his personality which attracted me also. With his sleek, black hair and his film-star-like good looks, his white flannels which always looked as if they had come straight from the laundry, he was always superbly smart, elegant and completely unruffled. He had such poise and natural dignity. He was always so completely imperturbable and untemperamental—an ideal man for a crisis because in Sutcliffe's philosophy there was no such thing as a crisis. Crises were just natural situations to be dealt with as efficiently and expeditiously as possible, like any other human situation. As R. C. Robertson-Glasgow has expressed it "Whatever may have passed under that calm brow—anger, joy, relief, triumph—no outward sign was betrayed on the field of play. He was understood over 2,000 years in advance by the Greek philosophers. They called this character megalo-psychic. It is the sort of man who would rather miss a train than run for it and so be seen in disorder and hard breathing."

Above all he was so utterly dependable. He always seemed to come off on the big occasions, or on the small occasions when big things were at stake. Don Bradman once said of Sutcliffe that he had the best temperament of any cricketer that he had ever played with or against and that together with his courage, infinite patience and tremendous powers of concentration his temperament was probably the explanation for his success.

For the experts are agreed that he was a great batsman as much by single-minded dedication and determination as by natural ability. The view is that Bradman, Hobbs, Hammond, Hutton and Compton all had greater natural gifts as batsmen—more of the raw materials from which cricketing genius is created. Sutcliffe was not a flashy player. He could slog when the occasion demanded and at Kettering against Northants he had 10 sixes in an innings of 113 and at Scarborough against the fast bowling of Farnes and Nichols he took his score from 100 to 194 in 40 minutes. But he was essentially a defensive player—cautious, careful, patient, meticulous, systematic. He gave the task in hand his complete concentration—whether it was scoring a century on the field or writing his business letters in a corner of the dressing room, in which he made an office, using his fitted writing case as a desk.

The two heroes of my boyhood, Herbert Sutcliffe and Maurice Leyland, pictured in 1932. I was much more nervous than they were as they went through the nineties!

J. M. Kilburn has in his book "Thanks to Cricket" written of this Sutcliffe concentration as follows: "His powers of concentration on the matter immediately in hand are astonishing. Not out at lunch time he could be found using a quarter of an hour before the resumption of play to write letters—in the neatest calligraphy of course. As the umpires returned to the field someone at the window would say 'They're out Herbert.' Papers would be folded, the writing case closed, the bat and batting gloves picked up and the innings resumed."

It is one of the most delightful features of cricket watching that over the years one gets to know the players one sees regularly so well that one feels as if one had known them personally for a long time. It is not only their cricketing prowess that one can assess and evaluate but their characters and peronalities. In some mysterious way which I don't profess to comprehend the cricketer reveals in his cricket the sort of man he is.

I never talked to Herbert Sutcliffe until some years after the war when I became a member of the editorial staff of the Yorkshire Post and met him in my professional capacity from time to time. I never knew him well in actual fact but I feel I knew him intimately. Perhaps I have merely assimilated all I have read about him in his own book "For England and Yorkshire" and in many other books by a variety of cricket writers. But I think there is more to it than that. Cricket is in many different ways a great revealer of character and personality as well as a great game and I fancy I had formed my opinions of Herbert Sutcliffe long before I had either met him or read about him. Indeed I had most of my opinions formed, even if I was not capable of articulating about them, by the age of 14 or 15. What I learned later when I got to know him personally merely confirmed what I had long ago instinctively apprehended.

Even most Yorkshiremen think Sutcliffe was a native of Pudsey, that famous little town between Leeds and Bradford which also produced Len Hutton and slightly lesser Yorkshire luminaries such as John Tunnicliffe and Major Booth. But he was not born there at all. He was born at Summerbridge, a village near Harrogate, and his parents moved to Pudsey while he was still a boy. He had a sad early life. His father, William Sutcliffe, from whom he inherited his love of cricket, was no mean performer and played for Pudsey St. Lawrence. He was a medium pace bowler of some accomplishment—it was said he could hit unguarded stumps four times out of six deliveries—and was good enough to be given a trial at the Yorkshire nets under the tutelage of George Hirst. He also played rugby football and while doing so sustained severe internal injuries. They were aggravated while he was playing cricket the following summer and he died within days. Herbert was only three at the time. Three years later his mother also died suddenly and Herbert was left in the care of three aunts who had the responsibility of bringing him up. They evidently made a splendid job of it.

It is perhaps appropriate that Herbert Sutcliffe was not born in Pudsey because although that town has always been extremely proud of him—even to the extent of once discussing whether he should be invited to be the mayor—he was far from being a typical Pudsey man. And although he had some strong Yorkshire characteristics such as his natural caution, his dourness and his intrepid determination never to give in, he was by no means a typical Yorkshireman—and certainly not a typical Yorkshire professional cricketer.

He did not speak with a Yorkshire accent and some typical Yorkshiremen who were members of the team, although they had great respect for him, have confessed that in secret they regarded him as a bit "la-di-da". He fitted into the atmosphere of Lord's and

Herbert Sutcliffe, aged 76, and his wife, Emmie, on their golden wedding day in 1971. With them is their dog, Susie.

the cricketing establishment just as well as he fitted in at Headingley.

The king of cricket writers, Neville Cardus, summed Sutcliffe up inimitably in his "Autobiography." "It is not known and will never be known," he wrote, "what Rhodes and Robinson in their hearts thought of Sutcliffe, who made his hair resplendent with brilliantine and wore immaculate flannels and on the whole comported with an elegance which in the Yorkshire eleven was unique and apocryphal. He did not speak with the accent of Yorkshire but Teddington. He would refer casually to the fact that he had yesterday "mootered" down from Pudsey to London. Witnesses could be called to testify that at Lord's Sutcliffe has held up fast bowlers in the middle of their approaches to the wicket and with a wave of his bat has removed some obstruction to his vision in the pavilion, probably a peer of the realm, who has bent double and crawled away into invisibility while members have gone red in the face at him and said 'Sit down sir, sit down!' Sutcliffe rose to the highest place amongst batsmen of his period and rose there as much by self-esteem as by technique. He simply refused to bow before the best bowler in the world. I have seen him beaten by five consecutive balls in a test match and at the end of the over he has crossed his legs, reclined on his bat and surveyed the scene with the air of one not to be touched by vicissitudes that affect common folk. In a Lancashire and Yorkshire match he was fielding close to the wicket on the leg side. The batsman hit a ball straight at him and it struck him a cracking blow on the ankle. For a second he was compelled to forget himself. For a moment he hopped about in undignified pain. But when one or two of his colleagues, including Emmott Robinson, came towards him to see how badly he was hurt he recovered poise and waved them from him as though saying 'Thank you, but we Sutcliffes do not have pain.' The county capable of containing a Rhodes, a Robinson and a Sutcliffe is, I should say, capable of anything besides having as many acres as words in the Bible."

Judged by his appearance, his temperament and his demeanour Sutcliffe should have been an amateur. He would have fitted into today's classless cricket environment much more easily than he fitted into the professional/amateur environment of the 1920's and '30's. For if any Yorkshire cricketer was suited to the role of walking out of a separate gate at Lord's or Old Trafford, that most tasteless of all pre-war cricket discriminations, it was Sutcliffe. He had far more appearance of aristocratic elegance than the Yorkshire skipper, Brian Sellers, who lumbered out onto the field with a gait which could only be compared to that of a slightly drunken sailor in a slightly choppy sea.

In fact Sutcliffe was at one time (before Sellers's day) offered the captaincy of Yorkshire without amateur status being involved. There are at least two versions of this incident. According to J. M. Kilburn in his "History of Yorkshire Cricket 1924–1949" there was a rare fluttering in the journalistic dovecotes when a suggestion of the appointment of Sutcliffe was first made known. After a committee meeting on November 2nd, 1927, a letter was sent to South Africa where Sutcliffe was on tour with the MCC team led by R. T. Stanyforth in the following terms: "Dear Herbert, At the committee meeting yesterday you were appointed captain for 1928 without your status being altered. It is hoped that this will be agreeable to you and that you will accept the same and be happy and successful in your new and honoured position. Best Wishes, F. C. Toone, Secretary." But Sutcliffe replied by cable addressed to Lord Hawke, the chairman, stating "Official invitation received yesterday. Many thanks/you and committee. Great honour. Question carefully considered. Regret to decline. Willing to play under any captain elected." A special committee meeting was promptly convened at which, by a unanimous vote, the captaincy was offered to William Worsley.

But according to Leslie Duckworth in his book "Holmes and Sutcliffe: the Run Stealers" it did not happen quite like that. He says that during November the Yorkshire committee met at Sheffield and afterwards announced that Sutcliffe had been elected captain in succession to Major Lupton, reportedly by a majority of two votes. Subsequently they had had second thoughts about the matter following complaints from members that if a professional was appointed captain it should be Wilfred Rhodes. They cabled Sutcliffe asking if he would consider withdrawing his acceptance of the position.

Mr. Duckworth says the Yorkshire Yearbook for 1928 does not relate that the committee sent a letter to Sutcliffe but merely that the trouble which threatened had been obviated by the action of Sutcliffe who cabled from South Africa a message expressing the honour done to him but declining the office and intimating his readiness to play under any other captain. "This," says Mr. Duckworth, "let the Yorkshire committee nicely off the hook and they then offered the position to Captain W. A. Worsley." He adds that he thinks Sutcliffe subsequently regretted his withdrawal and thought that he should have stuck to his original decision to accept the captaincy.

Whatever the truth of this, Sutcliffe remained a professional for the rest of his playing career. But if he was never an amateur he was always a gentleman and I have never heard a harsh word said against him. Bill Bowes said of him in a tribute on his death in January, 1978, aged 83: "He never did anything mean or underhand. His personality had the same characteristics as his batting. He was reliable. He was the first to admit that he had not the same ability as Hobbs, Wally Hammond or Len Hutton but he had concentration and the will to harness his ability. As a result he was England's most successful batsman of all time."

J. M. Kilburn referred to him in the following terms in the course of an eloquent tribute published in the Yorkshire Post and subsequently published in Wisden: "Courage and concentration were his basic attributes. No prospect daunted him, no difficulty dismayed him, no crisis upset him. He was an artist of the dead bat and an uncompromising hooker of fast bowling. He sought solution to his batting problems by taking them as they came, one at a time. He never allowed the present to be influenced by the alarums of the past or fears for the future. In the means and manner of his performances he raised enormous prestige for himself throughout the cricketing world. He was admired and respected wherever he played and by his refusal to depreciate his own value he raised the status of his profession."

My last sight of Sutcliffe was on the Headingley turf on which I had seen him score so many runs, on Saturday, August 13th, 1977, the third day of the England v. Australia test. I had seen Geoffrey Boycott on the Saturday score his hundredth century and he, with Hutton and Sutcliffe, the two other Yorkshiremen to make a hundred hundreds, had their picture taken together before the start of play. Sutcliffe looked his usual smart self with a large white rose in his buttonhole but he had been suffering from acute arthritis for some years and had to be brought onto the field in a wheelchair. It was a most moving occasion.

But my last personal contact with him was in November, 1976, when I sent him a copy of my book "Nowt So Queer As Folk" in which I had written briefly of my boyhood worship of him and concluded by saying "There may well be great batsmen still to walk down the pavilion steps at Headingley to cricketing glory but there will never be another Herbert Sutcliffe and as my letter to him at Melbourne 47 years ago was never posted let me take this opportunity of thanking him in print for all the joy he brought to me between 1928 and 1939. For I am glad to say that he is the only hero of my boyhood who is still alive, although now over 80."

I had a letter from him by return, written painfully by hand from the nursing home in Gargrave where he was detained, thanking me for my "supreme kindness" in sending him a copy of my book and telling me about the birthday party being arranged for him at which Fred Trueman was to propose his health. He added thoughtfully "I will ask Bill (his son) to get a dozen or so copies for my Leeds shop. Once again my best thanks. Yours sincerely, Herbert Sutcliffe. P.s. My arthritis gets no better." That letter gave me more pleasure than any other I received.

4 THE GOLDEN AGE

My guide, philospher and friend during my cricketing boyhood was my father. He was a player of no greater distinction than I proved to be, which is not saying very much, but his love for the game was lifelong. Apart from his family and his business it was his only interest. He and I, and later my younger brother, would go very regularly to practically all the grounds in Yorkshire where the county were playing, sometimes arriving for the start at 11.30 and sometimes, when the weather was doubtful, for the resumption of play after lunch at ten past two. And we were watching cricket and talking cricket the whole time.

One of the characteristics of the Yorkshire cricketing crowd which distinguishes it from most other cricketing crowds is that conversation is an essential part of the proceedings. Not just conversation with your own companion but with everyone else around you. This applies on the popular side as well as the members' enclosure but in the latter the sense of fraternity is deeper. The Yorkshire County Cricket Club today has around 12,000 members and yet they are almost as closely linked and as talkative to one another as the members of a small Rotary club or luncheon club. They have not much interest in the administration of the club or its finances and only in exceptional circumstances go to any of the meetings. But they have a tremendous common interest in the fortunes of the Yorkshire team and a partisan spirit of such unquenchable assertiveness that it is the despair of visitors from all other counties. All their sympathies are with their own team and all their support and encouragement, praise and censure, are lavished on them. A visiting player will be applauded politely when he reaches his 50 and applauded again when he reaches his century, but that is all. When a Yorkshire player reaches his 50 the cheers echo round the ground and when he reaches his century there is something approaching mass hysteria.

The only cricketing supporters who approach Yorkshiremen in their undisguised partisanship are those from the neighbouring county of Lancashire and the old story about the spectator at the Roses match at Headingley who shouted "well played" when a Lancashire batsman hit a boundary is no doubt founded on fact. His accent being unidentifiable a Yorkshireman sitting next to him demanded of him "Are you a Yorkshireman?" "No" was the reply. "Then are you Lancashire?" "No" was again the reply. "Then shut thi mouth. It's nowt to do wi' thee" was the rejoinder.

The main topic of conversation at Yorkshire county matches is the current performance of the team. In the 1930's when Yorkshire won the championship 7 years out of 10 there was general satisfaction in the members' enclosure. God was in his heaven and all was as it should be in the cricketing world. In the 1970's, when Yorkshire did not win a cricketing trophy once, the climate has been rather different and there has been an air of dejection and despair. The supporters at times have looked more like a crowd of mourners round the graveside than cricket lovers round the pitch. The constant inadequacy of the team's performance has meant that happiness has only been achievable by looking back to more prosperous times and this they have done with unrestrained zeal. If you go to a Yorkshire match today the conversation will not be so much of Boycott and Hampshire and other current players, but of Close and Illingworth and Trueman and the others who played when Yorkshire had a team worth talking about—when they last won the championship in 1968.

But this preoccupation with the past was also a feature of cricket watching conversation in the 1930's and my father always seemed to be talking with his neighbours about the players of former days. My father's cricketing boyhood had been at the turn of the century—now called the golden age of English cricket. He spoke lovingly of A. C. MacLaren and Tom Hayward, S. F. Barnes and L. C. Braund, J. T. Tyldesley and R. Abel, G. L. Jessop and C. B. Fry, P. F. Warner and K. S. Ranjisinjhi, B. J. T. Bosanquet and R. E. Foster, George Gunn and J. T. Hearne and his Yorkshire heroes during this period, J. T. Brown and John Tunnicliffe, David Denton and David Hunter, George Hirst and Wilfred Rhodes, Lord Hawke and the Honourable F. S. Jackson, Schofield Haigh and Edward Wainwright, T. L. Taylor and Ernest Smith, Major Booth and Alonzo Drake.

This was certainly the golden age of Yorkshire cricket. The team had been rebuilt from what had been described as a drunken rabble by Lord Hawke who took over the captaincy in 1883 and won the first championship victory in their history in 1893. They went on to win it five years out of seven between 1896 and 1902.

Lord Hawke was undoubtedly the chief architect of Yorkshire's greatness as a cricketing county and my father described him as an autocrat and a martinet but a man who did more to raise the standard and welfare of county cricket than any other of his contemporaries.

In this classless age it is difficult to realise how lowly the status of the professional cricketer was in the 1880's and 1890's. He was very poorly paid in the summer and received nothing at all during the winter. But because he was a public entertainer he was often the victim of misplaced generosity on the part of cricket supporters and frequently deteriorated into a hard-drinking, fast-living degenerate with little sense of self-discipline or self-control. When Lord Hawke (or the Honourable Martin Bladen Hawke as he then was) took over the team from the easygoing professional leadership of Tom Emmett in 1883, after playing under him for a couple of years, he realised that revolutionary changes were necessary and set about making them.

Since the formation of the county club in 1863 Yorkshire had achieved nothing under Emmett and his three predecessors, Ephraim Lockwood (1876–77), Joseph Rowbotham (1871–75) and Roger Iddison (1863–1870). They had plenty of talent in such batsmen as William Bates and Louis Hall, bowlers such as Edward (Ted) Peate and Robert (Bobby) Peel and all-rounders such as Tom Emmett and George Ulyett but their fielding was lackadaisical—they were said to be too polite to run anybody out!—and their general approach to the game was undynamic.

Hawke soon made changes. He set an inspiring example himself by his own dedicated approach and gave his professionals an incentive by introducing bonus payments based on a system of marks for meritorious performance. Fielding and general deportment rated as high as scoring runs and taking wickets. These rewards were distributed at the end of the season when all his players were summoned to a feudal gathering at his home, Wighill Park, Tadcaster. The biggest amount ever paid was £52 10s. to George Hirst.

Hawke also adopted a white rose as the county's emblem, acknowledging the borrowing

Four famous players in Yorkshire's Golden Age—top left Louis Hall, top right Lord Hawke, bottom left the Hon. F. S. (later Sir Stanley) Jackson, bottom right Schofield Haigh.

of the idea from Lancashire who had previously taken over the red rose. He also introduced winter pay for all professionals and—not an altogether characteristic move—stopped the use of separate gates for amateurs and professionals at all Yorkshire grounds.

In return for these privileges he insisted on high standards of behaviour both on and off the field and not all players were able to reach them. They were dispensed with ruthlessly even when talented and valuable members of the team. One of the victims of the Hawke axe was the first of the great Yorkshire left arm spin bowlers, Edmund Peate, who was sacked in 1887 at the age of 31 for over indulgence in alcohol. Peate's chief claims to fame, besides his ability to consume alcohol, were his eight wickets for five runs against Surrey in 1883 and his run of success against the Australian tourists in 1882, when he took 63 wickets for an average of 12.9.

His matches against the Australians included that at the Oval in which the tourists won the series and the celebrated mock obituary was put in the Sporting Times: "In affectionate remembrance of England Cricket which died at the Oval, 29th August 1882. Deeply lamented by a large circle of sorrowing friends and acquaintances. R.I.P. N.B. The body will be cremated and the ashes taken to Australia."

Hawke said to Peate that dismissing him was one of his saddest tasks. "But he bore no grudge," he added, "and whenever I subsequently ran across him invariably he greeted me with the old familiar smile and the same slow, spontaneous 'Good morning, my lord. I hope you are as well as I am'." Such was the respect for their superiors of 19th century professional cricketers!

Incidentally, Peate's successor as Yorkshire's main left arm bowler, Bobby Peel, another cricketing character of the period, was also sacked by Lord Hawke for insobriety just 10 years later. Apparently Peel, who was also an accomplished batsman, doing the double in 1896, came down for breakfast before a match at Chesterfield in a very well-oiled condition. George Hirst, realising what the consequence would be if the captain saw him, persuaded him to go back to bed. Hirst then went to the ground and reported to Lord Hawke that Peel was indisposed and would not be able to turn out that morning. Hawke accepted the explanation, lost the toss and led his team, including a substitute, onto the field.

As they went out Hirst observed to his horror that there were 12 of them—and that the twelfth was Peel, who was staggering about in a worse state than he had been earlier. Hawke took in the situation at a glance and ordered Peel to leave the field. Peel demurred and observed that he felt in fine form and to prove it seized the ball, took a run up to the wicket and bowled it in the direction of the sight screen. Then, according to one report, he urinated on the wicket. Hawke seized him by the arm and led him firmly from the field and out of first class cricket for all time. "Nothing," wrote Hawke, who was evidently something of a masochist, "ever gave me so much pain."

Lord Hawke captained Yorkshire for no less than 27 years from 1883 to 1910. During this period Yorkshire won the championship no fewer than nine times and in one period of nine years lost only 18 matches, 134 being won and 91 drawn. In 1900 and again in 1908 they were unbeaten. Yorkshire's establishment as the premier cricket county undoubtedly owed a great deal to him and so did cricket in general. After his retirement he occupied practically every important position in the game, including the presidency of Yorkshire and of the MCC. Besides being a remarkable captain he was also a very competent batsman. He had 679 innings for Yorkshire and scored 13,429 runs with an average of 19.7.

Although credited with abolishing the separate gates for amateurs and professionals he was not exactly a cricket democrat and one of his chief claims to fame was his famous observation "Pray God no professional shall ever captain England." This classic bit of reaction was expressed at the annual meeting of the Yorkshire County Cricket Club in 1925. He was commenting on an article by Cecil Parkin, the Yorkshire-born Lancashire bowler, attacking the leadership of A. E. R. Gilligan, then captaining the MCC team in Australia. Much of Lord Hawke's reputation for high-handed autocracy rests on this remark, which he must have lived to regret. But he was brought up in the age of the superiority of the amateur and even in 1925 his views were not as outrageous as they seem today. He was naturally conservative in his outlook and although he was responsible for so many radical changes in the organisation of county cricket he never welcomed any change that he did not personally inspire. It is one of the ironies of cricketing history that the first professional who became captain of England was a man who was not considered suitable to captain Yorkshire—Len Hutton.

Lord Hawke was one of several gifted amateurs who contributed to Yorkshire's success story in this golden age. It was, of course, the era of the amateur in cricket generally. Famous names included A. C. MacLaren, the captain of Lancashire, C. B. Fry, classical scholar and a triple Blue at Oxford, one of the greatest all-round athletes of all time who in 1901 scored six successive centuries (a feat only equalled by Bradman), K. S. Ranjisinhji, the Indian prince who became a legend in his own lifetime, and Gilbert Jessop, the Gloucestershire big-hitting batsman who, it was claimed, once scored 101 out of 118 in 40 minutes at Harrogate, smashing the pavilion clock and putting one six through the roof of a cab outside the ground, causing the horse to bolt and not stop running until arrested in Leeds, 15 miles away!

Yorkshire's quota of gifted amateurs was little less illustrious, including Lord Hawke, the Hon. F. S. Jackson, T. L. Taylor, Frank Mitchell, Ernest Smith and Clem and Rockley Wilson. Jackson, by far the most accomplished, was one of my father's boyhood heroes and was a member of what has been described as the best England test team ever to step out onto the field. It took part in the test series with Australia in 1902 which my father talked about most volubly because he was at boarding school at the time and recalled having the pictures of both teams decorating his study walls. He could recite them all without effort and did so on innumerable occasions. They included A. C. MacLaren, C. B. Fry, K. S. Ranjisinhji, J. T. Tyldesley, A. A. Lilley, G. H. Hirst, G. Jessop, L. Braund, W. H. Lockwood and Wilfred Rhodes.

Jackson certainly ranks with the greatest of English amateurs, although he is not particularly prominent in cricket records because, unlike the others, he was very much a part-time cricketer—a fact which makes his performances all the more remarkable. He was just as prominent in politics as he was in cricket, representing North Leeds as an M.P. and being at one time and another a financial secretary to the War Office, chairman of the Conservative Party, a Privy Councillor and the Governor of Bengal.

He did not even devote all his leisure to cricket, being also greatly interested in grouse shooting and golf, which he played to a handicap of one. C. B. Fry sang his praises very loudly and said that following the retirement of Arthur Shrewsbury of Notts., Jackson was the best batsman in the country on all wickets. "He had versatility," wrote Fry, "and what, for want of a better term, we call genius."

He was appointed captain of England in the series against Australia in 1905 and distinguished himself by heading both the batting and the bowling averages, scoring 492 runs with an average of 70.28 and taking 13 wickets at 15.46, and also by winning the toss in all five tests. He departed from the cricket scene to become Governor of Bengal and arrived in that country to become the victim of a potential assasin. He described this incident as the "quickest duck I ever made." In his latter years he succeeded his close friend Lord Hawke as Yorkshire president.

R. C. Robertson-Glasgow has written of him: "He had dignity without pomp; diplomacy with simplicity. He is a chapter in cricket history. For the amateur has passed from cricket and the pro-consul will soon be a story."

When he died a memorial service was held for him and was attended by a large congregation. The Bishop who conducted it recalled afterwards that there were hundreds of mourners at the service and that as he looked down on the rapt faces of the vast congregation he could see "how their hearts went out to that great man, how they revered him as though he were the Almighty, only infinitely stronger on the leg side."

My father ranked Ernest Smith as the next high in talent to F. S. Jackson although the records do not support this. But he was apparently an extremely attractive batsman to watch and a more effective bowler than his figures indicate. He was headmaster of a school in Eastbourne and was one of several amateurs who came into the Yorkshire team during the holidays.

Lord Hawke wrote of him that as a batsman he was an unknown quantity. "He might fail and, of course, did at times, but when he came off he made his runs more fiercely and faster than anyone else in the side and there was an audacity about the way in which he placed his scoring shots that completely perplexed opposing bowlers. He did not leap out like most hitters but stood firm footed. Like Jehu he drove fast and furious. On his initial appearance for Yorkshire he had the unusual experience of 'bagging a brace' though receiving only one ball, his partner running him out in the second innings before he had faced a ball."

In view of this commendation it is curious that the only place Ernest Smith has in the Yorkshire records is that of spending the longest time at the wicket without scoring. This occurred in a match against Essex at Leyton in 1905 in which J. W. H. T. (Johnny-won't-hit-today) Douglas had an inspired spell of bowling and took five Yorkshire wickets in eight balls, all clean bowled, including the hat trick. Yorkshire began the final day in a hopeless position and when Smith went to the wicket there was an hour still to survive. At the close he was still there and had not opened his score.

That Smith should hold the record for slow scoring is all the more surprising when one considers the competition he had from the man who was undoubtedly the most consistent slow scorer in Yorkshire's history—Louis Hall. He played during an earlier period—from 1873 to 1894—but I heard a great deal about him from my father because he came from Batley, which was our home town. Louis Hall must have broken more bowlers' hearts in his time than any other batsman there has ever been. He opened the innings with George Ulyett for many years and carried his bat through the innings much more frequently than any other Yorkshire player has ever done—no fewer than 14 times. Sutcliffe comes next with six. In 10 of these marathon innings Hall scored less than 100 and in five innings scored no more than 50. His lowest scores were 37, 34, 32 and 31.

Hall's run rate rarely averaged more than 15 an hour and sometimes dropped as low as 10. George Davidson, the Derbyshire bowler, once bowled 14 consecutive maiden overs to Hall before retiring fuming and frustrated. Some of his slowest innings were against Kent. In 1885 he spent 165 minutes getting 12 against them at Canterbury (including a runless spell of 70 minutes) and at Headingley in 1882 he spent 210 minutes getting 29. His slowest recorded innings was the 40 he scored in 4 hours and 25 minutes against Notts. in 1887.

Even Hall had wild aberrations at times, however, and my father gleefully recalled a charity match he played in at Batley in which the captain of the opposing side was none other than W. G. Grace. Hall amazed him as much as the crowd by hitting him for a six right out of the ground. My father also recalled the occasion when Hall was in the midst of one of his stone-walling marathons and an exasperated spectator shouted out to the man fielding at point "Get nearer, point, he wean't hurt thee if he hits thee wi' t'bat."

Hall was a tall, shambling fellow with a long, lugubrious face and was popularly known as "the Batley giant." In contrast to most members of the Yorkshire team in his day he was a strict teetotaller and non-smoker and a prominent Methodist lay preacher. His influence on the less self-disciplined players was said to be enormous and he was regarded with fond affection by everyone, including Lord Hawke, who often called upon him to lead the side in his absence.

Hawke has written of his indebtedness to Hall particularly during his early days as captain when he found the Batley player's shrewd knowledge of the game invaluable. Ulyett, his opening partner, known as "Happy Jack," was an admirable foil to Hall, being as adventurous in his batting as Hall was dour and as adept at beer-swilling as Hall was at bible-punching. Ulyett scored 15 centuries for Yorkshire and Hall 9.

By a rather odd coincidence Hall's successor as opening batsman, John Tunnicliffe, was also a teetotaller, non-smoker and lay preacher but that was about as far as the comparison went. He came into the side in 1891 with a reputation as an aggressive, swashbuckling batsman with Pudsey Britannia but, probably under Hall's influence, he learnt to curb his hitting instincts and formed with J. T. Brown an opening partnership which outshone that of Hall and Ulyett and in Yorkshire history is second only to that of Holmes and Sutcliffe. The most famous of their 19 opening partnerships of over 100 was the 554 they made against Derbyshire at Chesterfield in 1898—a record which stood until Holmes and Sutcliffe broke it against Essex at Leyton in 1932.

It is recorded that Tunnicliffe's contribution of 243 was made on an empty stomach and after a sleepless night. The match was being played at Chesterfield for the first time and Tunnicliffe had been given unsatisfactory lodgings where he missed the evening meal and also missed his night's sleep because he thought the bed was damp. He missed breakfast to catch an early train to the ground and after batting through to lunchtime found that there were no luncheon arrangements for the players and had to queue with the crowd at the refreshment tent. He had just been served with a sandwich when the bell went for the resumption of play.

Tunnicliffe, known as "Long John" because of his height, was as famous for his slip fielding as for his batting and in a career lasting 15 years took 678 catches—a total exceeded only by Wilfred Rhodes' 704 catches in a career spanning 34 years.

His partner, John Thomas Brown, was small and thick set and became the more

Back row: T. Mycroft, J. B. Wostinholm (Sec.), Rhodes, Tunnicliffe, Hunter, Whitehead, J. Hoyland (Scorer), A. Shaw.
Centre row: Wainwright, T. L. Taylor, Lord Hawke (Captain), Haigh, Hirst. Front row: Brown and Denton.

The Yorkshire team that won the championship in 1900, and again in 1901 and 1902.

aggressive of the two. He toured Australia with A. E. Stoddart's team in 1894/95 and contributed much to England's victory in the rubber with 140 in the final test at Melbourne. My father recalled going to his benefit match at Headingley in 1901. He was an extremely popular player and his benefit realised £2,282, easily a record at that time. But Brown's career was brought to a premature end in 1904 when he died from a heart condition at the tragically early age of 35.

Very often the mainstay of Yorkshire's batting in the golden age was David Denton, whose career spanned the period 1894 to 1920. A wonderful number three in the batting order he scored 33,608 runs for Yorkshire—a total exceeded only by Sutcliffe with 38,561. He scored 61 centuries for the county and ended his career with an average of 33.27. My father recalled Denton as an adventurous, attractive batsman and a very hard hitter. He was known as "Lucky Denton" because of his penchant for giving chances which were not accepted. He was also renowned as a great fielder in the deep and apparently hardly ever missed a catch. Denton made only 11 appearances for England but would undoubtedly have made more if his more celebrated Lancashire contemporary, J. T. Tyldesley, had not established himself as England's number three.

Three other golden age cricketers my father talked about were David Hunter, Edward (Ted) Wainwright and Schofield Haigh. David Hunter was Yorkshire's wicketkeeper from 1888 to 1909 and during those 21 years had 372 stumped and 965 catches. A quietly spoken, good humoured, unassuming individual, very tall for a wicket-keeper (over six feet), he was referred to by one cricketing historian as indisputably "the best wicket-keeper never to play for England." The reason for this was the same as it was in the case of other notable players during this period—they flowered at a time when the orchard of cricket talent was heavy with fruit.

Hunter did on two occasions what none of his distinguished contemporaries—A. A. Lilley of Warwickshire, Gordon McGregor of Middlesex and Storer of Derbyshire—ever did—he was responsible for six dismissals in an innings. In the 1891 season out of 3,500 runs scored while he was keeping wicket only 25 byes were conceded. He was not an outstanding batsman but usually could be relied upon in a crisis. When he went in last man against Derbyshire at Chesterfield in 1897, 16 runs were needed for victory and as he walked out of the pavilion he heard the Derbyshire secretary call for champagne to celebrate the home team's victory. "You can put those bottles away" snapped Hunter. He joined George Hirst at the wicket and, having got off the mark with a single, promptly hit three fours and a three off successive deliveries.

Hunter was a Scarborough man of diverse pursuits. He was a fine clog dancer, a keen follower of the hunt, a weight lifter of considerable local fame, a skilled bell ringer and a breeder of canaries. He was also, like Tunnicliffe and Louis Hall, a lifelong total abstainer—one reason perhaps why Lord Hawke invariably chose him as his deputy when absent.

Ted Wainwright, a tall, craggy Sheffield player, whose cricket career spanned the years 1888 to 1902, was one of only 13 players who have taken more than 1,000 wickets for the county—he took 1,173 at an average cost of 17.24. He was also an accomplished batsman and scored over 12,000 runs with an average of 22. He has been immortalised by Neville Cardus in his book "Close of Play." In Cardus's early days he was assistant coach to Wainwright at Shrewsbury School and Cardus gives an hilarious account of how he impressed Wainwright with his accurate bowling to one of the masters who insisted on having a net at a very innopportune time. Both Wainwright and Cardus were tired after a school practice. "I was furious," Cardus wrote. "Don't argue" said Ted "coom and get it over. There'll be half-a-crown for thee anyhow." I told him I didn't want the half-crown. "It's the principle" I argued. "Well" said Ted "if tha doesn't want to bowl at him tha knows what tha can do—hit him in't cobbles."

But, says Cardus, he was too young to know what was meant by cobbles and bowled his off breaks in his usual manner. The wicket had, however, become somewhat worn and dusty and one of his off breaks pitched on a very bare spot, "came back like a knife and sped upwards at an acute angle smack into the batsman's bladder. And he never wore a protector or box. He bent double with a stifled groan but before we could get down the wicket he drew himself erect and waved us away. But he decided he had better not continue practice that day. He tipped us and apologised for putting us to inconvenience. After he had departed and we were down again in the professional dressing room Wainwright chuckled richly. "By gum," he said, "tha's a sight better bowler than I though tha were. Anybody as can hit t' batter's cobbles when he likes is a bit of all right". Cardus protested in vain that he had hit the man in his vulnerable area purely by accident but Wainwright's reply was the classic Yorkshire declaration of unbelief. "Tha's tellin' me?" he said.

Schofield Haigh was the junior member of the great triumvirate which led and dominated Yorkshire's bowling attack in this golden age, the other two, of course, being George Hirst and Wilfred Rhodes. The contribution of these three players to Yorkshire's cricketing greatness between 1898 and 1914 cannot be overestimated. In their careers Haigh took 1,916 wickets at an average of 15.42, Hirst 2,569 at 17.86 and Rhodes 3,608 at 16.00. They are far and away the greatest wicket takers in Yorkshire's history and not one of the great bowlers of modern times, including Bowes, Macaulay, Verity and Trueman, took half as many wickets as Wilfred Rhodes. In the frequent absence of F. S. Jackson Yorkshire bowling strength was virtually confined to Haigh, Hirst and Rhodes and often only these three names appeared in the match analysis. In his early days a fast bowler with an unusually long run up, Haigh later shortened his run, reduced his speed and became a medium paced off spinner.

Haigh was renowned for his happy disposition and has been described by A. W. Pullin ("Old Ebor" of the Yorkshire Post) as "the stranger to despair, the enemy of long-faced misanthropy and for 18 years the sunshine of the Yorkshire eleven." C. B. Fry wrote more relevantly "Jaunty and springy, he runs up, flattens himself over the crease with a long drag of his back foot and the right arm slings through like a catapult. The ball comes low and swift in the air and then cannons in from the off with a little kick. So you may meet Haigh and regret it . . ."

He took 100 wickets in a season nine times for Yorkshire and although his performances are apt to be under-rated by being compared with those of his two great contemporaries he has the distinction of taking more wickets for the county than anyone except Hirst and Rhodes and no Yorkshireman has more hat tricks to his credit than the three he achieved.

Born in a country district near Huddersfield, Haigh remained a simple countryman at heart despite his prowess in the cricket field and had an admiration and affection for George Hirst which remained with him all his life. He always looked apprehensively at Hirst if he missed a catch or misfielded a ball. He was not very articulate and the story is told of an occasion after his county career was over when he had to accept a cup as captain of a league side which had won it. He began his speech of thanks with a long pause followed by the words "I'm uncommon glad we've won t'cup." There was then another long silence after which he said once again "I'm uncommon glad we've won t'cup." The next silence was even longer than the last but was eventually broken by a team mate who shouted from the back of the room "Hey, Schofield, tell 'em tha's reeight glad we've won t'cup."

Of Hirst and Rhodes, of course, so much has been written in so many different media that there can be little left in the world to say. They stand astride the history of Yorkshire cricket like the Colossus with which one of them shares a name. Rhodes in particular linked the ancient with the modern cricketing world in a mammoth playing career of 32 years—from 1898 to 1930. He was the only player in the world who bowled to both W. G. Grace and Don Bradman.

The question is sometimes asked "Who is cricket's greatest all-rounder?" And the trick answer is that he batted right handed and bowled left handed and came from Kirkheaton near Huddersfield. Both Hirst and Rhodes had all these three qualifications. And although Hirst is unique amongst all-rounders in being the only one who has ever scored 2,000 runs and taken 200 wickets in a season—a feat he performed in 1906—there can be little doubt that Rhodes was the greater of the two.

Although it may be a subject for argument whether Rhodes was the greatest all-rounder of all time, his batting and bowling record is certainly the most impressive. He scored a total of 39,788 runs with an average of 30.80 and he took 4,184 wickets with an average of 16.70. He did the "double" sixteen times and for 36 years held (with Jack Hobbs) the records for the highest first wicket stand and the highest last wicket stand in test matches against Australia. He was, among a variety of other things, the oldest player ever to play in a test match, playing at the age of 52—beating W. G. Grace by two years.

Not that Hirst's figures are unimpressive. He also had a career lasting 30 years—from 1891 to 1921—scoring 36,191 runs at an average of 34.14 and taking 2,723 wickets at an average of 18.75. And he did the "double" 14 times. But where Rhodes gained his superiority was in test cricket. Hirst played for England in 24 test matches, scoring 790 runs and averaging only 22, and taking 59 wickets at an average of 30. Rhodes scored 2,329 test runs at an average of 30.19 and 127 wickets averaging 26.96. And, lest these test figures may seem unimpressive compared with those of modern test cricketers, it must always be remembered when making comparisons between then and now that test matches in the old days were much less frequent than they are today and for the most part against much stiffer opposition—chiefly Australia.

Hirst was six years older than Rhodes and joined the Yorkshire team seven years ahead of him—in 1891. He left school at the age of ten and was employed in Huddersfield as a wirer for a handloom weaver and later as a labourer at a local dyeworks. He did not have the immediate success with Yorkshire that Rhodes did subsequently and it was not until he developed a "swerver" that he came to the top of the bowling averages. Hirst can claim to be described as the father of what is now known as swing bowling because his swervers were the precursors of what are now called in-swingers.

Hirst and his contemporaries did not understand the technique of swing bowling as it is understood today and when questioned about it he would reply modestly that he was not really sure how he did it—sometimes it worked and sometimes it didn't. Hirst's swing, like that of today's bowlers, depended more on the state of the atmosphere than of the wicket but whereas modern bowlers regard dampness and humidity as their main allies Hirst looked to wind for his assistance. With a headwind rather than a crosswind blowing the unnatural behaviour of the ball was said to be "bewildering" and the famous Somerset batsman, S. M. J. Woods, expressed the feelings of many when he declared "how the devil can you play a ball when it comes at you like a hard throw in from cover point."

Rhodes's mastery by contrast lay in flight and spin. He did not beat batsmen into cowering submission but tempted them into indiscretion. By altering the pitch and flight of successive balls he would draw the batsman further and further forward like an angler playing a trout and would eventually lure him to destruction—in the shape of either a catch or a stumping.

Rhodes was always the schemer, plotting his opponents' downfall with all the subtlety of a Jacobite conspirator. He would set his field with what appeared to be absurdly unnecessary precision, moving say cover point a foot or two to left or right, but very often it would make the difference between a catch that was catchable and one that wasn't. It was said of Rhodes that he could pitch the ball so accurately that he could hit a coin placed a yard or two from the wickets but he told me himself that this was nonsense—that it would take him all his time to drop the ball on a newspaper. Even so his bowling was as fine precision work as any bowling ever could be.

The precision of Rhodes's field setting is illustrated by Bill Bowes in his book "Express Deliveries." He tells how, in a match against Essex, Rhodes was bowling against Joe Hipkin, a left hander, and Laurie Eastman, a right hander. "This meant that I was alternately mid-on and mid-off, retaining my position even though the batsmen changed ends, standing in a slightly different place for Eastman than for Hipkin. Says Wilfred 'Go back a bit Bill.' I went back a bit. 'Too far' says Wilf. 'Come in a bit.' I came in. 'Now a bit to your right . . . no, too far. Come back a bit . . . now in a yard . . . nay, nay, nay.' Despairing of ever getting me where he wanted me Wilfred walked across, scratched a big cross with his spikes and said 'See lad, stand theer.' I stood theer and three balls later Eastman made a vicious swipe and connected right in the middle of the bat. Had I been a foot on either side of that mark I should never have seen the ball. As it was I either had to catch it or it would have gone clean through me. Fortunately I caught it. Wilfred walked across to me and the only thing he said was 'You see, lad, always go wheer tha's put . . .' This little episode made more impression on me than almost anything else in my cricketing career."

As batsmen neither Hirst nor Rhodes were great stylists and were workmanlike rather than theatrical. Hirst was more attractive to watch, famous for his sweeping hook to leg for which he went right down on one knee. Rhodes was naturally a bowler who became a batsman by dint of sheer determination and perseverance. He is quite alone in cricketing annals as the man who stepped himself up in a few years from England number 11 to England number two, and as I have already said held the record with Hobbs for the first wicket and last wicket partnerships.

The most famous joint appearance of these two giants was the final test against the Australians at the Oval in 1902—a match which has been described as frequently as the battle of Waterloo. Australia won the toss and scored 324 in the first innings against an attack consisting of Rhodes, Hirst, F. S. Jackson, Lockwood and Braund. There was rain in the night and the following morning England lost six wickets for 83 on a sticky wicket. The follow on seemed inevitable but, thanks chiefly to Hirst, it was avoided by nine runs. Australia were bowled out for 121 in their second innings, leaving England to score 263 to win. They started badly and lost five of their greatest batsmen for 48—McLaren, Palairet, Tyldesley, Hayward and Braund. At this point Gilbert Jessop joined F. S. Jackson at the crease and the position at once improved but when Jackson was out for 49 and Hirst came in to join Jessop there was still a long way to go. Jessop now began to play his natural game and a hurricane of hitting followed, taking his score to 104 in an hour and a quarter. But more wickets followed and when the last man, Rhodes, came in England still needed 15. The legend is that Hirst met Rhodes on his way to the wicket and said "Sitha, Wilfred, we'll get 'em in singles" but when I asked them both many years later whether this was authentic they replied that they did not remember. Suffice to say that they did in fact get 'em in singles, Rhodes making the winning hit off Trumble.

Hirst and Rhodes were the only members of the Yorkshire team in the golden age that I was privileged to know personally and I have the clearest memories of them both. I never saw Hirst play for Yorkshire because he retired in the year I was born—1921—but I saw him play seven or eight years later in a charity match at Dewsbury, of which one of the main organisers was a friend of my father's who for many years was the captain of Dewsbury and Saville cricket team—Henry Hill. Henry Hill himself played for Yorkshire on a number of occasions and he had been instrumental in getting Hirst to play for his team in a friendly match with the local police. The event was widely advertised and several thousand people turned up to see the great man in action. My father and I had seats in the front of the pavilion and to my great delight I was introduced to Hirst before he went out to open the innings with Henry Hill. But to the general dismay Hirst was given out l.b.w. in the first over. Mr. Hill was furious when he himself returned to the pavilion later. "We get all these people to come here to see the great George Hirst and that bloody idiot of an umpire gives him out l.b.w.," he said. "It would have been bad enough if he had been out but that ball was half a yard off the wicket."

The last time I was to see Hirst was when I interviewed him for the Yorkshire Post nearly 30 years later at his home in Huddersfield. He was now a bent, frail, immensely genial old man of 82 but there was still a sparkle in his eyes and his smile, which Lord Hawke once said "went right round his head and met at the back," was still infectious. He told me he spent most of his time in an armchair by the fireside and when he became nostalgic looked through souvenirs which he kept in a cupboard. He showed me them—there were silver trophies of all descriptions and enough cricket balls to stock a shop. The one he was most proud of was a mounted half cricket ball—part of the ball with which Yorkshire dismissed the Australians for a record low score of 23. The inscription read "Yorkshire v. Australia at Leeds, June 1902. Yorkshire won by five wickets. Australia all out 23, Hirst 5 for 9, Jackson 5 for 12."

As A. A. Thomson has written in his delightful book "Hirst and Rhodes": "His ultimate gift was the rare one of growing old gracefully and those who only met him in his later days were impressed by his gentleness and could not quite recognise the tremendous dynamo of energy and pulsing vitality this frail old gentleman had once been. This quiet and serene quality represented the final mulling and blending of his

Yorkshire's greatest all-rounders, George Hirst and Wilfred Rhodes. Hirst is still looking cheerful in his coaching days but Rhodes in his old age has a more pensive, far-away look as he sits clasping his white stick.

integrity, his sense of rightfulness and fair play. There were great cricketers before; there are great cricketers now; and hopefully there will be great cricketers again. But in the history of the game George Herbert Hirst will always hold his own shining place, a romantic but essentially robust figure. A noble game is the nobler because he played it."

Wilfred Rhodes was quite a different character and his dour approach to cricket had nothing in common with Hirst's geniality. They were never, in Rhodes's words, "buddies." Rhodes had many positive virtues and as his colleagues have almost universally testified he was a great team man. But he lacked Hirst's natural warmth and geniality and was a more austere, ascetic, introverted individual altogether. He never used two words where one would do and had a brusqueness of manner which some found disconcerting. My first encounter with him was as a schoolboy at Park Avenue, Bradford. I and my companion saw him on the way in to the ground one day and summoned up the courage to ask him for his autograph. But he pushed our books aside and told us cursorily to "Hop it." I reminded him of this many years later and he allowed a smile to creep out of the corners of his mouth "They always were a damned nuisance, autograph hunters" he recollected.

Rhodes was the complete cricketer. Cricket to him was much more than a game; it was an art, to which he brought not only talent, enthusiasm and dedication but a vast fund of knowledge and a shrewdness which only the closest application over many years could possibly have compiled. He kept a mental dossier of the habits and failings of almost every batsman he bowled against and was not averse to passing on extracts from it to new recruits on his own side. As a batsman came in he would say to the fielder next to him in the slips "Here comes so-and-so—he nibbles at 'em on the off." Or "Pitch 'em well up on his leg stump and you'll have him fumbling."

Writing of Rhodes in the closing stages of his career A. A. Thomson comments: "As a bowler he plotted his destruction strategy with inexhaustible skill. If he did not spin quite so viciously as of old there was still not a man in England to touch him for length, direction and craft, in both senses of the word. If knowledge is power then Rhodes was not far off omnipotence. After all he now had probably got out every man who had batted against Yorkshire or England over the past 30 years. He knew the weaknesses, foibles, phobias, indiscretions and suicidal tendencies of every batsman in England. In his head, you might say, he had a complete psychiatrist's case book of every batsman in the country and he went through the whole gamut of what we might without disrespect call fundamental guile; that is, he could lull them with flattery, tease them with increasing temptation and finally drive them into an act of insensate folly by pitiless persistence."

A. A. Thomson tells many stories of Rhodes's unofficial captaincy of Yorkshire in his later years, assisted latterly by Emmott Robinson. According to these stories the real captain, be he Major Lupton or Captain Worsley or an amateur without army ranking, took very little part in the tactical and strategic decisions on the field of play and off it. Rhodes, the uncrowned king, reigned supreme. There is a story of the captain who came in at his usual modest position of number nine in the batting order, made a nice shot past cover and started to run. But suddenly a bell rang in the pavilion and the batsman at the other end turned to the captain in mid-wicket and said "Don't bother, skipper, Wilfred's declared."

Another story is of Yorkshire having a very bad day in the field, their bowling being treated most contemptuously by the visiting batsmen. The language of the bowlers grew warmer and warmer until it passed all bounds and the umpire was obliged to protest "How can I hear your appeals with all this chatter going on like a bloody parrot house?" At this stage of the anecdote the innocent listener (preferably a southerner) is expected to ask "But what on earth was the captain doing while all this was going on?" "Ah," says the narrator, who has been waiting for just this question, "Wilfred had sent him into the long field so that he couldn't hear all the bad language."

One of the most romantic episodes in Rhodes's career was his recall by England for the final test against the Australians at the Oval in 1926 when he was on the eve of his 49th birthday. The selectors, headed by P. F. Warner, and with Jack Hobbs and Rhodes as co-opted members, had a problem in finding a left arm slow bowler. Yorkshire's Roy Kilner had filled the role in the fourth test but it was felt that there should be a change. Warner has described the scene at the final selection committee meeting. "Wilfred," said Warner, glancing at him across the table, "we think you should play. You're still the best left arm bowler in the country and in a match that is to be played to a finish it's likely that we shall need one some time or other. You can still spin 'em you know." "And your length," observed P. A. Perrin "is as good as ever." "Well I can keep 'em there, or thereabouts," said Rhodes modestly but insisted that they needed a younger man. "And," said Arthur Gilligan, "you're making runs for Yorkshire." "Aye," said Rhodes "I am getting a few." "And your fielding's all right" said Hobbs. Rhodes permitted himself a wry smile. "The further I run the slower I get"· he commented

Rhodes played in the match with distinction. He took two for 35 in the first innings and with 4 for 44 in the second was instrumental in bowling out Australia for 125 and leading England to victory and the Ashes by 289 runs.

"Aye," he said many years later when reminiscing about this match, "t'pitch was getting better all the time. They should have put me on sooner."

I had the distinction of seeing the last over he ever bowled. It was in 1949 and I went as a Yorkshire Post feature writer to Silcoates School near Wakefield to see him bowl a ceremonial first over in the school's new cricket field in a match between the school past and present and the Craven Gentlemen. He was now 72 and his sight was beginning to fail but he kitted himself out for the occasion in his white flannels, cricket boots and a Yorkshire cap and bowled six balls of impeccable length and direction to A. B. Sellers who was acting as captain of the Craven Gentlemen to the plaudits of a large crowd. It was a touching occasion.

The last time I met him was some years later when I went to Huddersfield to interview him and George Hirst about their cricket recollections. I went to see Hirst first but although he was keen enough to talk about cricket in general and said how much he was looking forward to the Australians coming that summer he was not keen to reminisce or to express his views on modern cricket. "I haven't got any views" he smiled. "Not for publication anyway. I had my day and I enjoyed it immensely but I've passed out of the picture. If old cricketers can't enjoy the game without finding fault with modern day players they want to stop it. They want to stay at home."

He shook his large, oval-faced head and his blue eyes twinkled. "But go and see Wilfred. He can't see much these days but his views are as sound as ever. I bumped into him yesterday and he was giving me a proper lecture. I'll bet he'll give you one too."

But Rhodes was not to be drawn at first. "What's the good of me talking?" he asked.

"I have had my day and I enjoyed it. My sight's gone now and I can't even see you properly in that chair never mind see a cricket match. And folk will only say that the silly old so-and-so wants to keep his mouth shut."

But keeping his mouth shut about cricket was very difficult for him and I was soon getting the lecture Hirst had promised me. I was absorbed by a closely reasoned and highly technical discussion on the inadequacy of the l.b.w. rules. He went on to talk about the Australians and said how temperament was all-important in test cricket. "I never used to notice the test match atmosphere until I got back and played for Yorkshire again" he said. "Then I noticed the difference."

He launched into another technical discussion about the virtues of playing off the back foot. "The Australians are better players off the back foot than we are. We are apt to over-coach forward and under-coach back."

He surveyed the matter from all angles and stood up to demonstrate more effectively. "The head needs to go out first you see and the leg follows."

I could see him in his mind's eye driving the ball crisply through the covers to the boundary and listening to the applause from the crowd. "But no-one wants my ideas" he said abruptly. "I've had my day."

He looked at me very keenly. "What did George Hirst tell you?" he asked—I had told him I'd been to see Hirst previously. "He told me" I replied "that you would probably give me a lecture."

He smiled and a faraway look came into his eyes. "Aye" he reflected. "It's a great game. We were talking about back play weren't we? I remember once in Melbourne . . ."

I was very late getting back to the office that afternoon.

Hirst died in 1954 at the age of 83 and Rhodes in 1973 at the great age of 95. His blindness was a remorselessly increasing disability as old age wore on and although he still went to cricket matches for a long time and could often be seen sitting in the corner of the pavilion at the Scarborough festival with his white stick by his side, looking as fresh-faced as a man of 60, he eventually had to resign himself to his cricketing memories. They must have been more extensive than those of any other cricketer in the history of the game.

5 THE ROSES MATCHES

Test matches were the main attractions of the cricketing calendar when I began watching cricket although there were precious few of them compared with now. In the whole of the 1930's only 36 test matches were played in England—15 against the Australians, 5 against the South Africans, 6 against New Zealand, 6 against the West Indies and 4 against India. Only the Australians and the South Africans qualified for the privilege of five tests in a season, New Zealand and the West Indies having three and India only one in 1932, although this was raised to three in 1936. And my home ground, Headingley, only got test matches when five were played in a series so throughout the 1930's there were only four tests at Headingley—against the Australians in 1930, 1934 and 1938 and against South Africa in 1935. Nowadays there is one every year.

I have already described the Bradman-dominated tests of 1930 and 1934. In 1938 the maestro only scored 103 out of Australia's total of 242, which was enough to give them a five wicket victory. It was not one of England's most distinguished performances, due perhaps to some extent to injuries. Only hours before the England team was due to be announced, and certain to include Hutton, Leyland and possibly Paul Gibb as a substitute for Ames of Kent who was injured, R. W. V. Robins won the toss for Middlesex in a match against Yorkshire at Lord's and put the visitors in to bat on a fiery wicket. The results were disastrous. Hutton sustained a broken finger, Leyland a fractured thumb and Gibb severe concussion.

In the emergency Hardstaff of Notts. was brought in to fill one of the batting vacancies and England, who won the toss, had to open with Edrich and Barnett and had two wickets down for 34. Hammond was top scorer with 35 out of England's total of 223. Australia replied with 242 and the match was evenly balanced. But England collapsed in their second innings and were all out for 123, O'Reilly taking five for 56 and Fleetwood Smith four for 36. Australia lost five wickets scoring the 107 needed for victory.

So, having so few test matches to get excited over, we had to expend our passions on other fixtures and the Yorkshire v. Lancashire Roses matches admirably filled the bill. Almost every Whitsuntide and August bank holiday in the 1930's I spent in the company of my father and eventually my younger brother at Headingley, Bramall Lane or Old Trafford. The Roses matches were always arranged at these holiday weekends, alternatively at one of the Yorkshire grounds and at Old Trafford in order to attract the crowds—and attract them they certainly did. If the weather was any good at all there were rarely less than 20,000 people present on the Saturday and the attendance on the Monday was often over 30,000. Sometimes the gates had to be closed and several thousand people would be locked out altogether. There is nothing remotely like it in county cricket today.

Why the fixture attracted this interest and produced these crowds is hard to understand because as cricket matches go they were far from exhilarating. Indeed they were often deadly dull. It was said as a joke that there was a traditional ban on boundaries before lunch but in my experience it was no joke at all. And there were precious few boundaries after lunch!

Many matches were essays in lethargy and inactivity. The object seemed to be not to score runs but simply to stay at the wicket all day—and hopefully all next day as well. Both sides seemed to work from the start on the assumption that there was very little chance of a result and that the purpose of the encounter was not to win but to avoid losing. It was a curious philosophy but the players of the period were thoroughly indoctrinated with it and any attempt at bright cricket was frowned upon. There have been various explanations given as to why a crowd of such magnitude turned up to watch these great sleeps, ranging from the triumph of hope over experience to downright masochism, but turn up they did.

Of course partisanship in these matches was so pronounced that if it were your side that were inflicting the boredom it was a good deal more bearable than if it were the enemy—and naturally no one not a Yorkshireman or a Lancastrian ever went near the fixtures. If Sutcliffe was as slow as a tortoise you made excuses for him—it was a difficult wicket, the light was poor or he was tired after his century the day before. But if it was Hallows or Makepeace who made 35 before lunch you tore him to shreds.

There were specialists in inflicting boredom on both sides. I shudder as I recall the agony inflicted by such people as Hopwood and Watson of Lancashire. And no doubt many Lancastrians shudder equally at the memory of Arthur Mitchell. Mitchell was one of the second tier of Yorkshire batsmen and never in the same class as Sutcliffe and Leyland, but nevertheless played for England on a number of occasions and was a very reliable number three in the Yorkshire team for most of his career, which stretched from 1922 to 1939.

The adjective to describe his batting is "dour." The crowd rarely derived any pleasure from it—and neither, to all appearances, did he. He had a long, narrow, lugubrious face and an expression which at best was a frown and at worst a scowl. He wore his cap slanted over one eye at an angle of 45 degrees, which gave him a slightly sinister air and altogether he would have looked more in his element at a graveside than on a cricket field. According to some of his colleagues he was never known to give a word of praise to anyone and it is recorded that when Ellis Robinson once made a spectacular dive and caught the ball brilliantly in his fingertips before rolling over and over Mitchell growled at him from the slips "Gerrup, tha's making a bloody exhibition of thisself."

It is quite probable that Mitchell derived as much enjoyment and self-fulfilment from the Roses matches as from any other activity he ever engaged in. He seemed to revel in playing the ball more with his pads than with his bat and competing with the long-dead Louis Hall in the time taken over scoring runs. Against Lancashire at Old Trafford in 1933 he took nearly seven hours to score a century and at the same ground in 1939 took over two hours to score 30. It was at this juncture of the 1939 match at Old Trafford that according to Neville Cardus the stillness was broken by a voice weary and outraged. "Every bloody year 'e cooms 'ere, this so-and-so Mitchell, and 'e spoils Bank 'Oliday. Every so-and-so year." Silence again, disturbed only by the sullen and muffled bat of Mitchell. More maidens. The voice, of a man in a hard bowler hat, was raised again: 'Every bloody year, every so-and-so year.' Thus far he had addressed nobody in particular; it was an apostrophe to abstract reason and justice and toleration. But now,

Arthur Mitchell (left), with his cap at its usual angle and his face set in its usual glum expression, ruined many a Bank Holiday for Lancastrians according to Neville Cardus. Emmott Robinson, right, another great Yorkshire cricketing character immortalised by Cardus.

he directed himself to the crowd around him.

'Every so-and-so bloody year 'e cooms 'ere. I said to my missus this mornin', "Ahm goin' to Old Trafford and what's more that so-and-so Mitchell'll stay in all bloody day, that 'e will. Every so-and-so year 'e does it, and 'e'll do it agen." That's what ah said to ma missus. And look at 'im; 'ere he so-and-so bloody well is.' "

I often had the same thoughts about Hopwood and Watson.

In all the glorious literature of cricket no-one has ever written or ever will write about the Roses matches with the depth of understanding and the humour of Neville Cardus. Indeed his writing on these matches almost constitutes a literature of its own. He invested them with a prose of such charm and distinction, and at the same time with such verisimilitude and wit, that they cease to be mere cricket matches and take on all the pomp and circumstance of an Elgar march performed by his beloved Halle.

He described the matches in his book, Autobiography, as "a play and a pageant exploiting the genius of the two counties."

"To watch it rightly you needed the clues; for years I lacked it and missed the point. There is slow play and slow play at cricket. There are batsmen who cannot score quickly because they can't, and there are batsmen who can score quickly but won't. In a representative Lancashire and Yorkshire match of 1924 to 1934 runs were severely discountenanced. No fours before lunch, on principle, was the unannounced policy; and as few as possible after. But fours or no fours, runs or no runs, the games touched greatness because of the North of England character that was exposed in every action, every movement, all day."

As a boy I always found the Old Trafford matches much more attractive than those played at Headingley or Bramall Lane, firstly because of the fun of getting there and secondly because of the thrill of being isolated in the heart of the enemy's territory.

Cunard, the shipping company, have or used to have as their motto the phrase "Getting there is half the fun." That was certainly the case with Roses matches at Old Trafford. My father was the most hopeless automobile navigator in the history of the motor car and we invariably took the wrong road. The journey across the lonely Pennine moors was not as simple in those days as it is now, with the M62 motorway linking Yorkshire and Lancashire, and there were several different routes to pick from. These were usually distinguished from each other by the name of the remote Pennine inns which one passed and my father's favourite route was past the Nont Sarah's. But invariably he would take a wrong turn going through Huddersfield, and although I would invariably advise him of this, he would invariably ignore me and finish up on the road leading past the Floating Light.

This would put him in a bad temper and for the next half hour he would complain bitterly that I should keep a better look out—it was no good expecting him to know which was which because he was concentrating on his driving. Although it is inconceivable to anyone who knows the road we would often get wrong again in going through Oldham and by the time we reached Manchester it felt as though we had travelled half way to Australia.

But my father's navigation was not the only cross there was to bear. If it was the Whitsuntide fixture we would invariably run into the Roman Catholic processions which were a great feature of Whitsuntide in the Manchester area. We rarely saw anything of the processions but we saw a lot of the masses of people attending them. There would be police on horseback controlling large crowds of onlookers en route and motorists

Four great Lancastrians: top left Ernest Tyldesley, top right Neville Cardus of the Manchester Guardian, bottom left George Duckworth, bottom right Eddie Paynter.

A view of Old Trafford, scene of many Roses matches in the 1930s at which the gates had to be closed, so big were the crowds.

were as popular as the plague. Indeed the main road was invariably closed and traffic would be diverted through a maze of side streets which probably would have succeeded in losing a good navigator, never mind my father.

"It's these damned processions again" he would protest as we ran into our first traffic jam. By now time was becoming critical, for it would never have done to miss the first ball of the day, and as we sped along the side streets searching for an exit my father's apprehension grew.

Over the course of several years these processions turned him from being a tolerant Protestant into a violent anti-Papist. "Blast these Roman Catholics" he would roar as 11.30 moved nearer and we went in circles round the labyrinth of side streets. I am sure that if we had ever missed Holmes and Sutcliffe coming out to bat he would have protested to the Pope in person about it but fortunately we never did.

It was the Catholic processions which persuaded him in about 1936 to find a new route to Old Trafford, avoiding the centre of Manchester altogether—which I imagine is what most Yorkshiremen had been doing for years. He got one of his Manchester business contacts to provide him with a detailed route and it became my job to read the instructions to him as we approached Manchester along the Oldham Road.

I remember the main things I had to watch out for were the Roxy cinema and a public house called Help the Poor Struggler which, believe it or not, was run by the judicial hangman, Albert Pierrepoint. I think we had to turn left at the Roxy and right at the Poor Struggler but it may well have been the other way around. Suffice to say that the new route was extremely complicated and that we never seemed to go the same way twice, with the result that when the war came in 1939 we were still getting hopelessly lost among the docks at Salford or in the burgeoning industrial estate at Trafford Park.

A great mental cheer went up when we eventually came within sight of the cricket ground, where we would run into the serious problem of getting rid of the car. There would be hundreds of cars and thousands of pedestrians milling round the ground and finding somewhere to park required both patience and parking skill, neither of which were qualities with which my father was over-endowed. By the time we had eventually found a berth for the day and got out our sandwich-bag, rug and cushions the gates had usually been closed to the masses and only members could now gain admission.

We, of course, were not members of the Lancashire club but as members of Yorkshire we were entitled to enter the pavilion once we had paid our ground admission. Most of the commissionaires and turnstile men were well aware of this and we usually had no trouble. But occasionally we would come up against a turnstile man who was difficult and there would be a long and acrimonious argument about our rights as Yorkshire members and sometimes a more senior official of the club had to be called to sort the matter out.

So by the time we had found ourselves seats we were, to say the least, a little frayed at the edges, and if Lancashire were batting it was essential we got one or two quick wickets to settle us down. If Yorkshire were batting it was essential for the same reason that they got off to a good start.

As I have said the partisanship at these matches was intense. Along with most of our confraternity we wore our white roses militantly in our lapels and rejoiced without reserve or diffidence in being Yorkshiremen. We'd show the old enemy how cricket was played!

Sometimes we did and sometimes we didn't. When we did we delighted in becoming objects of envy and hostility and when we didn't we smarted at having to expose ourselves to ridicule and disdain. When Yorkshire wickets were falling a red-faced Lancastrian would inevitably exclaim from three rows behind "These white roses seem to be wilting a bit. Haven't you wattered 'em or summat?"

Such remarks were treated by the Yorkshire contingent with the contempt they deserved. But despite all this fierce partisanship the two clans were quite well disposed towards each other at heart. There was no brandishing of bottles or other expressions of violence such as one gets at Manchester United football matches these days. The contest was on the cricket field and off it the only type of battle was verbal. Indeed sometimes we would become quite friendly with each other and indulge in harmless gossip about the weaknesses of our players and the failings of our respective county committees and there would be the inevitable exchange of reminiscences about past heroes—Hornby, Barlow, Brearley and MacLaren; Hirst, Denton, Jackson and Haigh.

Strangely enough I find that few details of the matches remain at all clearly etched in my memory. I can remember all the players vividly—Lancashire as well as Yorkshire. Makepeace, Hallows, Watson, Hopwood, the two Tyldesleys, Ernest and Richard, Macdonald, Paynter, Eckersley, Iddon, Sibbles, Pollard, Oldfield, Phillipson, Duckworth, Nutter, Green and Washbrook. But when I try to recollect the matches I cannot separate one from another. All blur into an amorphous picture dominated by an interminable partnership between Watson and Hopwood, or an interminable innings by Arthur Mitchell.

All except the Whitsuntide fixture of 1933. That I remember very clearly indeed. We had had our usual eventful trip over the Pennines—rather more hazardous than usual in fact, because we had run into patches of fog on the peaks and narrowly avoided the massacre of several sheep—but when we arrived, at the last minute as usual, it was to hear the news that Yorkshire had won the toss and had elected to bat. Holmes and Sutcliffe opened as always but Holmes was soon out and, as I read later, declared on returning to the dressing room that the wicket was so bad that the match would be over in a day. But he had not reckoned with Mitchell. Mitchell came in number three and batted for the rest of the day—practically six hours—scoring 123. The Lancashire crowd spent most of the day denouncing him and even we Yorkshiremen had to admit that he had not provided exactly stimulating entertainment. But we returned across the Pennines that evening well satisfied with our score of 341.

We battled our way through the Catholic processions on the Monday just in time to see George Macaulay open the bowling before a crowd of over 35,000. By now the wicket was in a very bad state indeed and Macaulay, one of the most aggressive cricketers who ever lived, evidently sensed that it was to be his day. He bowled his medium pace off cutters with an accuracy and a deadliness which made him virtually unplayable and as the Lancashire wickets clattered our excitement mounted and by mid-afternoon they were all out for 93. Macaulay had taken 7 for 28, including the hat trick.

Sellers, the Yorkshire captain, had no hesitation in enforcing the follow-on and in their second innings Lancashire could do no better. They were skittled out before close of play for 92, Macaulay taking 5 for 21 and Verity 4 for 41. Macaulay's match analysis was 12 for 49, his best bowling performance, and he is said to have commented on returning to the pavilion that he could have bowled 'em all out again before close of play!

It was the most magnificent day's cricket I had ever seen, just as it would have been the most disastrous if Yorkshire had been bowled out twice in a day and lost the match by the margin which Lancashire had—an innings and 150 runs.

6 PERCY HOLMES'S CIRCUS

If the 1900's were Yorkshire's golden age the 1930's were certainly their silver age. Indeed purely in terms of championship achievement the 1930's have a slight edge, Yorkshire being champion county seven years out of 10 compared with five in the 1900's. But in the other five seasons in the 1900's Yorkshire came second three times and third twice, whereas in the three seasons in the 1930's in which they failed to win the championship they came third twice and sank as low as fifth once. Compare this to the 1970's when they never won the championship once and in six years out of the decade were thirteenth, tenth, fourteenth, eleventh, eighth and twelfth and the contrast between then and now requires no further comment, unless it is that the 1980's could hardly be worse!

There were no doubt many secrets to Yorkshire's success in the 1930's. The first was undoubtedly the talent of the players. No team could win the championship seven years out of 10 without tremendous talent and Yorkshire's talents were prodigious in the 1930's.

The captain in 1930 was A. T. Barber who had distinguished himself at Oxford University and the regular twelve consisted of Holmes, Sutcliffe, Oldroyd, Leyland, Mitchell, Barber, Rhodes, Robinson, Macaulay, Wood, Verity and Bowes. Rhodes retired at the end of the 1930 season and Oldroyd and Robinson retired in 1931, Holmes in 1933 and Macaulay in 1935, and their places were taken by Wilf Barber, who became the regular number three, in 1931, Hutton, Smailes and Ellis Robinson in 1934 and Yardley in 1936. The captaincy changed from A. T. Barber to F. E. Greenwood in 1931 and from him to Brian Sellers in 1933. Others who played during the 1930's but were never regular members of the team were Dennis, Fisher, Rhodes (A. C.), Turner, Davidson, Gibb and Jacques.

Of the "regulars" no fewer than 12 played for England at one time or another—Sutcliffe, Leyland, Mitchell, Rhodes, Macaulay, Wood, Verity, Bowes, Barber, Hutton, Smailes and Yardley—and seven of them were regular test cricketers—Sutcliffe, Leyland, Rhodes, Verity, Bowes, Hutton and Yardley. With talent of this order Yorkshire could not fail to be a formidable force in the 1930's.

Perhaps the second secret of their success was brilliant captaincy in the person of Brian Sellers. He was "educated" by those three peerless professors, Wilfred Rhodes, Emmott Robinson and Herbert Sutcliffe, and led the Yorkshire team from 1933 onwards with a dedication and a zeal unsurpassed in the county's history. He brought to the task superb qualities of leadership, determination and resolution and in all the comments which have been made on him by the players who served under him I cannot recall one which did not regard his captaincy as being of the highest calibre.

From my own brief acquaintanceship with Sellers I could judge that he was not an easy man to work for and that beneath his hail-fellow-well-met ebullience and charm lay a belligerence which did not draw the line at ruthlessness if he considered it was necessary. He demanded the highest standards from those under him and spared nothing of himself.

Percy Holmes, the gay cavalier, who shared in no fewer than 69 century opening partnerships for Yorkshire with Herbert Sutcliffe.

He would put fieldsmen in suicidal positions and expect them never to flinch. But usually he would reserve the most suicidal position of all for himself. He would never regard a game as not winnable until it was lost and it was woe betide anyone who took a more compromising view.

He was not a great player but he exploited his competence as a batsman to the fullest extent possible and by the standards of Yorkshire amateur captains his career batting average of 23.18 over 386 innings and 8,949 runs is very good. It compares with Lord Hawke's average of 19.77 and Major A. W. Lupton's 10.27—to name probably the most undistinguished.

Like many of the Yorkshire players in the '30's Sellers was at his best with his back to the wall and the innings I shall always remember is one he played in a Roses match at Old Trafford in 1946. Lancashire were poised for victory on the third day with Yorkshire 216 behind on the first innings and five second innings wickets down before lunch for 120. When Sellers came in to join Maurice Leyland the home crowd were enjoying the debacle enormously and the stout, red-faced Lancastrians standing in front of the pavilion entrance with pints of beer in their hands were deriving sadistic entertainment from making derogatory remarks about the Yorkshire batsmen in voices loud enough to agonise the eardrums of every Yorkshire supporter within hearing. "No guts about 'em—no guts at all" one of them kept saying.

My father and I listened to them with growing desolation as our white roses drooped and I think we both prayed to the Almighty to make the impossible happen—as He sometimes did in cricket matches. Our prayers were answered. Leyland and Sellers dug themselves in with unflagging resolution and stayed at the wicket together for the rest of the day. Nothing Lancashire could do could shift either of them. They did not score many runs but runs were superfluous anyway. The sole object of the grim battle was to prevent Lancashire gaining the victory they had felt absolutely certain of gaining at lunch-time. As the Lancastrians in the pavilion doorway sank from disappointment to despair and descended from raillery to abuse the Yorkshire spirits soared. They were Sellers' and Leyland's finest hours.

But as I say the greatest tributes to Sellers' captaincy are the observations of the players who served under him. Probably the best book ever written by a Yorkshire cricketer is Bill Bowes' "Express Deliveries" published in 1949 and with Bowes the only survivor today of the team of 1930—and with only Hutton, Robinson and Yardley left of those who joined the team during the 1930's—Bowes' recollections are a unique and irreplaceable record and I am greatly indebted to him for giving me permission to quote extensively from his book in this chapter.

Of Sellers he writes very shrewdly as follows: "Sentiment had no place in Sellers' make-up; a man could either do his stuff or he could not and if he could not then he must go. I have so often seen him come into the dressing room, look round the players and say 'I trust you are all fit.' The man with aches and pains would grin. The man who was nursing a pulled muscle would say 'Well, not too fit, skipper.' 'Do you want to play or not?' skipper would demand. 'If you can do your stuff play and if not you're resting. No-one knows better than the man himself.' Never did he say to the outfielder 'Do you think you can manage if you field in the slips?' Never did he suggest that a man should play under hardship. The side came first and in all cases of doubt the player was dropped.

"This feeling for the side was perhaps the only factor which prevented him enjoying his cricket to the full. Even on his greatest days he always wondered if he was pulling his weight. In his prime he was one of the best fieldsmen in England. He was a dynamic captain, a keen student of the game and the rules and he would bring an umpire to order as easily as a player. At times he was a martinet but he loved the team as cricketers and always one could detect that modest trait in him which made him constantly question his own ability.

"When he took over the captaincy he came 'in his stockinged feet.' His average with the second team in 1931 had been 14.7 and although in 37 innings with the first eleven in 1932 he averaged 25 he wisely continued to seek the advice of his senior professionals on matters of policy. What Rhodes, Robinson, Sutcliffe & Co. didn't know about the game was hardly worth knowing and in Sellers they had an apt pupil. Gradually he assumed the full mantle of captaincy and by 1938 he was unquestionably the best captain in the world. He made fewer mistakes than most and would listen to advice.

"Brian Sellers did a grand job. We shall always cherish the memory of that dominating, self-assertive figure whose personality made him the most colourful of captains."

But although the talent and the captaincy were two of the secrets of Yorkshire's success in the 1930's there was a very important third—the indomitable, inimitable, irrepressible team spirit. All the members played always for the team, never for themselves—neither for their own glorification nor their own pockets.

First class cricket in those days was not the attractive commercial proposition it was to become in later years and although Yorkshire players were well paid in relation to most other cricketers it was by no means a lucrative profession, even for the stars such as Sutcliffe and Leyland. No T.V. advertisers paid them for promoting their products and no Sunday newspapers paid them for their ghost-written comments on the game. The most they had to look forward to was a benefit of a few thousand pounds after at least 10 years' service. It would no doubt be untrue and unrealistic to say of 1930 cricketers that they were not interested in money, but it was certainly not their god. Their god was cricket and they worshipped it as a team.

Bill Bowes describes in "Express Deliveries" how the team became known as the Yorkshire "circus". They arrived late one night at an Oxford hotel and the girl at the reception desk told them all the rooms were taken. "By whom?" demanded Percy Holmes. "Jack Hilton and his band" replied the girl. Percy took out his pen and signed the book. "We're the same sort of party" he said. "Percy Holmes and his circus." "Why didn't you say so at once?" the girl said. "That described us perfectly . . . a circus," Bowes comments.

In another part of the book he is a little more explicit. "Somebody once said to me that it was an education to watch the Yorkshire team in the field. They had a smoothness and precision which was a delight not only to the spectators but to the players. All of us who played in tests—myself in particular, having played so often in mixed MCC teams—noticed afresh each time we returned to Yorkshire the closely-knit cohesion of our own team. Automatically after each delivery the Yorkshire fieldsmen would glance at the bowler and skipper. A glance, a nod or an almost imperceptible movement of the finger was enough to move a man ten or fifteen yards; a wave of hand would send the fine leg or third man round by as much as fifty yards. Every man was a specialist fielder for a particular bowler. Wilf Barber was always my deep leg man, Maurice Leyland third man and Herbert Sutcliffe first slip. Arthur Mitchell was my slip on the leg side, Brian Sellers was short leg or gulley if I was bowling with two gulleys. Most important

Holmes and Sutcliffe in front of the scoreboard at Leyton, Essex, in 1932 when they broke Brown and Tunnicliffe's record partnership for the first wicket.

of all, no fieldsman was ever permitted to become heartily tired of one particular position.

"We had a captain moreover who was something of a slave driver. He never permitted himself to give in and woe betide anybody else who did. The new ball must never be bounced because the shine had to be kept on it as long as possible. Bowlers must never need to stoop or run after the ball. When fielded the ball must go back from hand to hand to the bowler. It was ridiculous, Brian felt, that a succession of fieldsmen should have to bend to pick up the ball. Experimental throws could be made at the bails to see if the wicket-keeper was awake but only after the umpire had called over, otherwise a bad throw might give byes. Attention to these and many other small details all contributed to the smooth performance of the team."

Bowes goes on to say that the Yorkshire players were at all times students of the game. They lived and talked cricket. Most remarkable was the unity achieved by eleven vastly different characters. "Think of them. There was George Macaulay, a fiery temperament with a rapier wit; Sutcliffe, immaculate and orderly; Leyland, pleasant and easy-going; Verity, studious and careful; Percy Holmes the irresponsible; Arthur Wood the irrepressible."

But Bowes' most illuminating comment on the Yorkshire team spirit is earlier in his book when he describes his induction into the mysteries of county cricket by Wilfred Rhodes and Emmott Robinson. "If I found that playing with Yorkshire had now become more remunerative I also discovered that it meant much more mentally and physically. 'Now that you've got your cap and you're one of us' said Emmott Robinson 'you have to study this game.' I was recommended to get a book and keep a cricketing ledger. Primarily I had to study the strong points and weaknesses of batsmen and to make notes about wickets. Indeed so thoroughly did the Yorkshire team study the game that we knew all about the umpires too.

"To Wilfred Rhodes and Emmott Robinson—and I am not forgetting the early encouragement and help of Walter Brearley—I owe most of what I learned of first class cricket—and Hedley Verity shared my debts.

"Every night at about 10.30 those two would come and collect us in the hotel lounge and off we went to a bedroom. There the shaving stick, toothbrush, hairbrush and contents of a dressing case would be pushed around the eiderdown to represent the fieldsmen as all our mistakes of the day were discussed in detail.

"They were hard and exacting task-masters but they were right, always right. On the night after Hedley Verity took his seven wickets for 26 runs against Hampshire we found Emmott and Wilfred awaiting us in the lounge when Hedley and I returned from the pictures. "We've been waiting a long time—we'd better go, else it'll take 'till midnight" Wilfred growled.

"What, I wondered, had I done wrong? But there was no comment as we filed from the lounge to the quiet regions upstairs. We entered Emmott's room and with a skill born of practice and a thorough appreciation of the job in hand the masters placed the fieldsmen—the customary toilet articles—in position on the eiderdown. I obviously must be the culprit. My bowling figures for that day had shown 20 overs, 4 maidens, 43 runs and only one wicket. Hedley could rest assured. He was all right—with 24.4 overs, 11 maidens, 26 runs and seven wickets. Yes, seven wickets for only 26 runs. Hedley was as delighted as any youngster might be at such success.

"But as the toilet articles were placed in position I saw that they did not represent the field I had been using. "Now then, Hedley," said Emmott "what did you do today?"

"Hedley stuck both his hands into his pockets, stuck out his chest and did a little pleased bend at the knees like a contented father with his back to the fire talking to his son, smiled and replied "Seven for 26 Emmott."

"Emmott smote the woodwork at the foot of the bed in his disgust. 'Aye, 7 for 26 and it owt to 'a been seven for 22. Ah nivver saw such bowlin'. Whativver wa' tha doin' ter gi' A. K. Judd that fower?"

"According to Emmott and Wilfred the batsman would have had many more fours too if they had only given the thought to their batting that they expected Hedley to give to his bowling. It was a good performance in figures only.

"So far as I was concerned they wanted to know why, even after the new ball had lost its shine, I had persisted in giving all my attention to getting the opponents out. I had given too many runs away and generally speaking runs should be conceded only at the end where the wickets were falling or when runs played a secondary part in winning the match. I escaped much more lightly than Hedley.

"How could any young man coming into such an atmosphere get a swollen head? Yet they were not ogres and they believed the best time to tell a lad his failings was when he was riding on top of the world, not when he was down. Discussions in the dressing room, criticisms of players and events while sitting on the veranda, reference to fieldsmen and the qualities of their throwing—all this became part of the flow of our cricket knowledge. Often they joked but there was a good deal of truth in their jestings. The last thing they desired was to undermine our confidence and they had divers methods of restoring faith to the player who was down. With a transparent sincerity they desired everyone to do well, they played for the side to win and felt that the failure of one required a little bit of added effort from the others. It was a grand atmosphere in which to learn the game and appreciate colleagues and opponents."

My own memories of those Yorkshire players of the '30s are far sharper and clearer than those of any subsequent decade. This is not surprising because these memories were implanted on virginal material, so to speak, unmarred by critical perceptions and judgements. I was lyrical in my appreciation and unbounded and unwavering in my enthusiasm. The Yorkshire team were gods, every single one of them, and as such could do no wrong.

Now, 50 years later, as I indulge myself on that inexhaustible digest of cricket nostalgia, the Yorkshire County Cricket Club Yearbook, I am sometimes surprised to find that my boyhood heroes were perhaps a little nearer to common cricket mortals than I had imagined. It came as a shock the other day, for instance, to discover that Emmott Robinson scored no more than 9,444 runs for the county with an average of no more than 24.53 and took no more than 892 wickets for an average of 21.97. Good perhaps, but not quite the breath-taking all-round performance I had remembered.

Taking them in the "order of going in", to use the stock phrase which the familiar portly score card seller with the rolling gait at Headingley always employed as his theme song, Percy Holmes was, according to Bowes, the ballet master of the Yorkshire circus. This description was a tribute to his quickness on his feet which was probably his most outstanding characteristic. His movements as he positioned himself for a shot to fine leg or a square cut from a ball well outside the off stump would, says Bowes, have done credit to Pavlova. "He never fielded in boots, always pumps, and his dainty heel-toe walk gave him the appearance of bouncing over the ground. There was a daintiness

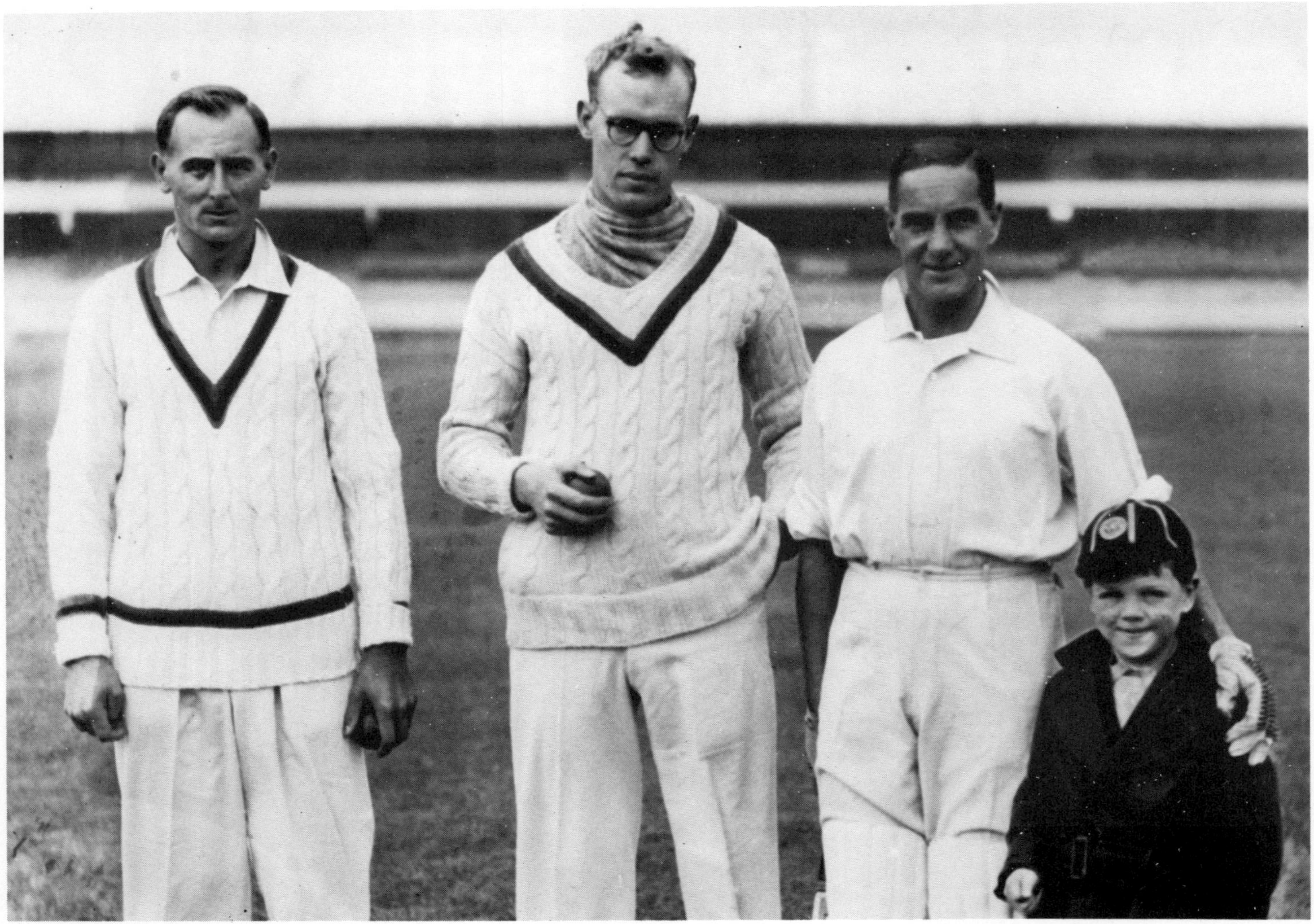

Hedley Verity, Bill Bowes, Herbert Sutcliffe and son Billy, a future captain of Yorkshire, pictured in 1933.

about all his cricket. A century by Holmes was an experience to remember for life."

Holmes had a remarkable capacity in an opening batsman for never being dull. No matter how devastating the opening attack or how critical the situation Holmes always started off as he meant to go on—briskly, bouncily, rather impertinently. By nature he was an incurable optimist and had an air of jaunty self-confidence and a disdain for all bowlers, whether fast, medium or slow. He was quite convinced of his power to make mincemeat of them and if they succeeded in getting him out he invariably attributed it to an unfortunate error on his own part rather than any inherent quality in the bowling.

Holmes was eight years older than his famous partner, Sutcliffe, and preceded him into the Yorkshire team by six years, making his debut in 1913. But the first world war took up four of these years and when Sutcliffe joined the team in 1919 Holmes had made little impact. The two of them first met, it is recorded, on the top of a tram on the way to the nets at Headingley. They noticed each other's cricket bags and got into conversation. For many years they believed they shared a birthday—November 25th—and always celebrated it in some way. It was not until Sutcliffe happened to look at his birth certificate quite late on in their association that he discovered that he had been born on November 24th.

When county cricket recommenced in 1919 Holmes and Rhodes opened the innings but Sutcliffe soon rose from number seven to take the place of Rhodes, whose primary value following the war-time deaths of Major Booth and Alonzo Drake was as a bowler. Their first partnership produced exactly nothing. Towards the end of June they had produced the first of their record 74 century opening partnerships—a massive affair of 279 against Northants.

They were a beautifully matched although very contrasting pair—Holmes full of dash and daring, Sutcliffe calm, stolid and imperturbable. Holmes was always thrusting aggressively in search of runs; Sutcliffe dour and determined and content to let runs come. That brilliant master of metaphors, R. C. Robertson-Glasgow, described Holmes as looking as if he were off to Aintree or Harringay, merely incidentally in cricket flannels, and Sutcliffe as if about to lay with a golden trowel the foundation stone of some hostel for deserving cricketers.

In his excellent book about these two, "Holmes and Sutcliffe—the Run Stealers," Leslie Duckworth says that both of them were masters of the technique of playing on difficult wickets, of knowing which balls must be played and which left alone, especially the latter, and of the art of playing with a dead bat which killed the lift and spin of a dangerous ball. He goes on: "Both loved the smell of battle. They would rather make 35 on a sticky wicket—and when did any modern batsman last play on a really sticky wicket anywhere?—than a hundred on a billiard table and neither knew when he was beaten, especially Sutcliffe."

But there was a tremendous rapport between the two players and this was nowhere better demonstrated than in their running between the wickets. Those who did not see the two of them bat together very often considered that the understanding between Hobbs and Sutcliffe was supreme but most Yorkshire supporters would have plumped for the Yorkshire pair. The statisticians have computed that in the 15 seasons they batted together one or other of them was run out only 22 times—an average of 1½ times a season. Holmes was the victim on 14 occasions and Sutcliffe on eight. This is a striking record for such a long association.

Holmes' misfortune as a cricketer was that he was a contemporary of Hobbs and Sutcliffe. Holmes had good claims to being the third best opening batsman in the country during his palmy days but because of the consistent prominence of Hobbs and Sutcliffe he played in no more than seven test matches and only once against Australia. Yet only a handful of other English batsmen have higher career averages than his 42 and when he retired he was among a select group of 36 who had scored more than 30,000 runs. Hobbs' opening partner with Surrey for many years, Andy Sandham, suffered the same deprivation. He appeared in only 14 tests, although he scored over 40,000 runs in his career with an average of 44.

There was a suggestion that Holmes blighted his chances of playing for England by causing offence to the Lord's establishment by backing away from the fast bowling of Macdonald and Gregory in his only test appearance against the Australians at Trent Bridge in 1921. No less an authority than Walter Hammond reported that "a famous cricket authority" seeing Holmes allegedly flinch declared "that man shall never go to Australia." This is an astonishing story because in the match in question against Australia Holmes opened the England innings with D. J. Knight of Surrey, Hobbs being unfit, and defied the full fury of the Australian pace attack for an hour and a half and was top scorer with 30. But Holmes was dropped for the second test and never played against Australia again.

If he did flinch against Macdonald and Gregory it was certainly completely out of character and it is far more likely that if he offended the Lord's establishment he did so by not sounding his aitches as clearly as his colleague Sutcliffe. There is no doubt that there was in the '30's—and probably still is—a certain antipathy towards cricketers born north of the line between the Wash and the Bristol Channel and Holmes is by no means the only Yorkshireman to have suffered because of his bluntness of manner. In later years Fred Trueman and Brian Close were both to be victimised for their refusal to touch their forelock.

Holmes bore his exclusion from international cricket with philosophic calm but that it rankled deeply inside him was indicated at the Oval in August, 1928, when, with an average for the season of 58.42, he expressed his disappointment at not being selected for the forthcoming Australian tour in an interview with the cricket correspondent of the Bradford Telegraph and Argus. He was reported as saying "I shall never play in a representative match again. In future all my first class cricket will be played for Yorkshire. Time after time I have made big scores when chosen for trial matches but however well I play I am persistently ignored when it comes to the test match. The only tour really worth going on is the Australian trip but they always pass me over for it and send me on the others which don't really matter. I have never complained before although since they left me out of the England side in 1921, after getting top score in that memorable first innings at Nottingham, I have felt sure that someone with influence is keeping me out of the honours. I am tired of the continual disappointment so I have decided to refuse any future invitations in these representative games. I shall be quite content to play for Yorkshire."

Holmes' career ended on a similarly sad note in 1933 when, after being third in the Yorkshire averages in 1932 with an average of 47, he had a disastrous season and finished with a total of 783 runs for an average of only 19. He was much troubled by a knee which an operation had not restored to full strength and it was felt in some quarters that he should have been given another season to prove his viability, so to speak. But the Yorkshire committee, then as now, were not noted for their generosity and announced in the July that at the end of the season his services would no longer be required. They evidently felt that they were giving adequate reward to Holmes for his 20 years of yeoman service by saying a few kind words about him in the Yearbook and giving him a parting grant of £250. It would have been more fitting if, like Hirst and Rhodes, he had been able to choose his own time of departure.

The Yorkshire committee were probably not stricken by remorse when the following advertisement appeared in the Yorkshire Post early in 1934 but they should have been. "Percy Holmes, first wicket batsman for Yorkshire. Too fit and young to retire. Engagements required for the season." The Daily Express to its credit answered the advertisement and Holmes was engaged to scout for new cricketers and to act as coach.

Thereafter it was back to league cricket with the Ebbw Vale and Swansea clubs until the second world war broke out and he went back to the sort of work he had started out on at the age of 13—in the mills. He worked in no fewer than nine mills in the Huddersfield area during the war and afterwards, until he was 70, coached at Scarborough College. By then he suffered badly from arthritis and he was obliged to use a couple of sticks to enable him to walk. Ironically Sutcliffe was to suffer severely from the same condition. Holmes attributed it to "too much standing on damp grass."

"Summers are not like they used to be" he told a correspondent of the Shefield Morning Telegraph on the eve of his 80th birthday. "I don't get to many matches these days. Now and again I read a bit of Cardus' stuff but reading books about cricket isn't the same when you're not playing it. My career is old history now. Cricket belongs to someone else, another generation. These days they can make some money out of the game. We got £5 a match and we had to pay all our own expenses when we were playing away and staying in hotels. It took me three years to save up £100 and I was a non-drinker at that." He died in 1971 aged 84.

Edgar Oldroyd, a small, rugged man who batted number three for Yorkshire for most of the years between 1910 and his retirement in 1931, was perhaps a more typical Yorkshireman than either Holmes or Sutcliffe. Holmes was too cheerful and ebullient and too lacking in the caution which is the watchword of every true Yorkshireman, while Sutcliffe was altogether too grand and lah-di-dah. Oldroyd expressed the essential spirit of Yorkshire, both in his batting, which was dour and painstaking, and in his personality, which was dogged to an extreme. Like that other scintillating run scorer, Louis Hall, he came from Batley where, when he was not playing cricket, he ran a successful rag business.

Most southerners are under the misapprehension that rag merchants are a variety of rag and bone men who collect old clothes from housewives in exchange for small sums of money or goldfish or balloons for the children. Yorkshire people know that rag merchants are the backbone of the shoddy trade, which has brought great wealth in its time to the towns of Batley and Dewsbury. Edgar Oldroyd, I am sure, made a great deal more money out of buying and selling rags than he made out of cricket and while Percy Holmes spent his old age working in a mill, Oldroyd spent his retirement in a detached house in Horsforth in comparative affluence.

Some friends of mine lived opposite him and were always curious as to why such a small man always drove such a large car. They also told the story of Edgar's nocturnal adventure when he was roused in the middle of the night by a wailing noise. According to Mrs. Oldroyd he bounded out of bed thinking it was an air raid warning and, donning his tin helmet, got out a bicycle he kept for the purpose in the garage and pedalled furiously off to his Air Raid Precautions post where he had been a keen air raid warden during the war. The point of the story was that this happened in 1947, nearly two years after the war had finished!

But although Edgar was comparatively affluent he took money very seriously, as every good Yorkshireman should. Bill Bowes tells a fascinating story of some tram rides by members of the Yorkshire team to the Leyton cricket ground during a match against Essex. "The first morning Edgar Oldroyd and Emmott Robinson joined me on the tram I bought the three penny tickets. When the three of us returned that night Emmott was most zealous that the penny debt should be promptly sorted out. "I'll get these" he said. "Tha' can buy mine on Monday, Edgar, and now gi' Bill a penny for t'fare this morning." "No, no, that's all right" I said, but Edgar gave me his penny saying "Nay, we'd better be reight." At that time I thought 'There's nowt so queer as folk,' but I found that this precision was customary between these two and when one became used to it one liked it."

My father, who was also in the rag trade in Batley, knew Edgar Oldroyd quite well and when we ran into him occasionally during the intervals in the Yorkshire matches they would exchange greetings and discuss the state of the shoddy trade. This personal contact with one of my gods thrilled me profoundly and when we walked round the pavilion enclosure at lunch and tea time I would pray for Oldroyd to emerge from the dressing room in his blazer. He was far from being a romantic figure but to me at the age of nine he personified some of the heroic qualities of Yorkshire cricketers. For Oldroyd's abiding claim to fame in my reckoning was that he had been knocked unconscious by a bumper from the Australian fast bowler who later played for Lancashire, E. A. McDonald. This incident had occurred at Old Trafford in 1926 and what struck me as the most tragic feature of the incident was not that Oldroyd had remained unconscious for some considerable time and indeed was out of cricket for the rest of the season. It was the cruel fact that it was discovered as he was carried off the field that he had touched his stumps as McDonald felled him and the bail had been disturbed, thus making him out, hit wicket. Incidentally Bowes reports that Oldroyd's first words on recovering consciousness in hospital were "Don't forget to let me have the insurance form."

Apart from this dramatic happening Oldroyd was never a spectacular batsman but he was always reliable and dependable and an outstanding player on bad wickets. He made 37 centuries for Yorkshire and scored 15,876 runs with an average of 34.6.

He was followed in the batting order by the stocky, broad-beamed, lion-hearted Maurice Leyland, undoubtedly one of the most popular Yorkshire cricketers ever to walk out of the Headingley pavilion. Next to Herbert Sutcliffe, Leyland was my greatest hero in the 1930's and many were the times I literally shivered with apprehension as he travelled through the nervous nineties to get another of the 62 centuries he made for Yorkshire in a career extending from 1920 to 1947.

I am sure Leyland very rarely joined me in this expenditure of nervous energy because, like Sutcliffe, he had an ideal temperament for the big occasion—complete self-confidence and complete imperturbability. He proved this by scoring 137 in his first test match against Australia and by his average of 46 in the 65 test innings he played for England, five more

Back row: M. Leyland, E. Robinson, A. Mitchell, F. Dennis, A. Wood, W. Barber, W. Ringrose (Scorer).
Front row: E. Oldroyd, G. G. Macaulay, W. Rhodes, Captain W. A. Worsley, P. Holmes, H. Sutcliffe.

The great Yorkshire team of 1929, the year I started watching Yorkshire cricket.

than his average for the 26,180 runs he scored for Yorkshire. He was a born fighter and the greater the crisis the greater his dependability.

I loved to see Leyland bat because, like so many left handers, he always hit the ball hard and almost always scored his runs quickly and effortlessly, not hesitating to lift the ball in the air and score sixes if the circumstances permitted. He was a delightful batsman to watch and although he had a wide range of strokes all round the wicket he was, again like many left handers, particularly strong on the leg. Of the many centuries I saw him score I remember above all others the first I witnessed—his 211 not out against Lancashire at Headingley in 1930—the biggest individual score in a Roses match.

If Edgar Oldroyd typified the cautious, shrewd, calculating, lugubrious, money-conscious Yorkshireman caricatured mercilessly by southerners, Maurice Leyland represented the warm, genial, magnanimous, happy-go-lucky type of Yorkshireman who is just as typical of the county although less eagerly publicised. He shared with Oldroyd certain qualities such as courage, fight, determination and utter dependability—but his character, like his batting, was much more colourful and more appealing altogether. I did not get to know Leyland until many years later when his playing days were over and even then I never knew him well. But what I learned when I met him and talked to him merely confirmed what I had always instinctively sensed about him—that he was a most lovable man—as straight as a die and not an ounce of guile, deception or malice in his whole make-up.

That he was above all an honest cricketer was communicated by his twinkling blue eyes. He was boyish in his appearance until quite late in life and when he spoke to you he looked you straighter in the eye than any other man I have ever known. Neville Cardus picked out this optical directness when he likened Leyland to those two other Yorkshire "laughing cavaliers", George Hirst and Roy Kilner. "His arms were long and after driving a ball straight for four he would stand quite still, arms down by his legs, and he seemed to be looking into the far distance. His eyes were frank and open. When he spoke he looked straight at you exactly as he looked at the fastest bowler. His face was boyish and he wasn't tall. His shoulders sloped a little but, as he said, he was broad in the beam. I don't think he had, or has to this day, any powers of deception. His cricket was like the man himself, absolutely honest."

He was a splendid team man and I am sure never had an enemy in his life. J. M. Kilburn, who is sparing with his praises, had this to say of him in his book "Thanks to Cricket": "Overseas or at home Maurice Leyland was the best of team companions. He accepted obligation and inconvenience with comforting imperturbability. In the phrase of his time he was invariably ready to 'make one' when delegates were required for a social function or other representative occasions. He would go without demur to a race meeting or a municipal banquet, join a darts match or a fourball at golf. In all circumstances he would enjoy himself and let his enjoyment be known."

Leyland had a great sense of humour and a ready wit. He did not believe in isolating himself from the spectators and many stories exist about his exchanges with barrackers while fielding on the boundary—as he usually did. He particularly relished his duels with spectators on the famous Hill at Sydney and perhaps his best rejoinder was to the man who said of a catch he had just missed "I could have caught it in my mouth." "Aye", replied Maurice, "and if my mouth were as big as thine so could I."

He did not always spare his team mates from his barbs of wit and it is recorded that when Arthur Mitchell once told Neville Cardus in Leyland's presence that he didn't think much of his writing because it was too "flowery" Leyland chipped in with the observation "Well, nobody can say that about thy batting, Arthur can they?".

This may have been the occasion when Cardus wrote a bitterly sardonic piece in the Manchester Guardian about Mitchell's marathon six hour innings in the 1933 Roses match at Old Trafford, to which I have already referred. Cardus recalls that the next day he met Leyland before the resumption of the match. "Tha's written a funny article in t' Guardian this morning, Mr. Cardus, about Arthur Mitchell," he said in his blandest tones. "Thanks Maurice" Cardus replied. "Aye," said Maurice, "and tha'll have to write a funnier one tomorrow." George Macaulay, as I have already reported, bowled Lancashire out twice that day for 93 and 92!

But perhaps Leyland's most widely-quoted observation to Neville Cardus was that on very fast bowlers—which, Cardus was later to complain, was often misquoted and attributed to the wrong player. "It was Maurice Leyland, let me say yet again," writes Cardus, "who during a discussion about very fast bowlers and bouncers summed up the session by saying 'The fact is that none of us likes fast bowling—but some of us doesn't let on.'"

Leyland's chief contribution to Yorkshire cricket was his batting but he was by any standards no mean bowler and if he had played for a team with less bowling resources than Yorkshire in the '30's he would have been employed far more than he was in that capacity. He took in all 409 wickets for Yorkshire in his 21 playing years for an average of 27 and was really much more of an all-rounder than he was generally thought to be. He was usually called on to try to break long partnerships and his bowling always added a little levity to the proceedings because nobody seemed to take it quite seriously. He had a peculiar little run up to the wicket and a rather odd action and he made great use of the Chinaman—the left hander's off break to the right handed batsman. But batsmen who did not take his bowling seriously often paid the penalty.

Leyland was one of the old brigade who turned out for Yorkshire in 1946 when cricket resumed after the six years of war and he helped Yorkshire to win the championship. But he was by now nearing 50 and at the end of that season he retired. He subsequently became a coach to the county but in his later years was afflicted by Parkinson's disease. I last saw him at his home ground in Harrogate in 1965 or '66 and although his blue eyes were as piercing as ever they seemed to have a faraway melancholy look in them instead of their earlier twinkle. When I read in London that he had died on New Year's Day 1967, aged 66, I felt as though I had lost a lifelong friend, whereas in fact I had had only a few desultory conversations with him in my life. Such is the relationship one forms with one's boyhood heroes!

I have already written of Mitchell and Rhodes who followed Leyland in the batting order in that season of 1930 and my next man in is the inimitable Emmott Robinson. I am never quite sure how much of Emmott Robinson is fact, created by God and Emmott's parents, and how much is fiction, created by his biographer in chief, Neville Cardus. For Cardus, Emmott Robinson was the original, archtypal Yorkshireman. He writes of him affectionately in many of his books and articles and sums him up succinctly in his 'Autobiography'. "Emmott Robinson was a grizzled, squat, bandy-legged Yorkshireman, all sagging and loose at the braces in private life but on duty for Yorkshire

Frank Smailes who joined Yorkshire in 1934 as the team's only all-rounder and Arthur Wood, wicket-keeper and team jester.

Left: Edgar Oldroyd, the dourest of number threes, and (right) Maurice Leyland, the brightest of number fours.

he was liable at any minute to gather and concentrate his energy into sudden and vehement leaps and charges and scuffles. He had shrewd eyes, a hatchet face and grey hairs, most of them representing appeals that had gone against him for leg before wicket. I imagine that he was created one day by God scooping up the nearest acre of Yorkshire soil to hand then breathing into it saying 'Now lad, tha's called Emmott Robinson and tha can go on wi' t'new ball at t'pavilion end.'

"Emmott cherished the new ball dearly; he would carry it between overs in person to the next bowler needing it after himself; and he would contain it in the two palms of his hands shaped like a sacred chalice. If some ignorant novice unnecessarily threw the new ball along the earth Emmott gave him a look of wrath and pain. He was not a great cricketer in technique but by passion, by talking and by taking thought he became so. But for me he will be remembered for the Yorkshire stuff in him. He had no use for the flashing bat school, 'brighter cricket' and all such nonsense. He dismissed it with one good word. 'Swashbuckle' he called it. Life had taught him to take no risks. On a cold, winter evening a member of the committee of the Yorkshire County Cricket Club was hurrying along a pavement in Bradford when out of the fog emerged Emmott carrying a black portmanteau. 'Hey. Good afternoon Mr. Holdsworth' he said. 'Ah'm pleased to meet you.' 'Good evening Emmott. How are you?' Neither had seen the other since summer. 'Hey' said Emmott. 'Ah'm a bit poorly Mr. Holdsworth. I've got a pain.' He indicated a place in his stomach. Mr. Holdsworth expressed anxiety. 'Now listen, Emmott' he said, 'you mustn't neglect it. Go to the hospital. Find out what it is. You needn't worry about expense if any is incurred. The committee will see to that.' Emmott pondered. 'Well maybe you're right Mr. Holdsworth. It's been hurting me weeks now. Maybe I will try t'hospital but . . .' He paused and then announced decisively once and for all 'Ah'm 'avin' no knife.' "

That really says, in the most brilliant way, all there is to say about this great Yorkshire cricketing character. Cricket was his whole life although strangely enough he came into the Yorkshire team quite late—at the age of 35, a time when most county cricketers are thinking about retirement. Despite his grey hair he kept himself remarkably fit and did not retire until he was almost 50.

This was not quite as old as his guide and mentor, Wilfred Rhodes, who played until the eve of his 53rd birthday, but in view of the fact that he bowled no fewer than 670 overs in his last season, taking 48 wickets for an average of 24, and scored 386 runs for an average of 25, it was certainly no mean achievement. When Emmott bowled an over he did not walk up to the wicket to deliver the ball as Rhodes did. He leapt off from his mark like a greyhound out of a trap and hurled himself into action in a veritable maelstrom of bandy legs and flailing arms and shoulders, into which a strange little hop, skip and jump were inexplicably woven.

Emmott was a perfectionist and was never satisfied with his own performance. Roy Kilner said of him that if he had taken all 10 wickets in an innings he would have wanted to dismiss the not out batsman to complete the job. No-one put more into his cricket than Emmott, whether he was batting, bowling or fielding. He was not uniquely gifted in any department unless it was fielding—where he revelled in occupying suicidal positions, such as silly mid off, silly mid on, short gulley and short leg, and his courage was unlimited.

Bowes has recalled how a batsman would often drive hard at him, trying to move him.

"But Emmott's anticipation was always quick to the emergency. He would rub his hands with glee. 'Just what I want him to do' he murmurs. 'We'll get him out if he tries that sort of thing.' His remark to a 'varsity batsman who said to him 'You're a bit near, old boy. Don't you think you might get hurt?' was a classic. 'Thee get on wi' thi' laikin; I'll tak' care o' misself' he growled."

Emmott never took kindly to University players, particularly those who wore fancy caps. The story is told of one such fashionably equipped student whom Emmott bowled neck and crop with a beautiful yorker. Passing the glaring bowler on his way back to the pavilion the batsman turned to him and said sportingly "Good ball, Robinson, good ball." Emmott regarded him with undisguised ferocity and contempt. 'Aye" he observed. "A pity it were wasted on thee."

Nor did Emmott restrict his brusqueness to undergraduates. Famous captains of England also came under the lash of his tongue, among them D. R. Jardine of Surrey who made his reputation as the leader of the England team which toured Australia during the bodyline controversy. Bowes recalls how Jardine was backing up a little too eagerly while Emmott was bowling to his partner in a match against Surrey, leaving his crease before the ball was bowled. Emmott refused to put up with this even from someone as prestigious as Jardine. He suddenly stopped in his tracks while swinging his arm over to bowl and stood with the ball poised above the bails while Jardine advanced at least four yards up the pitch. Jardine turned in amazement to see Emmott standing ready to run him out. "Nah then, 'ave I to do it?" Emmott demanded aggressively, making a threatening gesture with the ball. "Tha's been pinching a yard or two every time ah've bowled. If tha does it again I shall do thee." Jardine walked majestically back to the crease. He did not say anything but he did not offend again.

Emmott was unsurpassed as a trier and a fighter and he never recognised defeat, even when it stared him in the face. This was quite surprising really because he was by nature a pessimist rather than an optimist. He was a born worrier—a characteristic which expressed itself in his grizzled, hatchet face. "Tha's always nattering, Emmott," his team mates would tell him. But, as Bowes commented, "His cautious approach to the game never succeeded in dimming his enthusiasm and they shared a warm regard for his abilities."

He did, however, sometimes take caution to extremes and this is perhaps best illustrated by his reaction to one of the most remarkable innings ever played in a Roses match at Bramall Lane in 1947—16 years after Emmott had retired. A Yorkshire colt called Gerald Smithson, playing in his first Roses match, went in to bat with the first Yorkshire wicket down for only a dozen runs. Emmott—who although long retired could not keep away from the Roses matches—gave him some stern advice before he left the pavilion: "Nah lad, what tha' has to do is to shove thi' bat in thi' block hole and keep it there, choose how."

But far from taking this advice young Smithson treated it with a contempt only exceeded by his contempt for the Lancashire bowling. I was present at this match and I had never seen anything approaching his innings in a Roses match before, nor am I likely to again. Like a man possessed he drove and pulled the bowling of the Lancashire opener, Philipson, to every corner of the field and, with lunch still some time away, took his score to an incredible 98 before being dismissed, flouting the Roses 'no fours before lunch tradition' outrageously by hitting four boundaries in one over. Emmott witnessed this sacrilegious behaviour in sorrow rather than in anger and after suitably reprimanding the culprit was heard to mutter to himself "We'll never learn this lad."

This was not Emmott's only intrusion into the Roses matches after his playing days were over. In the season following his retirement he was called upon in an emergency to act as a substitute fielder and had not been at short leg more than a few minutes when he appealed for leg before—a thing which, of course, no substitute is allowed to do. The umpire said to him sharply "Not out—and keep thi' mouth shut, Emmott, tha's not playing in this game and it's got nowt to do wi' thee."

It was the same umpire, Arthur Morton, who, having suffered a constant battering of appeals from Robinson and Macaulay in one game, commented that it was like umpiring a match in "a bloody parrot house."

Emmott in his retirement had a short spell as an umpire himself, but it soon became apparent that he was far too partisan to be a hundred per cent successful in that sphere. Umpiring in a match against the Australians at Trent Bridge in 1938 he so far forgot his impartiality as to congratulate Charlie Barnett on scoring a century, shaking him vigorously by the hand to the amused surprise of the thousands of spectators.

Emmott, of course, had his weaknesses and among them was the common one of not always recognising his own faults as clearly as those of other people. He once ran Rhodes out at a critical point in a Roses match and as Rhodes walked dejectedly to the pavilion Robinson sank down on one knee, head bent and hands clasped over the top of his bat handle as though in prayer. A voice from the crowd shouted out "It's too late for that Emmott" but, according to the wicket-keeper, George Duckworth, he was not asking for forgiveness from the Almighty for his egregious error but muttering to himself "Nay Wilfred, nay Wilfred, what were tha doing?"

On another occasion he was bitterly critical of a team mate, Abe Waddington, who in a fit of madness in a Roses match ran out to a ball and was stumped. "Getting stumped wi' t'match in this state," Emmott cried in distress. "Ah'd have died first before they'd have stumped me."

Like Edgar Oldroyd, Emmott had a keen interest in money and was frugal by nature. Bowes said he suspected the roll-up that was always noticeable in his trousers was to allow for shrinkage. He always counted the pennies. It was said he had worked out exactly what the gate money would amount to during his benefit match and when it fell a few shillings short of his estimate he complained bitterly "it ain't enough" for the rest of the day, shaking his head in disbelief that his calculations should be wrong.

Southerners think sometimes that this sort of attitude is tantamount to meanness but, as that great Yorkshireman, J. B. Priestley, once pointed out, Yorkshiremen are less ashamed of their interest in money than people in the south and are therefore less reluctant to talk about it. Emmott talked about money a lot but this did not in any way imply that he was mean. As Bowes has recorded, Emmott offered five shillings reward to new players who scored 50 and insisted on handing it over to them. Bowes has also revealed that he turned up at Bowes' house one day shortly after the fast bowler's marriage with a parcel under his arm containing a barometer. "I've bought you a weather glass as a wedding present, Bill" he announced. "It's same make as mine and tha wants to look at it night and morning. It's seldom that I've been let down and it's nice to know when there's a sticky wicket in t'offing."

But perhaps Cardus should have the last word as he had the first on this great character.

"His cricket was of a kind that could never be estimated by the averages, by statistics; it was an activity that came out of his own being. Robinson was always in the game passionately. Indeed it was in moments of frustration that he was at his most impressive. He had an eloquent droop of the body in his hours of impotence. You see he expected to take a wicket every ball."

George Gibson Macaulay, who followed Robinson in the batting order, and formed with Robinson and Waddington the mainspring of the Yorkshire opening attack until the advent of Bill Bowes, was also a bowler of controlled passion and fury who, like Fred Trueman in a later era, regarded all batsmen as not his opponents in a game of cricket but his deadly enemies in a battle. A native of Thirsk, Macaulay began his career as a fast bowler but under the guidance of George Hirst reduced his pace to medium and produced a deadly off break or what nowadays would be called off cutter which made him, on a wicket which suited him, one of the deadliest bowlers in the country. He shares with Trueman the distinction of the most hat tricks for Yorkshire (4) and with Rhodes, Hirst and Appleyard that of taking 200 wickets in a season. In his 15 year career between 1920 and 1935 he took 1,773 wickets at an average of 17.08.

Macaulay had the reputation of being one of the finest fielders to his own bowling the game has ever seen and, in my experience of him, must also have had the reputation for appealing for l.b.w. more than any other bowler in the game. As someone once put it he made far more appeals than Dr. Barnardo! Bill Bowes summed him up when he says "He knew all the dodges. He glared at the batsman and thought nothing of bowling a fast 'un straight at the head. He would pounce on the ball as light as a panther and hurl it back at the wicket fast and true. There was devil in everything he did . . . He glared and muttered under his breath (his tongue was bitingly caustic) and although he was always filled with a devilish energy I swear that he put another couple of inches into his stride to the wicket when he saw the ball turning after pitching. We used to tell him that his ears flapped and his eyes darted fire . . . George Macaulay was devilish. From a few feet away he was devilishly good-looking too—but coming closer you saw lines and wrinkles which should not have marred the face of a man of his years. His wit, always devilish, had a razor edge which sometimes cut deep into his victim. As a bowler there was no harder trier in the world but he expected no less from his fieldsmen and when he sent them into suicidal positions they had to choose between their fear of sudden death by decapitation or Macaulay's tongue. They preferred sudden death but never experienced it—at least not from Macaulay's bowling—for I have only known one other bowler, Tom Goddard, who could equal Macaulay in bowling so accurately that fieldsmen crouching at short leg could have complete faith in their safety."

My outstanding memory of Macaulay was his 12 wickets for 45 against Lancashire at Old Trafford in 1933 which I have already described. Maurice Leyland has recorded walking off the field with Macaulay after Yorkshire had won by an innings and observing that his face was as black as thunder. "What's up?" I asked him. "An easy win and you got twelve wickets. What more d'you want?" "Oh Maurice," he groaned, "if only the buggers had to go in again."

Macaulay served in the Forces in both world wars and died in 1940 on active service with the R.A.F. aged only 43.

Arthur Wood, who kept wicket for Yorkshire in 225 consecutive matches and missed scarcely a day's cricket from the time he succeeded Dolphin in 1928 to his enforced

Brian Sellers leads the Yorkshire team onto the field at Park Avenue, Bradford in 1939. Left to right: Leyland, Verity, Yardley, Mitchell, Wood and Sellers.

retirement on the outbreak of war in 1939 (although he played in a few games in 1946) sometimes went in before Macaulay and sometimes after him. He had a better career batting average than Macaulay—21 against 18—but only scored a single century for the county while Macaulay scored three. He was a very useful man to come in at number nine, however, and played many distinguished defensive innings in that position.

Wood was the principal comedian of the Yorkshire circus. A portly, almost rotund figure of a man with a face which can only be described as beery, he would have looked far more at home with a pint in his hand behind a bar than behind the stumps in pads and wicket-keeping gloves. He looked about as agile as a retired alderman of a rural district council but appearances deceive and he could hurl himself into breathtaking dives down the leg side to take catches which many more athletic-looking wicket-keepers would not even have attempted, although it must be admitted that some of his dives and somersaults were contributed more for effect and entertainment than from sheer necessity. He always believed in keeping the crowd happy with a little drollery and always succeeded in doing so without losing dignity or being merely farcical, which is never very funny on a first class cricket field.

Wood came from Bradford and was as solid as Bradford Town Hall. He had the earthy, spontaneous wit and wisdom so often manifested by the inhabitants of that city. When the great Frank Woolley of Kent hit Hedley Verity for repeated sixes onto the red slate roof of the football stand at Park Avenue, Wood observed that it was like a boy scout band going by—rat-a-tat, rat-a-tat, tat. When the South African, H. B. Cameron, hit the same bowler for three fours and three sixes in one six ball over—30 runs in all—Wood said to Verity as he despairingly took his sweater "Keep at him, Hedley, you've got him in two minds. He doesn't know whether to hit you for fours or sixes." When he himself came back into the pavilion at the Oval in 1938 having scored 53 in his first test match out of England's colossal total of 903 for seven wickets declared (of which Hutton had contributed 364, Leyland 187 and Hardstaff 169) he threw his bat across the dressing room in simulated anger and declared "Just like me. Always lose my head in a crisis." He had taken a taxi all the way from Scarborough where Yorkshire were playing on being urgently summoned to play for his country and often recalled his horror when the driver wakened him up on arrival at the Great Central Hotel in London and told him how much was on the meter. "I could have bought t'taxi for less" he complained.

If Macaulay could be likened to a swashbuckling hero from a novel by Henty or Alexander Dumas and Wood could be compared to a mediaeval court jester, the last two members of the Yorkshire 1930 eleven, Hedley Verity and Bill Bowes, had the appearance and the manner of a couple of erudite dons who had wandered onto the cricket field by mistake on a rare excursion from the cloistered seclusion of a Cambridge college. Both were very tall and langourous and while Verity expressed his academic appearance by a grave, almost sepulchral expression which some people would describe as a poker face—it never seemed to change whether he was proving completely unplayable or (much more rarely) being hit to every corner of the field—Bowes expressed his scholasticism by his unruly mop of blonde hair and a pair of large horn-rimmed spectacles which he was never seen without. Even when dressed in cricket boots and white flannels they looked very little like serious cricketers and certainly not remotely like the most devastating bowling combination in Yorkshire's cricketing history.

Verity was the elder by three years, but Bowes first played for Yorkshire in 1929 and Verity in 1930. Bowes, however, had commitments to the M.C.C., with whom he began his cricketing career, and although they topped the Yorkshire bowling averages in 1930 it was not until 1931 that they got into their stride and again topped the averages with over 100 wickets apiece. And then, right through to the war, the same pattern was repeated every season, Verity heading the averages four times and Bowes three. In their careers Verity took 1,558 wickets for an average of 13.71 and Bowes, who played a couple of seasons after the war, took 1,351 wickets, average 15.68. Only Rhodes, Hirst, Haigh and Macaulay took more wickets than Verity and only these players plus Illingworth and Wardle more than Bowes.

These two great bowlers, so different in their styles—Verity with his slow left arm spinners and Bowes with his fast medium swingers—and yet in many ways so alike in their personalities—were the closest of friends and undoubtedly contributed more to Yorkshire's reign of success in the 1930's than any other two in the team, Sutcliffe and Leyland, the best batsmen, being their only challengers. There is a cricketing tag which says laconically that catches win matches. This is an exaggeration because if all a team could do was take catches it would not get very far. Bowlers win matches is a more accurate maxim and Verity and Bowes certainly won a great many for Yorkshire.

Before the opening of the 1932 season Lord Hawke in his presidential address made some pertinent comments about these two bowlers. "I still maintain," he declared, "that these two bowlers may prove to be the mainstay of the English bowling in the future." They certainly did. Verity took 144 wickets for England with an average of 24.31 and Bowes 68, average 22.33.

Both Bowes and Verity had a disastrous war, Bowes being taken prisoner by the Italians at Tobruk in 1942 and spending the rest of the war behind barbed wire and Verity being wounded in action at Caserta and dying of his wounds. Bowes tells of hearing of Verity's death in his prison camp at Chieti. Two Canadian airmen were among a new batch of prisoners and during the course of conversation one of them referred to "some cricketer guy" they had had in the hospital at Caserta . . ." what was his name . . . Verity . . . yea, that's right, Verity."

"Do you mean that Hedley Verity was in hospital at Caserta?" Bowes asked eagerly.
"Yea, that's the fella. But he's not in hospital now. He was buried yesterday."

"Buried?"

"Yea, he must have been some important guy. The Italians gave him military honours."

Bowes, stunned, walked up and down the desolate roadway through the camp sadly recalling all the hours they had spent together. He was roused from his reverie by a tug at his elbow. "Say fella," came the Canadian voice again, "I'm mighty sorry. I'd no idea that Verity was your cobber. Would you like to hear all about it?" The airman fell into step beside him and told him the story. He ended "He seemed a great guy."

These, then, were the professional performers in Percy Holmes' circus as they were listed on the score card in 1930—Holmes, Sutcliffe, Oldroyd, Leyland, Mitchell, Rhodes, Robinson, Macaulay, Wood, Verity and Bowes. One of these had to be dropped to make room for the amateur captain, who in 1930 was A. T. Barber, and as Oldroyd, Rhodes, Holmes and Macaulay retired, in that order, the replacements were Barber, Hutton, Smailes and Ellis Robinson.

Wilf Barber, "Tiddly" to the team, was one of the most modest, unpretentious,

Back row: B. Heyhirst (Masseur), C. Turner, E. P. Robinson, H. Verity, W. E. Bowes, L. Hutton, T. F. Smailes, W. Ringrose (Scorer).
Front row: A. Mitchell, A. Wood, H. Sutcliffe, A. B. Sellers, N. W. D. Yardley, M. Leyland, W. Barber.

The Yorkshire team in 1939, the last season before the holocaust.

diffident, self-effacing men ever to have played for Yorkshire. He was always the understudy and never the star but frequently stole the limelight nevertheless. He came into his own when the two batting stars, Sutcliffe and Leyland, were on test duty and filled the breach admirably. A slight man with closely cropped hair he had a very orthodox style and I remember him for his nervous, hesitant little pats with his bat as the bowler ran up to the wicket to deliver the ball. They were more frenetic than any other batsman I have ever seen. He scored 15,289 runs for Yorkshire with an average of 34.51, including 27 centuries, and was an excellent boundary fielder who rarely dropped a catch. On the occasions when he did it must have made him very miserable for weeks, for he was in all ways a most sensitive man.

My main recollection of Frank Smailes has nothing to do with cricket at all. He happened to be staying at a Blackpool hotel where, as quite a young boy, I had gone with my family for Easter. This was at the time when all Yorkshire cricketers were demi-gods and my younger brother and I were greatly excited by the presence of one of them in our midst and debated for hours as to whether we might offend him if we asked for his autograph. We decided it would not be proper to do so while he was on holiday and gained what satisfaction we could from watching him eat his dinner. But one afternoon—I believe it was raining—my brother and I were playing table tennis alone in the games room when Smailes came in. I rather fancied myself at table tennis. After watching us play for some time he asked "Would either of you care to give me a game?" As the elder I at once agreed and to my everlasting satisfaction I comfortably beat him. It was one of the proudest moments of my life!

Like Barber, Smailes was also always an understudy and never a star, but following the retirement of Rhodes and Robinson he was the team's leading all-rounder and with his right arm seam bowling and forceful left hand batting he was a most useful player. His career spanned the years 1932 to 1948 and he scored 5,683 runs with an average of 19.19. He took 800 wickets with an average of 20.72. He is one of only four Yorkshiremen to take all 10 wickets in an innings. Smailes served in Italy during the war and it was he who located Hedley Verity's grave and arranged for a tombstone to be erected on it.

Although he was in the team purely as a slow right arm off spin bowler, I remember Ellis Robinson chiefly for his hurricane hitting as a number 10 or 11 batsman. He was always greeted with loud cheers by the juvenile section of the crowd for his known entertainment value. He disappointed more than he pleased but when he did get going the power in some of his shots was tremendous. I have seen him lift a ball right over the top of the football stand at Park Avenue and onto the roof of the new stand at Headingley. His batting average was no more than 12 but he took 735 wickets for Yorkshire between 1934 and 1949, when he lost his place in the team and went to play for Somerset, at an average of 20.59.

The other two entrants into the Yorkshire team in the 1930's were Norman Yardley, who first played in 1936 after a very successful few years with Cambridge University, and Len Hutton, who first played in 1934 at the age of 17 and who had already been acclaimed by Herbert Sutcliffe and others as a potentially great batsman. The careers of Yardley and Hutton spanned the war to a greater extent than those of any other members of Percy Holmes' circus and will be discussed in a later chapter.

The year 1939 brought Yorkshire the championship again for the third year running. It was the final triumph for one of the greatest county cricket teams of all time. There was no chink in its armour. Led by an outstanding captain, Brian Sellers, it had wonderful batsmen in Hutton, Sutcliffe, Leyland, Mitchell and Barber, it had the best new ball bowler in the country in Bowes and the best left arm bowler in the country in Verity and it had outstanding close-in fielders in Mitchell, Sellers and Turner. No fewer than six batsmen scored over 1,000 runs in that season—Hutton, Sutcliffe, Leyland, Barber, Mitchell and Yardley—and Bowes, Verity and Robinson between them took 363 wickets. Verity headed the national averages with 191 wickets at a cost of 13.13 and Bowes came second with 122 wickets at 14.48.

In many ways this last season before the deluge was remarkable. I recall particularly a match against Hampshire at Sheffield in which Sutcliffe and Hutton put on 315 for the first wicket and, after Sutcliffe had been dismissed, Hutton and Barber took the score to 490 for one before the declaration. They proceeded to dismiss Hampshire for 174 and 90. There was another remarkable match at Sheffield against Derbyshire. Four men—Hutton, Wood, Verity and Bowes—were out of the team on test duty and Yorkshire with their depleted resources were all out for 83, the two Pope brothers bowling unchanged. But the depression in the Yorkshire camp soon disappeared when Derbyshire went in and were promptly dismissed in 40 minutes for a total of 20. In their second innings Yorkshire made 310 and won the match easily, Smailes taking all 10 Derbyshire second innings wickets for 47.

But perhaps most dramatic of all was the Roses match at Headingley where Lancashire gained a first innings lead of 54 but were skittled out for 92 in their second innings by Ellis Robinson, who took eight wickets for 35 runs. Yorkshire needed 147 to win and went for them after lunch on the third day with rain clouds gathering in all directions. Two wickets were down for 20, three for 83 and the fourth also went down at 83, when Turner was caught at slip first ball. Yardley was out at 106 and at 129 Sellers miraculously avoided a run out. Only Hutton stood firm and reached his century with the score at 142 for seven. With five runs needed for victory the gods of Old Trafford arrived on the scene in the shape of a violent thunderstorm and in a downpour of rain Hutton twice skied Pollard into the covers in his frantic search for quick runs. Two runs were taken off the first mis-hit and the second mis-hit gave Yorkshire victory. Had Washbrook held a difficult catch, the ball swirling at him through the downpour, the match would have undoubtedly been abandoned as a draw, for the players were already soaked to the skin and within five minutes the ground was under water.

But there were blacker clouds gathering over the horizon than any Headingley could produce and as the Yorkshire team set off on their final southern tour with matches at Dover, Bournemouth and Brighton, the outbreak of war was imminent. Cricket was far away from most people's minds, players or spectators. Herbert Sutcliffe who was on the reserve of officers received instruction from the War Office to report to his unit and left the tour at Bournemouth, and news was received that the Scarborough Festival, which ended the season, had been cancelled. There was talk of abandoning the Sussex match but Sellers was adamant that they should carry on. "We are public entertainers and we must carry on until we receive instructions not to" he told his team. So the match in Sussex was played in an atmosphere of bleak despondency and Yorkshire once again reaffirmed their superiority by dismissing Sussex for 33 in their second innings and winning by 9 wickets. Hedley Verity bowled the last overs in his life as it sadly turned out, and took seven wickets for nine runs.

The trains were crowded with children being evacuated from London and the Yorkshire party had to hire a coach to transport them home. The black-out was in force and they broke their journey at Leicester and there had their last dinner together. It included champagne and oysters. A cricketing era had ended.

7 AFTER THE DELUGE

Between the end of the summer of 1939 and the beginning of the summer of 1946 I did not see a ball bowled in cricket of any description. I spent most of those seven years in the Merchant Navy. The nearest I ever came to seeing a cricket match was when one of my ships called at Port of Spain in Trinidad in 1943 or 1944. I was informed that a "test match" was currently being played between Trinidad and Barbados and if we had tarried there I should certainly have gone to see it—although the rumour was that half Trinidad were present and the only accommodation likely to be available was in the top of the trees overlooking the ground.

I was not completely divorced from cricket, however. Whenever I got home from a trip—which usually happened two or three times a year—I always spent part of my short leave collecting 50 or more books to take aboard with me on my next trip. I always took considerable pains to ensure that the collection was varied and, in addition to novels and biographies for entertainment, embraced one or two esoteric subjects which I knew nothing about but which had a certain appeal for me. In every selection I always included three or four books which had unlimited scope for study—just in case the trips lasted longer than expected and I exhausted my private library. These books always consisted of the Concise Oxford Dictionary, the Bible, the collected works of Shakespeare, Wisden's Cricketers Almanack and a Yorkshire County Cricket Club Yearbook. I frequently got round to Wisden and the Yorkshire County Yearbook but only on one trip—when homeward bound from Halifax, Nova Scotia, we were diverted to Bombay and Calcutta—did I tackle the Bible, Shakespeare and the Oxford dictionary!

I often used to cheer myself up during the depressing times by turning my mind to cricket and I often said to myself that I should never really feel that the war was over until I sat once again in the new stand at Headingley and watched a Yorkshire match. That to me was the sweetest symbol of peace I could imagine.

That day was an unconscionable time in coming, but come at last it did and I remember it distinctly, though strangely enough I have no recollection of who Yorkshire were playing, or of any details of the match. All I remember is sitting there in the sunshine in a golden haze of contentment, enjoying that soporific two hours between lunch and tea when so often nothing at all seems to happen and one is reminded of the foreigner who said that the English, not being a religious people, invented cricket to give themselves an idea of eternity.

The scene was exactly as it had been in 1939 and even most of the players were present—Sellers, Hutton, Barber, Turner, Yardley, Leyland, Smailes, Robinson and Bowes. Only Sutcliffe, Mitchell, Wood and Verity were missing, the first three having retired. But this was only a temporary reproduction. Six seasons had gone by and all these pre-war players were six years older. And six years are a long time in a county cricketer's life. Any player who had reached his middle thirties before the war was now drawing close to retirement and in the years immediately following the war Yorkshire's loss, like that of all other counties, was severe. Leyland, Barber and Turner retired at the end of 1946, Bowes and Sellers at the end of 1947 and Smailes at the end of 1948. In three seasons Hutton and Yardley had become the sole survivors of the great team of the 1930's and the only players whose careers had really spanned the war years.

It was, of course, the same pattern over all the counties. A few of the great pre-war players—Hammond being the most famous—battled on for a few seasons but the only survivors from the pre-war period who made any notable contribution to English cricket in the post-war era in addition to Hutton and Yardley, were Denis Compton and Bill Edrich of Middlesex, Cyril Washbrook of Lancashire, Joe Hardstaff of Notts., and Freddie Brown of Surrey. In the party of 17 which sailed under the MCC colours to Australia in the 1946/47 series 11 were pre-war test players—Hammond (captain), Yardley (vice-captain), Compton, Edrich, Fishlock, Gibb, Hardstaff, Hutton, James Langridge, Voce and Washbrook—and six were not—A. V. Bedser, Evans, Ikin, Pollard, T. P. B. Smith and D. V. P. Wright. By 1950 only Hutton, Washbrook, Edrich, Compton and Yardley remained as England players. The post-war generation, of course, were ousting them, headed by Bedser, Evans, Laker, May, Cowdrey, Shepherd, Lock, Trueman and Statham.

It is not without significance that all the five players who spanned the war years with their glory undimmed, so to speak, were batsmen. Edrich and Compton reached their remarkable zenith during the 1947 season when they both broke Tom Hayward's 1906 record of the most runs ever scored in a season in England—3,518. Compton scored 3,816 with an average of 90.85 and Edrich 3,539 with an average of 80.43.

I saw these two bat in a number of test and county matches and they were almost always a delight—although because they played for Middlesex they were never very popular in Yorkshire. Yorkshiremen have a chip on their collective shoulder about men from Lord's—who, it is always claimed, with more emotion than logic, are prejudiced against northerners and never include them in test teams unless they have to. But why they should express that sense of grievance by being uncharitable to players like Edrich and Compton I don't know. Edrich, admittedly, had a succession of test failures but he was always attractive to watch whilst I would rate Compton among the best batsmen to watch that I have ever seen. There was a dazzling quality about his stroke play which seemed to reflect his film-star-like appearance and the natural ebullience of his personality and behaviour at the wicket. Even in the grimmest situation he gave the impression of enjoying himself enormously and it is not surprising that he was every schoolboy's hero—except in Yorkshire where schoolboys reluctantly conceded his abilities but dubbed him as the "Brylcreem Boy" and regarded him as "nowt like Hutton."

In fact Compton was superior to Hutton in some ways. He was more daring and adventurous and much less easily subdued. It was not always difficult for a bowler at least to contain Hutton; it was virtually impossible for any bowler to contain Compton. Compton had much more of the Bradman touch than probably any other English batsman of modern times. Edrich by contrast was more the earnest craftsman than the erratic genius and got his runs by sheer determination and hard graft.

The differences in this famous Middlesex pair were, strange to relate, as much demonstrated in their bowling as in their batting, for both of them were no mean exponents of the bowling art. Compton tossed up his left arm leg breaks and Chinamen

Len Hutton and Cyril Washbrook, the most successful of England opening partnerships in the post-war era.

with every appearance of careless nonchalance, getting through an over at breakneck speed and with the minimum of effort, while Edrich took an enormous run at an exhausting speed and hurled himself down the pitch almost as fast as the ball—as though (as Cardus once wrote of him) he was blown half way down the pitch "by the draught caused by his own velocity." "I expected," says Cardus, "to see dust and newspapers eddying in the air wherever he bowled—like the tremendous atmospheric disturbance which happens on a railway station platform as an express thunders through. At the close of play I expected that the groundsman would find trouser buttons on the wicket and torn bootlaces."

Many people have written about Edrich's remarkable courage on the field—a courage only equalled in my experience by the two Yorkshire Brians—Sellers and Close. Edrich would bat for hours on wickets which caused the ball to come off at all angles and hit his body as much as his bat and once at Melbourne he received a blow on the kneecap while he was fielding close to the wicket at short leg, the crack of which was said to echo all round the vast enclosure. He was carried from the field and the expectation was that he would be out of action for at least a fortnight. But next morning he opened the English bowling, hurling himself into action as though nothing had happened.

His powers of recovery were remarkable, as I once experienced at first hand at the Scarborough Festival. Edrich was playing for the MCC against Yorkshire on the Saturday and arrived at the Grand Hotel at two o'clock in the morning, having driven all the way from London. I know because I let him into the hotel. I was with a party having drinks in the lounge as private guests of the hotel manager and when Edrich arrived at the front door the night porter was doing the vacuuming in the corridors. I saw Edrich trying to enter and released the catch for him. When the manager was told who his late guest was he at once invited him to join the party and he did so with some enthusiasm and did not go to bed until about an hour and a half later, rather the worse for wear. "I'll bet he's out first ball in the morning if MCC win the toss" someone said. MCC did win the toss and Edrich opened the innings. He scored a century!

Cyril Washbrook, whose test career extended from 1933 to 1956 and whose opening partnership with Len Hutton in the immediate post-war years stands comparison with those of Hobbs and Rhodes and Hobbs and Sutcliffe, was produced in the same mould as Denis Compton but lacked his genius. He was aggressive, adventurous, daring and always a joy to watch but never seemed to be able to realise his full potential. This was the case in many of the innings I saw him play as well as in his career as a whole. Opening with Hutton he would often put the master completely in the shade, scoring freely from an opening attack which reduced Hutton to grim defence and only an occasional scattered single. But just when he looked certain to make a big score he would throw even commonsense as well as caution to the winds and attempt a fierce hook off Lindwall or Miller and land the ball straight into the hands of the man at deep square leg. Hutton, eschewing such shots like the plague, would stay behind and make a century. But Washbrook, with his red-rosed cap set four-square on his head, his chin and his chest thrust forward like a pouter pigeon, and his general air of jaunty indifference to everything around him, was always one of my favourites despite his Lancastrian base.

An unidentified member of his team during the years of his captaincy (1948 to 1955) once said of Norman Yardley that he was too nice a man to be captain of Yorkshire and that is profoundly true. As a player he was undoubtedly the best amateur captain

Yorkshire have ever had—he played in 20 test matches for England and captained them in 14—but as a leader his qualities did not compare with those of Sellers. Yorkshire shared the top place in the championship with Middlesex in Yardley's second season as captain, 1949, and were second in 1951 and 1952 but in 1953 they dropped to 12th in the table, four places lower than ever before in the history of the club.

Yardley was perhaps unfortunate in having some difficult personalities to deal with but he did not assert his authority nearly as much as he should have done and appeared to be largely indifferent to the strife and unrest in the Yorkshire dressing room which spread like a disease in the 1950's, rather than seeking to uproot it. Yardley, with all the qualities of the true sportsman and a tolerant, understanding, forgiving nature, could not easily have undertaken the role of ruthless disciplinarian which Sellers would have revelled in and the result was that the Yorkshire team deteriorated into an undisciplined rabble, which took several years to sort out—if, indeed, it ever has been sorted out, which some of the county's sternest critics would question. But if Yardley's legacy was not that of Sellers, his name is still an illustrious one in the county's annals.

Of the final member of the group of five England cricketers whose test careers spanned the second world war I write with exceptionally nostalgic pleasure. Leonard Hutton was the hero of my young manhood just as his predecessor, Herbert Sutcliffe, had been the hero of my boyhood and as I wrote in another book which included Yorkshire cricket in its contents, "Nowt So Queer As Folk," if I had a fairy godmother who would grant me one cricketing wish before I died it would be to see Hutton again make one of his exquisite cover drives for four. For me, for all the years I watched him, Hutton was the supreme cricketing artist and his stroke play represented the apotheosis of grace and symmetry. Because I had more understanding of cricket and more appreciation of its artistry when I watched Hutton than I had possessed as a boy watching Sutcliffe I can truly say that Hutton gave me more pleasure than any other player I have ever seen. Bradman and Sutcliffe and possibly even Compton and Leyland may have given me more excitement and stimulation but for sheer sensual cricketing pleasure Hutton stands supreme. His batting roused in me the same aesthetic emotions as I imagine music lovers derive from a Beethoven symphony or a Brahms sonata and art lovers derive from a Turner or a Rembrandt painting. To use a cruder metaphor his batting represented for me cricket champagne of the finest vintage and I enjoyed every glass of it I ever had.

Among the batsmen who have scored more than 25,000 runs, only the averages of Bradman (95.14) and Hammond (56.10) stand higher in the records than Hutton's 55.51 and only six players have exceeded his total of 129 centuries—Hobbs (197), Hendren (170), Hammond (167), Mead (153), Sutcliffe (149) and Woolley (145). And of England players only Hammond (58.45), Hobbs (56.94), Duleepsinjhi (58.52), Paynter (59.23) and Sutcliffe (60.73) have higher averages in test cricket than Hutton's 56.67. Hutton also, of course, holds the record for the highest innings in test cricket against Australia with his 364 at the Oval in 1938. This total was beaten by Sobers who scored 365 not out in a test at Kingston in 1957 but it was against a minor test side—Pakistan.

But what of Hutton the man? Some journalists regarded him as rather remote and unapproachable but what was seen as standoffishness was, I am sure, his natural reticence; and when others said he was inarticulate they were probably misinterpreting his essential modesty and diffidence. Even his knighthood left him completely free of airs

Wilf Barber and Maurice Leyland taken near the end of their careers in 1946 and Bill Bowes coming out for his last innings for Yorkshire in 1947.

and graces and he had no pretensions whatever. I frequently had the job of interviewing him for the Yorkshire Post in the post-war years—on his returns from tours of Australia and on other notable occasions—and he was always most friendly and helpful.

Not that he was an easy man to interview. He was rather like Wilfred Rhodes in that respect. He did not waste words—indeed like all true Yorkshiremen he wasted nothing—and he did not enthuse about anything very easily. I remember once trying to get him to say something when his native town of Pudsey were giving a big reception in his honour after he had captained the team which won back the Ashes from the Australians in 1953.

I described the scene in Pudsey that day as Pudsey's finest hour and wrote that it was more like a civic coronation than a civic reception. "Several thousand people thronged the market place and the frontage of the gaily beflagged public baths and there were men selling favours and souvenirs. The mayor, Alderman Walter Ward, described it as 'A gathering such as we have never had in Pudsey before' and that other famous Pudsey cricketer, Herbert Sutcliffe, called it 'historic.' The MP for the borough, Colonel Cyril Banks, said it was one of the most exciting things that could possibly happen to a Member of Parliament."

What I didn't report was what Hutton said about it when I asked him for his reactions to this remarkable example of civic enthusiasm. He pondered the question deeply and said "Well, I suppose, it's all right if you like this sort of thing." He clearly didn't!

One of Hutton's many claims to cricketing immortality was the fact that he was the first professional to captain England—an ironic choice in view of Lord Hawke's famous comment, and a courageous one in view of the fact that Hutton had never been the captain of a county team. In this capacity he had the satisfaction of winning the Ashes in 1953 and giving the Australians one of their biggest drubbings in that country in 1954/55, winning three tests and drawing one. And these successes, it must be remembered, were in the hey-day of Lindwall and Miller, one of the most ferocious opening bowling attacks the Australians have ever produced.

Although it was the last thing he sought, Hutton was a controversial captain inasmuch as tactics and strategy were concerned, his inbred Yorkshire caution leading him to adopt safety-first attitudes which although generally successful, were not always popular. He was also accused of lacking firmness in his handling of difficult players like Trueman and Lock, who were alleged to be the cause of some of the high feeling which was produced by Hutton's West Indian tour in 1954. But the English skipper could not possibly be held responsible for the riots which culminated in the bottle throwing episode at Georgetown which were political in origin. Hutton's classic reply when asked if he and his fielders wanted play to be abandoned in the melée was hardly an indication of lack of firmness. "Not likely," he replied, "I want another wicket before the close."

He was also accused of ruthlessness in the incident in which he made a difficult decision to leave Alec Bedser out of the second test match against Australia in Sydney in the 1954/55 tour. Bedser, who had been the spearhead of England's attack for years, was in the 12 selected for the match, but had not been bowling particularly well and in the first test at Brisbane had only taken one wicket for 130 runs. The choice of who should be dropped lay between Bedser and Tyson—who was much the faster of the two of them, although he lacked Bedser's accuracy. Hutton made a last minute decision in favour of speed and it was a decision amply justified by results, Tyson taking

10 wickets for 130 in the match. But Hutton omitted telling Bedser personally about the decision and the first Bedser knew about it was when the team manager pinned the team list to the dressing room door.

Colin Cowdrey has defended Hutton in his book "MCC—An Autobiography of a Cricketer" by saying he understood his dilemma completely. "On his batting days," Cowdrey writes, "Hutton retired into a world of his own. He neither spoke to anyone nor appeared to hear them if they spoke to him. That morning he was in a trance. He returned from the toss but the damage was done. Bedser was deeply hurt; this was the end of his great career overseas." Other players in the England team were not so charitable and Denis Compton in particular attacked him for his "ruthlessness."

The whole Australian tour of 1954/55 proved an immense strain for Hutton, physically and emotionally, and although he was hailed on his return to England as a conquering hero and paid the signal honour of being invited to be captain for the whole series of tests against South Africa in 1955 he dropped himself from the first test because of lack of form and then resigned the job completely in favour of Peter May.

It was hoped he would have recovered his form and fitness by 1956, when the Australians were due over here, but in January of that year Hutton ended all speculation by announcing his retirement from first class cricket at the age of 39. How much this was due to the strain of the England captaincy, all the greater because of his inexperience in captaincy—and how much to the contentious atmosphere in the Yorkshire dressing room at this period it is impossible to say, but it was a tragedy that his career, already shortened by six years of war, should have been further attenuated by the pressures which were imposed upon him both in test and county cricket.

For he not only carried the chief burden of responsibility in the England team but also in the Yorkshire team, where so often if he failed everyone else seemed to fail. The very least the Yorkshire committee could have done to recognise his outstanding contribution was to offer him the captaincy of Yorkshire in succession to Yardley and by doing so they may have persuaded him to stay for several more seasons. But, so far as I am aware, no such suggestion was made. The MCC may have accepted change by making a professional captain of England but the Yorkshire committee stuck to the tradition of having an amateur captain and invited Herbert Sutcliffe's son, Billy, to take the job.

So on this sad note ended the career of one whom Colin Cowdrey, among others, ranked as one of the four or five greatest batsmen of all time. Of all the tributes that have been paid to him I rate E. W. Swanton's the highest because he is not predisposed to eulogistic assessments of Yorkshire cricketers and has had some very harsh things to say about some of them. But of Hutton he wrote in his admirable book "Sort of a Cricket Person" as follows: "I do not doubt that Hutton, like the rest of us, if he had his time again, would have ordered some things differently. But what has he not got to show on the credit side? He brought England back to the forefront of world cricket and showed to his fellow players a perfection of technique and a dedicated example that were faithfully followed by his young disciples, Peter May and Colin Cowdrey. Both of them likewise saw in their first touring captain and followed in their turn the dignity and reticence he brought to the job. These attributes did not desert him when, after retirement, came the blandishments of newspapers and publishers to 'reveal all.' Len felt the lure of brass keenly enough, but unlike most of his professional contemporaries,

Back row: D. B. Close, F. S. Trueman, J. V. Wilson, A. Mason, W. H. H. Sutcliffe, F. A. Lowson.
Front row: E. I. Lester, L. Hutton, N. W. D. Yardley, D. V. Brennan, E. P. Robinson.
The Yorkshire team of 1949 with only Yardley, Hutton and Robinson (Ellis) left of the pre-war team.

he never yielded to the temptation to depict his career and times in the sort of language that the ten per cent agents could have made a small fortune from."

The disparagement of Hutton which infuriated me most in his post-war playing days was that he lacked courage against fast bowling. For this to be said of the man who opened the England innings for so many years against the fast bowling of Lindwall and Miller is like saying that Bradman was always uncomfortable at Headingley. It was Maurice Leyland who said of fast bowling "None of us like it only some of us don't let on" and Hutton was certainly in the second category. His courage was all the more notable in view of his vulnerability due to his permanently shortened left arm, which he fractured in a wartime accident and would probably have ended his cricket career had it not been for the skill of a Leeds surgeon, Reginald Broomhead, who was made an honorary member of Yorkshire County Cricket Club for his services.

Hutton once referred to this alleged fear of his in a public speech in Yorkshire, saying he had never feared Lindwall and Miller nearly as much as he had feared one Bill Hudson, the demon bowler of Pudsey St. Lawrence. I was writing feature articles for the Yorkshire Post at this time and, always on the lookout for ideas, was intrigued by this speech and set off for Pudsey in search of this legendary character. I have described this in my book "Nowt So Queer As Folk" and I think it is worth recording here again because it provides a pretty telling comment on the view that Hutton was frightened of fast bowling. "Bill Hudson" I wrote, "turned out to be a 53-year-old Pudsey coal merchant, standing 6 feet 3 inches tall and weighing 16 stones 10 lbs. He frightened me with a lump of coal in his hand, never mind a cricket ball.

"'Can't you see I'm busy?' he snapped, looking down on me belligerently from the top of his lorry. 'I've more to do than talk about Len Hutton.'

"'But Mr. Hudson' I protested 'you're the bloke whom Len Hutton feared more than Lindwall and Miller put together and yet few people outside Pudsey have ever heard of you.'

"He grunted non-commitally and went on loading his coal from a wagon in a windswept railway siding. 'He were t'only one I could bowl to' he ruminated, lifting a sack into position with effortless ease. 'T'others wouldn't stand up to me—not even t'big 'uns.'

"He laughed grimly. 'Mind you, I could chuck 'em down a bit in them days. I could throw a ball across the St. Lawrence ground and twenty four yards into t'next field. And I'm not saying I couldn't lay 'em out. There were often a couple lying dead in t'pavilion when I'd been on.'

"'And yet young Hutton stood up to you' I said, getting him back to the point.

"He put down his coal, sat on his coal bags and prepared to talk cricket at length. 'Aye,' he said reminiscently, 'he did. And, think on, he were nobbut a lad of thirteen.'

"He shook his head in wistful admiration. 'A wonder, he was. A real wonder. He would hook balls into t'tennis ground off his chin. T'gardener would come next morning with half a dozen of 'em.'

"'How did it all start?' I asked.

"'Well,' he said, 'it were this way. Leonard were only a schoolboy and the first and second team players, including his brothers, considered him a damned nuisance. They used to let him field for 'em but Leonard wasn't satisfied with that. He were no darned good at fielding anyway. 'Can't I have a bat' he was always moaning. 'No tha can't' they'd tell him, 'we've got to get our practice in for Saturday.'

" 'Well, I reckon I took pity on him. Or maybe I wanted somebody to bowl to. I got old George—he was our groundsman until he was ninety—to put a special net up where I could bowl to him on his own. And then when we'd finished I'd buy him a fish and a pennorth because he was never flayed of owt. Mind you, I did used to try and bowl on the off.'

" 'And then I suppose he got into the team?'

" 'Aye. It was about 1930. I had a bull-nosed Morris Cowley and because we were one short against East Bierley I went off to fetch him and he got 36. A good innings. But the best he ever played was his 115 against Bradford in the Priestley Cup. Far better than his 364 against Australia at the Oval. Think of it, 15 years old and playing against veterans! There was a bowler called David Luckhurst and he was the best bowler in the district. 'I've tried everything I know on him, Bill' he told me. 'He's an absolute bloomin' master.'

"Warming to his memories, Mr. Hudson went on to recall other great boyhood innings of the potential cricketing genius. 'There was that 85 he got against Sydney Barnes. He wasn't sixteen then but I remember it well because I gave him a sweater—he'd only got one of his father's.'

" 'And then,' I said, 'he played for Yorkshire and England.'

" 'Aye,' he said. 'He did.'

" 'And yet some people still go on saying he was frightened of fast bowling.'

"Mr. Hudson gave a derisory guffaw and went back to work again on his coal bags. 'Him frightened of fast bowling!' he repeated ironically. 'That's a laugh if ever there was one.' "

As for Hutton's alleged ruthlessness Colin Cowdrey tells a story about the departure of the 1954/55 English team to Australia. It hardly supports this contention. Cowdrey, a callow and nervous youngster, was off on his first tour and he writes of the events at Tilbury docks that morning as follows: "Len Hutton as captain was much in demand that morning and yet he still found time to move in among the crowd of reporters and relatives to find my father, draw him aside and talk to him earnestly for some twenty minutes. The tone of it, I gathered later, was that there was no need for my parents to worry. 'I'll look after him' he reassured him again and again. Which suggests that he knew a good deal more about how I was feeling than I gave him credit for at the time. My father was immensely impressed by Hutton's thoughtfulness and concern and indeed looking back now there was something almost uncanny about the care he took to put my father's mind at rest. I was never to see my father again. Three weeks later he was dead."

That is the Hutton I have had the privilege of knowing.

8 REPORTING DAYS ON THE YORKSHIRE POST

The article I wrote for the Yorkshire Post on my interview with Bill Hudson was one of scores of cricket articles I wrote for that distinguished newspaper during the 10 years I was on the editorial staff—from 1946 to 1956. Indeed looking through my cuttings books, cricket seems to have been one of my main inspirations, particularly during the years I was given a roving commission and turned out what features I liked, for a long time under the heading "Such is Life."

It is a tribute to the catholicity of my news editor, Frank Snape, and my editor, Sir Linton Andrews, neither of whom was a cricket fan, that I was allowed to consume so much valuable space with my sketches and musings on all sorts of cricketing phenomena—from the traditional test and Roses matches at Headingley and Bramall Lane to all kinds of eccentricities, such as women's cricket, village cricket and cricket played in snow showers on Boxing Day.

The only brand of cricket writing I never attempted was straight-forward match reports which, so far as the Yorkshire Post was concerned, were in the capable hands of J. M. Kilburn. Kilburn covered all the test matches and most of the Yorkshire county matches and what he thought of my frequent excursions into his hallowed territory I will fortunately never know. For Kilburn was essentially a purist and did not, I think, consider cricket to be a subject for lighthearted and humorous observations. He wrote very serious and very polished prose about it himself and, I fancy, took rather a poor view of his erudite reports of the test matches in the Yorkshire Post being accompanied by my irreverent sketches on another page, often, to make matters worse, the front page. I very rarely ventured into the press box—the sanctum-sanctorum of the professional cricket writers—for fear of being immediately ejected as a 'non-unionist' and gathered the material for my contributions chiefly from sitting and listening in the crowd.

The test against the Indians at Headingley in July, 1952, was a match to which I paid great attention because it was the first match to be televised at that ground. I wrote a long description of how the T.V. pictures were relayed from the cameras to a mobile control van and thence into a transmitter van carrying a 90-foot high aerial which in turn transmitted the signals to another aerial on top of the water tower at Cookridge and from there to the main transmitter at Holme Moss.

I also wrote about the crisis concerning Freddie Trueman's special steel toecap, which he had to have fitted to his right boot because a normal boot would not stand up to the strain as he dragged it over the crease. Since the beginning of the season, he told me, he had gone through nine pairs of boots. Fred discovered to his dismay on the eve of the match that a member of the ground staff had forgotten to take his boot to a cobbler's shop near the ground and there were rumours that he would not be able to play without it.

> "So," I wrote, "in the interests of English cricket I immediately volunteered to take the boot—size 9½—to the cobbler myself. The cobbler was just leaving his

shop but when he heard whose boot it was he immediately agreed to do some overtime and an hour later the boot was back with Trueman, complete with a shining steel toecap. Trueman examined it closely and, glaring in the direction of the Indian dressing room, said "I think this will do the trick."

This was a prophetic utterance if ever there was one for this was the match in which Trueman, playing in his first test, so demoralised the Indian batsmen that in their second innings they had four wickets down without a run being scored, Trueman taking three of them. I wrote of this dramatic happening as follows:

"Unless something very unexpected happens the first test match of the present series will end at Headingley today with a convincing victory for England. At one time—when the demoniac Freddie Trueman was knocking wickets down in all directions—it looked as if it would end on Saturday and the wild joy of the crowd was only equalled by the blank misery of Mr. Pankaj Gupta, the normally jovial little manager of the Indian team and the uncrowned king of Indian sport. As one of his best batsmen after another walked dejectedly back to the pavilion Mr. Gupta's face was a study in horrified bewilderment. 'It is terrible, terrible' he told me sadly. 'The tour is going to cost £35,000 and there are four wickets down for nothing. I am very distressed. This Trueman man is terrifying them.'

He added that the tour had been a financial disaster up to date and Saturday's crowd of 28,000 was the only one to reach normal test match dimensions. Many people felt the reason for this was the fact that a 3s. 6d. entrance charge was too much for a test match! The main diversion of the day, I reported, was a black and white dog which held up play for over five minutes while it won a running battle with a member of the ground staff, a stout special constable, both umpires and half the Indian team.

Another diversion for me, I reported, was picking an English test team out of the distinguished ex-players in the press box or on the players' balcony. My final selection was: Hobbs, Sutcliffe, Hammond, Leyland, Ames, Rhodes, Wyatt, Peebles, Gover, Root and Bowes. "I'm sorry to report" I went on "that probably the greatest player of them all, Wilfred Rhodes, is now almost blind and can see next to nothing of the play, but he enjoys sitting out on the players' balcony reviving old memories and he can pick up a lot that you and I would miss. 'They've taken the new ball' he commented at one point.' 'How do you know that?' asked his neighbour. 'Oh,' he replied, 'I can tell by the sound of it on the bat.' His late partner, Jack Hobbs, who is five years his junior, looked in very fine fettle and fit to go out and bat at any moment."

I also wrote extensively on the thrilling test match against the Australians in July, 1953. The first day was one of tribulation for the crowd of 30,000, England scoring only 142 for seven in five and a half hours.

"The tribulation began" I wrote "when the second ball of the morning, a vicious yorker from Lindwall, hit Hutton's stumps and reduced the crowd to a state of shocked incredulity from which they never really recovered. "He's out!" gasped the talkative man in front of me who had just been saying that Lindwall's limbering-up routine was all for show. "He's out!" They were the last words he spoke before lunch. This disaster was, however, only the beginning. Edrich was out l.b.w. to Miller—a grinning, exultant Miller who added insult to injury by clapping his hands wildly. And ten minutes later Compton was also back in the pavilion. 36 for three. Most of us felt like going home.

A shy youth called Fred Trueman talking to one of Yorkshire's Golden Age batsmen, David Denton, at the dinner held in Sheffield in 1949 to celebrate the centenary of Lancashire v. Yorkshire matches.

A more mature Fred Trueman comes out to bat with the same determined expression he displayed in his more familiar role as demon bowler.

> "It was Watson, the hero of Lord's, in now and as Lindwall walked back to his mark the tension was spread like a blanket over the ground. Watson missed the first ball and the second struck him on the pad. There was a roaring appeal from Lindwall, answered by a far louder roar of disapproval from the crowd. We lived nervously till lunch. During the afternoon as Watson and Graveney held the fort we gradually took a more cheerful attitude. But then it was back to tragedy with a jerk. The Headingley hoodoo struck again. Within an hour Graveney was caught out, Watson bowled out, Bailey run out and Simpson laid out. 110 for six and that horrible man, Miller, grinning more broadly than ever."

England were all out for 187 on the following day, Friday, and the Australians passed their score with only three wickets down. "And then" I wrote "with the swiftness that is half the joy of cricket, Harvey was out l.b.w. to Bailey—a Bailey who went down almost on his knees in supplication to umpire Frank Chester—and the crowd came noisily to life. In the next dramatic hour five more wickets fell in rapid succession and the day ended with Australia all out for 266."

There was a tremendous turnout on the Saturday. I reported that hundreds of people slept in the street and by eight o'clock in the morning the queues stretched all round the ground. Most of the gates were closed long before play began. And when it did begin 33,000 had been admitted. But it was a bitterly disappointing day, with a downpour ending play a quarter of an hour before lunch with England 62 for one, Hutton being out just before the abandonment for 28.

There was an even bigger crowd on the Monday—36,000—but there was more rain and they got only four hours' cricket, including a disastrous evening session, in which Watson and Simpson were out in successive balls and Bailey survived the hat trick. At the close England had a paltry lead of 78 and only five wickets left.

There was, however, adequate compensation for the lucky 22,000 who were present on the Tuesday.

> "I don't know if any umbrella handles were chewed off at Headingley yesterday" I wrote "but as the Australians just failed in their race for victory there was more nail-biting and handkerchief-chewing than had been seen there for many a day. There was excitement of one sort and another all day and it did not reach its thrilling climax until about a quarter to six when the Australians needed 66 runs to win with 45 minutes in which to make them. The tension was hard to bear. Watches were consulted after every over and there were 22,000 appeals for l.b.w. every time the ball hit the batsman's pads. Would they do it, or would we stop them? It was a question which had everyone almost shivering with suspense and in the new stand balcony where I watched for the agonising answer there were eminent men of business and the professions (not to mention a few famous ex-cricketers) shuffling in their seats like schoolboys, hardly daring to watch. The Australians failed in the end by 30 runs but such is the English temperament that escaping from defeat was hailed as a great victory. The hero of the day was Trevor Bailey, who not only batted grimly for four hours but bowled so accurately that the Australians could score only nine runs off him in six overs. When the match ended thousands of spectators swarmed onto the field and he had to run a gauntlet of cheers all the way to the pavilion."

The next test at Headingley was against the South Africans in 1955, which South Africa won by 224 runs. Hutton did not play, having turned down an invitation to captain England in the series because of loss of form. He was to retire at the end of this season. His successor as captain was Peter May and although he had strong batting support in Compton and Graveney, Lowson of Yorkshire, Bailey and D. J. Insole, and strong bowling in Statham, Loder, Bailey, Wardle and Lock he was unable to give much distinction to the English performance and faced with the South African second innings total of no less than 500, including centuries by McGlew and Endean, they could only muster 256, May being the top scorer with 97.

Although played in excellent weather before big crowds, reaching a peak of 36,000 on the Monday, it was an extremely dull match, the only notes of comedy being introduced by Johnnie Wardle, the Yorkshire left arm bowler and natural comedian, who imitated South African Tayfield's bowling. Tayfield had a number of eccentricities both in his batting and his bowling. When batting he would tap the ground with his right foot while awaiting the bowler's delivery, as though he were keeping time to his heartbeats, and before starting every over he bowled he would ostentatiously kiss his cap before handing it to the umpire. This was presumably to secure some fluency with the ball. I lamented in my sketch that there was not even the traditional Headingley test match feature of play being held up for five minutes while a stray dog emerged from the popular side pursued vainly by umpires, fielders and at least a couple of policemen.

Indeed I was so stuck for something to write about on the third day that I decided to try to get into the scorebox to find out why the fieldsman indicator was not working while the South Africans were in the field—a source of widespread dissatisfaction among the vast crowd. The light had flickered with unfailing regularity while England were in the field—which was not nearly so necessary because most of the players were well-known—but for the South Africans there had not been a gleam.

I soon discovered, however, that getting into the scorebox at Headingley was like getting into the Kremlin in Moscow. I could not get in at all without the right authority and this was difficult to obtain. I did eventually convince the Yorkshire county officials that I was not a spy from Old Trafford or Lord's and was told I could go in for 10 minutes provided I did nothing to distract the scorers from their work. I was, therefore, let in and after a little difficulty identified the operator who was supposed to identify the fieldsmen by flashing a light on his particular number on the board. I asked him why it was that the indicator was not lighting up and thus not providing 36,000 spectators with the satisfaction of knowing who was fielding each ball. He looked at me in some surprise. "Isn't it?" he asked. "I've been pressing my buttons all day just as usual." "Then I'm very much afraid" I said apologetically "that you've been completely wasting your time." "Well I'll be buggered" was his caustic reply. "You'd have thought someone would have told me, wouldn't you?" I explained that communication with the custodians of the scoreboard was not easy.

I then interviewed the chief scoreboard operator and gently voiced other criticisms which were being made by the crowd—chiefly the fact that it was often very slow in recording runs, with the result that the last runs had not always been recorded when the next runs were made. The chief operator did not say anything—he just showed me how the mechanics worked. And after seeing them in operation I was amazed that runs were registered at all. The Headingley scoreboard was a frightful monster which, I wrote, must have been old fashioned when W. G. Grace was a lad. I went on:

"The mechanics consist of three tremendous drums with numerals painted on the outside, and every time a run is scored the drums have to be revolved by hand. One operator watches the game with a pair of binoculars and shouts to another man standing on a sort of gallery above him that a run has been scored and that batsman number so-and-so has scored it. The man on the gallery has then to push round the drum registering the total score and run across the gangway to the other side of the scoreboard to push round the drum accrediting runs to the batsman.

But although recording each run is complicated enough it is the essence of simplicity compared to recording the fall of a wicket. Then the monster really comes to life and a variety of plates have to be put in position to record the number of wickets that have fallen, the last player's score, who caught him out and so on. Standing in the score box and watching this frantic activity in progress is almost a terrifying experience. With the men rolling the drums in the loft above me I felt like the Hunchback of Notre Dame—who I seem to recall had a similar experience. It was grand to get out into the fresh air again and discover by looking behind me how the match was getting on. For all its rigours, however, operating the scoreboard at Headingley is apparently a healthy life. I was informed that the last man who rolled the drums round did the job for about 50 years and was still going strong at 90.

Alas, it is not the same to-day. There is a new inhuman electronic scoreboard which provides you with much more information, much more quickly. The only trouble is that when the sun is shining the light is reflected in such a way that you can't read any of the information the board is dispensing. But the sun doesn't shine very often at Headingley!

My final test match so far as writing for the Yorkshire Post was concerned was that against Australia in 1956, a match which was notable for giving England their first victory ever against Australia at Headingley. They won by an innings and 42 runs, the deadly Surrey combination of Laker and Lock proving match winners in conditions ideally suited to them. England batted first and scored 325, May again being top scorer with 101 and he and Washbrook putting on 187 for the fourth wicket, and the Australians were skittled out for 143 and 140, Laker having a match analysis of 11 for 113 and Lock seven for 81. The Australian team were strong enough on paper including Lindwall, Miller, Johnson, Harvey, Benaud, Burk and Burge but 1956 was a very wet summer and batting on wickets to which they were not accustomed the Aussies had a very unsuccessful tour. They had not defeated a single county when they came to Headingley for the third test in July and had been humiliated by a 10 wicket defeat by Surrey.

For me as a columnist this match provided a tricky problem because I had agreed to write my "Such is Life" column for Monday morning's paper on the Saturday's play at Headingley—and to my dismay (and that of approximately 30,000 other people) there was not a ball bowled. With Australia having lost 6 wickets for 81 in their first innings in reply to England's 325, this was a most frustrating situation for cricket lovers in general and for me in particular and I spent most of the Saturday speculating on what to write. I thought of recalling other test match washouts—for this could hardly be the first—and of doing some interviews with members of the two teams but neither prospect excited me. I eventually settled for a description of the frustration as I had experienced it and wrote as follows:

"You've got to be philosophic about it," I told my friend as he gazed lugubriously through the window at the sodden lawn with a stiff gin in his hand and a reserved seat for the test match in his pocket. "Just try to imagine you're a water works superintendent watching your reservoirs fill up."

He growled as only men with reserved seats for test matches can growl when rain is teeming down and the Australians are 81 for six. "They shouldn't have altered the date" he said bitterly. "It's a fortnight earlier this year than it's been every year since the war and this is what happens. We've got the Manchester weather—and it serves Headingley right. I hope they lose thousands of pounds."

The only woman present shook her head disparagingly at such a contemptible attitude, no doubt reflecting that cricket brings out the worst in men. "I don't know what you're all making such a fuss about" she observed, after telling us that we should have to eat all the sandwiches for lunch. "It's not the end of the world."

You could certainly have been excused for thinking it was the end of the world in Leeds and district on Saturday. Never do I remember trying to plumb such infinite depths of gloom and depression. Even in the bread shop—usually the most cheerful of places—you would have thought they were catering for a funeral tea.

"He's gone" the proprietor's wife announced solemnly and portentously, as though her husband had set off by rocket for the moon. "He said he could see some specks of brightness over Kirkstall and he's gone. What he'll have to say when he comes home I dread to think."

The lugubrious company in front of the counter shook their heads—either in admiration for such boundless optimism or in sympathy for such incredible stupidity.

"I wish my Albert had seen some specks of brightness over Kirkstall" said one stout woman with a basket. "I haven't had a civil word out of him all morning. Like a bear with a sore head he is. We had a proper row at half past seven. He wakened me to tell me it was chucking it down." "Well" I said "what about it? The ceiling's not leaking is it?" "What about it" he said—as nasty as owt—"what about my test match?" "Oh" I says "you and your blinkin' cricket. Fancy waking me up for that . . . "Yes, and I think I'll take half a stone of potatoes while I'm here."

The news at the tobacconist's after lunch was that the proprietor and his son had returned home dejectedly from Headingley after queuing in the rain for several hours. "A lot of them left together in a bus" the tobacconist's wife explained. "The ones who went on waiting called them cissies. Personally I think they all need their heads looking at for going at all."

By teatime, of course, the test match had faded out of the picture and it was just the weather in general. To relieve wounded feelings it was being denounced with astonishing venom. "Filthy climate" everyone was declaring. "The worst summer in living memory."

And yet are we ever satisfied? It is exactly a year ago that I wrote an article in the Yorkshire Post under the heading "And now they are grumbling about the heat".

My Yorkshire Post articles also embraced a number of Roses matches and the memorable dinner at the Grand Hotel, Sheffield, in 1949 to mark the centenary of these matches. This was a gathering of the rival clans such as had never happened before in history. The oldest ex-player present among nearly 100 was 79-year-old E. B. Rowley of Lancashire who had played in a Roses match in 1896 and the youngest was 18-year-old Fred Trueman, who first played in 1948. Trueman, incidentally, was a very shy, rather gauche youngster who seemed to be completely overawed by the occasion. I tried to have a chat with him whilst he was drinking a glass of orange juice during the interval but he had little to say for himself. I was to meet him on a number of other occasions later in his career and shy would be the last adjective I would apply to this ebullient character.

Scarcely a season between 1896 and 1948 was without its representatives. There were familiar faces wherever one looked—Wilfred Rhodes, David Denton, Ernest Tyldesley, Emmott Robinson, Herbert Sutcliffe, Maurice Leyland, Cyril Washbrook, Jack Ikin, Reggie Spooner, Len Hutton, Percy Holmes, Harry Makepeace, C. S. Marriott—these and dozens more. And reminiscence flowed. My article on the occasion was published in the Yorkshire Post the following morning, together with a picture of Emmott Robinson and David Denton, and read as follows:

> "Sheffield Friday night. It was a schoolboy's dream come true at the Grand Hotel here tonight where a dinner was held to mark the centenary year of the Yorkshire and Lancashire cricket matches. The tables were filled with past and present stars of the famous game—41 from Lancashire and 52 from Yorkshire—and the uniqueness of the occasion was well illustrated by the fact that the cricketers themselves were busily collecting autographs. As the chairman, Sir William Worsley, remarked "If a team to beat the world was wanted it could be found in this room tonight."
>
> The surprise of the evening was when Sir William wound up the proceedings by presenting a flag to the Lancashire club—"to be flown at Old Trafford whenever Roses matches are played."
>
> The flag contained a white rose and a red rose with their stems crossed and bore the figures 1849 to 1949. It was accepted on behalf of Lancashire by Sir Francis Joseph.
>
> Reminiscence flowed. I found Ben Blomley, the old Lancashire wicket-keeper, reminding David Denton of the match in 1890—Lancashire having been set to get 240 odd to win and were 100 for one wicket at the end of the second day. "But rain came in the night and Lancashire were out for 148" added Ben. "You always had the luck, you know."
>
> Herbert Sutcliffe was talking to Albert Rhodes, the Lancashire amateur all-rounder, about the match in 1924 when Yorkshire wanted 55 (or was it 58?) to win—and were bowled out for 33. "I remember I got a duck in the first innings and three in the second" Sutcliffe recalled. "No, Herbert, you're wrong" Rhodes corrected, "you got 5 in the second inmings. I remember it distinctly. Dick Tyldesley bowled a perfect leg break and you played forward and missed it . . ."
>
> There was Maurice Leyland with a great white rose in his buttonhole leaning back and saying to Cyril Washbrook "Aye, they all thought we were deadly enemies but really we were the best of pals."
>
> And Len Hutton telling a Lancastrian too old for me to recognise that a Roses match was the next best thing to an England v. Australia test.
>
> The speeches flowed with reminiscence too. Mr. Miles N. Kenyon, a former Lancashire captain, recalled the time when Lancashire batted more drearily than usual at Bramall Lane. "I remember it because I was stoned by some small boys as I left the ground" he said amid loud laughter.
>
> Lord Scarbrough, proposing the health of the Lancashire County Cricket Club,

said the matches between the two sides had done three things. They had created in a rather material age a kind of chivalry between the two counties in which the characteristic courage, energy and courtesy had been splendidly displayed; they had provided a special spice of interest at Whitsuntide and August bank holidays for almost every human being in the two counties; and they had given a healthy inspiration to every boy.

The health of the Yorkshire County Cricket Club was proposed by Sir Francis Joseph and responded to by Sir William Worsley. Sir William referred to several who were unable to be present and said he particularly regretted the absence of the chairman of the Yorkshire club, Mr. Tom Taylor. "He would have loved to have been here" said Sir William.

They were also extremely sorry that George Hirst was not present. He had been hoping to come but ill-health had prevented him.

Telegrams of good wishes were read out from the MCC, the Surrey County Cricket Club, Mr. H. D. G. Leveson-Gower, Sir Pelham Warner and others."

Lord Scarbrough could well have added that the characteristics of torpor had also been rather splendidly displayed in these matches and it was not altogether inappropriate that the centenary Roses match at Headingley that year was one of the dullest ever. Five hours' batting on the Saturday produced 211 runs for Yorkshire and the crowd justifiably gave them the slow handclap. I wrote in the Yorkshire Post:

"Yorkshire copied the railwaymen in their match against Lancashire at Headingley on Saturday and went slow. Occasionally they went one better and stopped altogether. Five hours batting produced 211 runs—42 an hour.

The crowd of 16,000 did not like it. They clapped slowly, cheered ironically and swore they would never go again. Perhaps they did not realise that it was the centenary of these Roses duels. To ask Yorkshire, or for that matter Lancashire, to score at more than 40 an hour on such an occasion would have been asking them to ignore a grand tradition. It would have been like asking the organist to play rag-time at the harvest festival.

The day started tragically. Before we had got our score-cards from the little man with the white hair, a dejected Hutton was walking back to the pavilion, run out from the third ball. Gloom struck the Yorkshire ranks and there was not a single small boy to clap him on the back as he walked up the gangway and only the Lancastrians to applaud. They enjoyed it immensely. One of them was so excited that he lost his return ticket to Manchester and its discovery later had to be announced over the loudspeakers.

But Lowson and Halliday came gallantly to the rescue and it was half past two before another wicket fell. It was a grand partnership between sharply contrasting personalities—the serious Lowson, who always looks ashamed of himself, whether he has scored a duck or a hundred, and the happy Halliday, who smiles broadly at a bowler when he spreadeagles his wickets with his score at 96.

It was the afternoon that dragged interminably. The only time Wilson swung his bat was when he was practising at the bowler's end and Halliday didn't even do that. He merely leaned on it and thought about the theory of relativity or something.

The women did their crosswords and discussed Princess Elizabeth's dresses and the men argued fiercely about who should be dropped from the Yorkshire team. Only Hutton apparently was worth his place—and even he would have to do something in the second innings.

The tea interval arrived without anyone's noticing that the players had left the field and then at 4.20 a boy reading a detective story looked up and said "Something's happening, dad." It was. It was raining. So 12,000 people got up gratefully and went home.

It stopped about five o'clock and we martyrs who were left gathered in front of the pavilion to inform the umpires and players that they could start again. But we had to wait until twenty five to six before they made a reluctant reappearance. "Why haven't you all gone home?" they seemed to say.

Watson came in at five to six and showed his annoyance at being disturbed by getting two in the first half hour. "He's scoring at the rate of 24 a day" a statistician announced. "He should just reach his 50 before close of play on Tuesday."

And so we homeward plodded our weary way. And the funny thing about it is that we shall all be there again today. These English . . ."

But even this was better than the match at Headingley in 1954. I wrote two articles on the match, the first headed "For most it was an experience in monumental patience" and the second "More than 1,000 wait in rain-soaked desert: Roses match fails to bloom." They read like this:

"A crowd of 20,000, 12,000 of whom paid £1,395 at the turnstiles—spent one of the most exasperating bank holidays of their lives at Headingley yesterday waiting for play in the Roses match to start.

Most of them were in the ground by 11.30 am and the last did not leave until play was finally abandoned for the day at 5.30 pm. The rewards for their monumental patience and perseverance were long looks at the umpires and groundsmen as they repeatedly mopped up the pools on the wicket and shorter looks at the rival captains as they came out to inspect it. A ball or a bat they never saw.

It was a study in frustration. The weather was unbelievably perverse. A decisive downpour—such as washed out the Roses match at Old Trafford last Whit Monday—could have been taken with a stiff upper lip. We could have packed up our sandwich bags philosophically and gone off to queue for the pictures but there was no such happy release. The weather played with us like a cat with a mouse. It first drenched us to near despair and then held its fire while the wicket was dried and inspected. Then just as the players were about to appear it put down another barrage. It was never sufficiently dry to play—and never sufficiently wet for the real enthusiasts to go home.

The patient thousands, if patient is the right word, crouched under bicycle capes, umbrellas, raincoats and sodden newspapers and looked intently for breaks in the skies. The optimists saw them repeatedly but the pessimists looked without hope. They were declaring there would not be a ball bowled all day at half past eleven and presumably stayed until five thirty just for the masochistic satisfaction of proving themselves right.

The women were the only people who enjoyed themselves at all. They got much sardonic pleasure out of commenting on the stupidity of men. "You wouldn't believe it, would you?" they kept saying as their husbands refused to give up.

Not, of course, that there was a total lack of entertainment. Cricket grounds do not go in for playing music over loudspeakers (or any other such vulgar amusements) but there is always the more indigenous variety provided by the groundsman and his staff. The march of science seems to have passed cricket grounds completely by and the methods of drying the wicket yesterday (although doubtlessly highly efficient) must have been in vogue when W. G. Grace was a boy.

The operation was heralded by two men and a wheelbarrow containing sacks and blankets—some of which the moths had badly got at. These were placed on the pitch and stamped upon and then wheeled off to dry. There was some delay before their return and one man in the crowd said they were having difficulty finding a house with a wringer. That, however, I dispute. I am sure Headingley has a wringer of its own. Test matches, after all, are played there.

It wouldn't have been much use, however, if science had been employed. The weather was determined to win—and win it did. Some people were saying as they walked disconsolately home that it was time county cricket clubs started giving spectators their money back, or at least pass-out checks valid next day.

The women, of course, had no sympathy. "You would come" I heard one of them telling her husband as he groused on these lines. "I wish they'd charged you double."

It will, however, all be forgotten today—particularly if the sun shines."

But the sun didn't shine and I wrote the following day:

"There were four things that were proverbially considered to be wonderful to behold—the way of an eagle in the air, the way of a serpent upon a rock, the way of a ship in the midst of the sea and the way of a man with a maid. With due humility I would add a fifth—the way of a cricket supporter at a Roses match.

I went up to Headingley at 2 pm yesterday just out of idle curiosity. There might, I thought, be one or two incurable optimists who had got dry from Monday's soaking and come back for more. They would, I thought, be worth interviewing, if not for the Yorkshire Post then for the Lancet, but lo and behold there were more than one thousand armed with sandwich bags and binoculars and, in some cases, even sun glasses.

The gates were firmly shut but there were two queues, each more than one hundred yards long at the Kirkstall Lane entrance and nearly as many in St. Michael's Lane. And in the ground itself there were fully 500 members sitting hunched over their sandwiches in the pavilion discussing the prospects of bowling Lancashire out twice in four hours. Macaulay had apparently done something similar at Old Trafford in 1933—and there was no reason why Appleyard, (with the assistance of Wardle, Close and Trueman) should not do the same in 1954.

The presence of these incurables was putting the ground officials in rather a quandary. With prospects of play hopeless the staffs of all the refreshment rooms and bars had been sent home at ten o'clock and now a call for reinforcements was being considered.

"It's incredible" a girl in the secretary's office told me. "We're getting telephone calls from all over the place—including Manchester and Sheffield. They all want to know when we're starting."

Of course I will admit that at this precise moment it was fine—and that according to the experts the wind was "drying". It was also clear that the ground staff were working with superhuman energy, if not surgeon-like precision, on the wicket. They were stamping on their blankets with what can only be described as reckless abandon.

What everybody seemed to ignore, however, was a tremendous black cloud which was lurking over the boundary at deep fine leg. That cloud had spite and venom written all over it. It was clearly waiting for the right moment to pounce.

The feverish preparations went ahead. The umpires came out to inspect the wicket, prodded it and eyed it from all angles. The faithful gathered to greet them as they returned to the pavilion. "Any hope?" they asked in hushed, sick-room voices. The umpires gave noncommital nods and said there would be a further inspection with a view to play at three o'clock.

The glad news spread. More members arrived with sandwich bags, binoculars and sun glasses and the queues outside lengthened. Meanwhile the great black cloud—apparently invisible to all but me—was moving slowly in towards the wicket. Soon drops of rain began to fall—big drops which hit the sandwich bags with a resounding ping before rolling into the puddles on the floor. But still no-one noticed anything amiss.

Then at a quarter to three perception dawned. "It's looking bad" said a member as the rain streamed like Niagara off his hat. "I'm beginning to think we've had it."

His companion frowned at such unwarranted gloom. "Nobbut a shower" he said. "And, sithee, it's looking brighter over there."

The cloud moved off, roaring with laughter, at quarter to three but the damage—the irreparable damage—was done. And although, of course, no spectators thought of leaving I think in their hearts they knew it. The officials seemed to sense it too and the waiting queues outside the ground were admitted free. They swarmed in joyously to view the body.

Before the corpse could be interred, however, the proprieties had to be observed. Cricket is nothing if not decent. The umpires came out and solemnly examined the wicket. They prodded it with the right foot, prodded it with the left foot and stamped all over it.

But still no certificate of death could be issued. The rival captains, Yardley and Washbrook, were summoned. They solemnly felt the corpse's heart and Yardley shook his head and made a tragic gesture with his hands. Washbrook seemed to shed a silent tear.

"The match" boomed the loudspeakers two or three minutes later "has been officially abandoned."

And then the sun came out. Yes, I'm not inventing it—the sun came out. It spread its beneficence all over the ground and warmed our saddened hearts as we departed.

"It's Somerset at Bradford tomorrow" I heard one member observe to his companion. "Are you going for the start?"

The 1955 August bank holiday match was played at Bramall Lane and although Yorkshire dominated it from the start, any satisfaction they gained was forfeited by a display of popular side ignorance and ill manners on the Monday, which made nonsense of the proud assertion that the Sheffield crowd was the most knowledgeable in the country.

They revealed themselves on this occasion to be yobs of the first magnitude and I wrote an angry article in the Yorkshire Post the following day which appeared under the heading "Bramall Lane crowd blots its reputation."

"When the popular side crowd left the Roses match at Bramall Lane, Sheffield yesterday I hope they had the common decency to clothe themselves in sackcloth and ashes. For thus, and only thus, could they hope to redeem themselves for their outrageous conduct on Bank Holiday Monday.

It was conduct which almost every London newspaper from The Times downwards was yesterday at pains to condemn. It was conduct which will, when they hear about it, make living Yorkshiremen wince and dead Yorkshiremen turn in their graves. For Sheffield's shame is Yorkshire's shame and none of us can ignore it.

It all started when Lancashire's number 11 batsman, Tattersall, joined Lancashire's number six batsman, Grieves. Lancashire needed 28 runs to save the ignominy of following on and Grieves set about getting them in an orthodox and well approved way. He proceeded to farm the bowling. That is to say (for the few old ladies who do not understand the phrase) he kept as much of the bowling as possible himself and exposed his weaker partner to it only when it could not be avoided. To do this he refused to run singles, even easy ones.

On the pavilion side we silently nodded and agreed that it was the best thing to do. For a moment (only a moment) we even had a sneaking sympathy with Grieves in his mission.

And then the incredible happened—over on the popular side, beneath a large metal awning advertising somebody's beer, there were cat-calls and slow handclaps and impatient cries of "Ger-on-wi'-it Grieves."

We assumed at first that there was a sound and logical explanation for it—that the omniscient Sheffield crowd had spotted something we had missed. But as the slow hand clapping continued the awful truth dawned. Incredible as it seemed these people were barracking Grieves because they didn't understand what he was doing and merely thought he was wasting time.

We on the pavilion side blushed with shame and if there had been any room I think we would have crawled under the seats. Because, you see, there were odd Lancastrians sitting around us and as Lancashire wickets had been crashing we had lost no opportunity of rubbing their noses in the dust. That is to say we had sadly shaken our heads and regretted in stage whispers among ourselves that Lancashire cricket had sunk to such a deplorably low ebb.

We were, of course, powerless to do anything but ignore this monstrous barracking completely and pretend it didn't exist—and I felt we accomplished this difficult task rather well. I think we even inveigled the Lancastrians around us into thinking it didn't exist. At any rate I didn't hear any of them commenting on it and I know there were some sitting near me because they had all scowled together when Washbrook was out.

And yet I had a sneaking feeling we should not get away with it altogether—and that probably explains why I opened my papers yesterday morning with a strong sense of disaster. There was, of course, no reference to it whatever in the Yorkshire papers and, to my great relief, no mention of it in the Manchester Guardian. But, alas, those London papers had printed the lot and paraded our shame quite unmercifully before the world. That, needless to say, is the only reason why I am drawing attention to the disgraceful business now.

"The crowd of 28,000 at Bramall Lane are part of the old tradition although it is to be regretted that their cricket wisdom is not what it used to be" one paper commented. "The Bramall Lane spectators are slipping from their once proud title of most-knowledgable-crowd when they start slow handclapping a number 6 batsman who is trying to farm the bowling when the last man in is his partner."

Other papers wrote in similar vein and some of their comments stung like salt in open wounds. One paper even went so far as to suggest that the Sheffield crowd (and by implication all Yorkshire cricket followers) should wear dunces' caps.

It would not have been quite so deplorable if it had happened at Leeds or Bradford but at Sheffield it was inexcusable. A drastic remedy is obviously called for and the Yorkshire committee must study the problem at once. The only suggestion I can make is that no-one is ever allowed into Bramall Lane again until he has passed an examination on the elementary principles of cricket at the gate."

In 1956 it was Lancashire's turn to dominate and they won the Whitsuntide match at Headingley by 153 runs. This was only their second Roses victory since the war but it was two too many for the demanding Yorkshire supporters and they were still complaining bitterly about the team's performance when I went to the Yorkshire and Middlesex game at Bramall Lane the following Saturday. I wrote in the Yorkshire Post as follows:

"With the humiliating defeat by Lancashire at Headingley still rankling Yorkshire cricket supporters turned up for the Middlesex match at Bramall Lane, Sheffield, on Saturday in a mood of bitter reproach. You might think that the season is yet too young for any judgements on Yorkshire's performance but they could not be more complete if it was the middle of August. Dissatisfaction is profound.

"Did you see t'Lancashire match?" I was asked by a man on the pavilion in the very early stages of the Yorkshire innings.

I replied that I had been there on the Saturday and the Monday but had missed the final obsequies on the Tuesday.

"You were lucky" he said grimly in the Al Reed manner. "It were enough to break your heart."

He shook his head bitterly. "T'batting's no backbone" he said. "In the old days if a few of 'em failed it were a challenge to t'rest. You could bet that if Holmes and Sutcliffe were out for ducks Oldroyd and Leyland would get fifty apiece. But now? They've no fighting spirit. No backbone. They collapse like a pack of cards. Aye, like a pack of cards."

This, as I say, was when the Yorkshire innings had barely begun. I looked for the man on the pavilion again when Yorkshire had been ignominiously skittled out for 99 but presumably he had gone home long ago in disgust.

There were plenty of others lamenting Yorkshire's batting inadequacies, however. They stood in solemn little groups outside the tea tents behind the pavilion looking for all the world like sorrowing mourners at a graveside.

"No fighting spirit" I kept hearing. "If one fails they all fail. Now when we had people like Maurice Leyland and Brian Sellers . . ."

Brian Sellers was being invoked all over the place, not only for his fighting spirit but also for his qualities as a disciplinarian. "He'd have had 'em all out there this morning" said one elderly gentleman indignantly, pointing with his stick to the practice net.

"Nay" replied his friend. "You can't blame t'captain for that. They want overtime for practice these days."

Some, of course, went much further back than Brian Sellers in search of the missing inspiration and fighting spirit. One old gentleman was talking about Lord Hawke and F. S. Jackson and another about T. L. Taylor. A third was vainly trying to recall an incident which occurred at Bobby Peel's benefit in 1894. The past is all glory to Yorkshire cricket supporters—and the further away it is the brighter it glows.

Not that it is all carping criticism. Even the few critics who make an effort to be unbiased about the past seem to think that Yorkshire's fighting spirit is not what it was. Even old players do not seem to be greatly impressed by their youthful counterparts.

"What do you think of 'em?" I asked that famous character of the cricket field Emmott Robinson, who at the age of 71 looks good for at least a dozen overs at the pavilion end.

He didn't pass any comment of course. It would not have been politic. He merely shook his head and sighed like mourners do as the coffin is being lowered. "Nice day, isn't it?" he said, looking up to the sunlit heavens.

The phase will pass no doubt. Three or four victories in a row and Yorkshire will be Yorkshire again. Not, of course, that they will ever be like the Yorkshire they used to be . . ."

This remorseless self-criticism was still going on when the Old Trafford match came along in August that year (1956) and for my final contribution to the Yorkshire Post on Roses matches I had this to say under the heading "Please be discreet at Old Trafford."

"When Yorkshire cricket supporters pull the Yorkshire team to pieces at Park Avenue, Bramall Lane or Headingley I don't much mind. If I'm feeling that way out I will join in myself. "And what about so-and-so" I will say bitterly. "If ever a man wanted dropping it is him."

I can even regard it with moderate equanimity when Yorkshire supporters pull the team to pieces in the correspondence columns of the Yorkshire Post.

When Yorkshire supporters pull the team to pieces on the pavilion at Old Trafford, however, I feel it is going too far—much, much too far. Quite frankly I was disgusted with some of my compatriots on Saturday.

It started as far as I was concerned when one of those familiar Lancastrians, ruddy of face and bright of eye, emerged from the pavilion bar in mid-afternoon breathing beer and benevolence all around him.

"No, I'm not sitting with you, Fred," he said in a loud voice to his friend. "I want a Yorkshireman to sit next to. I'm feeling like an argument. Now where are all these white roses?"

There was a general chortle of amusement as there so often is on the pavilion at Old Trafford—a pavilion which is not just a place to sit in as at Leeds or Bradford, but a place which has all the intimate friendliness of a club—including that most convenient bar. "There aren't none, Fred," chuckled another ruddy faced individual who looked to be on the verge of a stroke. "They've all wilted."

Fred, however, identified a Yorkshireman by his blue and yellow county tie and squeezed himself laboriously into the seat next to him. "Now then" he said belligerently, just spoiling for a fight, "you've got a bloomin' awful team this season, haven't you?"

The Yorkshireman looked up glumly—the score at that particular moment was Yorkshire 97 for five. "Aye," he said laconically, "we have. We're all thoroughly disgusted with 'em. I don't know what the heck we've come for today."

The Lancastrian looked at him in blank amazement. Never in all the long and glorious history of Old Trafford had such a damning admission been elicited from a Yorkshireman before. It took the wind completely out of his sails. He found himself in the absurd position of defending Yorkshire against the white rose detractors.

"Nay" he said slowly "t' bowling's not so bad. It's t' batting that's letting you down. 'Course I suppose t'trouble is you're missing Hutton."

"Aye," said the Yorkshireman dourly, "and Holmes, Sutcliffe, Oldroyd, Leyland, Mitchell, Barber and a good few more. Wilfred Rhodes could bat a lot better than any of this lot. It's the most disgraceful bloomin' side we've ever had. They've got better batsmen in t'Sunday school league."

"Nay, I don't know" said the Lancastrian generously. "Watson's not so bad."

"Watson?" growled the Yorkshireman. "Don't you mention Watson to me. Haven't you seen what he's just been and done? Run Padgett out when he were just getting going and then run himself out as well."

The Lancastrian busily studied his card. He had evidently missed this bit of excitement when he was at the bar—as Lancastrians at Old Trafford have a habit of doing.

"How many did he get?" he asked.

"Seven" said the Yorkshireman bitterly. "Not that I'm grumbling about that. It's a good score for Yorkshire is seven. But if he hadn't gone and run himself out he might have gone and got ten." He laughed sardonically. "And then I suppose they'd have given him talent money."

The Lancastrian shook his head. It still obviously struck him as uncanny. "So you don't think you're going to beat us this time?" he asked.

"Beat you?" said the Yorkshireman bitterly. "We couldn't beat the old age pensioners this season. Did you see what we scored in the first hour? Twenty. Twenty bloomin' runs in sixty blinkin' minutes. If I'd my way I'd put Lowson and Billy Sutcliffe on a charge."

They sat in silence for some time, the Lancastrian mournfully shaking his head and the Yorkshireman scowling darkly. Suddenly Brian Close disturbed the cloistered calm by hitting a six and there was a round of applause. The Yorkshireman did not join in. "Marvellous" he said ironically. "Six off one ball. They'll be putting his name forward for a place in t'test team after that."

The Lancastrian could stand the denigration no longer. These were the things he should be saying—had been saying at Roses matches at Old Trafford for 30 years. He got slowly to his feet. If this was the white rose attitude watching the cricket was obviously pointless. He sighed with frustration and walked back to the bar.

As I say I felt disgusted about it. It is taking things much too far and I appeal to Yorkshire supporters to try to put matters right. Let us all take our places on the pavilion at Old Trafford this morning with large white roses proudly displayed in our buttonholes. And if things follow their usual pattern, well let's just pop them in our pockets and keep quiet. And leave playing pop until we've crossed the Pennines!"

Even in Yorkshire's relatively successful years in the 1950's—and they came second to Surrey in the championship in 1951, 1952, 1954 and 1955 and won the title in 1959—the team's supporters were not sparing in their criticisms. I wrote an article early in 1955, for instance, mildly protesting against the chorus of disgruntlement which expressed itself at the annual meeting of the Yorkshire County Cricket Club, held perhaps rather appropriately in the Leeds City Museum, which greeted entrants with a large placard proclaiming "The meteorological record for 1954". This recorded that the sunshine had been the lowest since 1920, the rainfall the highest since 1951 and the "highlight of the year" was the fact that rain fell on 181 days.

Under the heading "Field day for cricket critics" I wrote:

"It may have been the lack of inspiration in the museum posters which induced in the members a disgruntled mood. At any rate although they expressed themselves as completely satisfied with the way the club was run and accorded votes of thanks to the president, secretary and other officials with hearty unanimity they took leave to express some doubts about the team's performance. The team had had the temerity last season to finish as low down the championship table as second—and something obviously needed to be done about it. One member called for desperate remedies.

"There was a lack of the proper spirit in some matches, Mr. President," he protested. "A lot of members were very disappointed. I hope that if the same lack of spirit is shown this year you will show less tolerance and drop 'em."

There were strong murmurs of approval to this merciless proposal and although no names were mentioned publicly, private lists were rapidly compiled. "So-and-so wants dropping for one" a member behind me whispered to his neighbour. "He should never have been in t'team anyway." "Aye," came the reply, "and what about so-and-so? He can't even bend down to pick t'ball up, never mind do owt wi' it."

There was nothing new about this, of course. Dropping all the players except Hutton is one of the Yorkshire members' favourite recreations. They spend hours fixing the dropping order at every match—with the tempo increasing after rain has stopped play. But coming up as it did at the annual meeting gave it a new and more sinister significance. The members obviously mean business and if I were in the Yorkshire team next season I should see to it that I got a century or took ten wickets in every match.

It was perhaps unfortunate that while this shock treatment was being billed for the future an official should return members' minds to the past. He got up to propose the re-election of Mr. T. L. Taylor as president and he recalled in doing so that Mr. Taylor played for Yorkshire as long ago as 1899. He also recalled that Mr. Taylor took part in "the memorable match at Leeds in 1902 when Yorkshire beat the Australians by about 20 runs."

There could have been no better way of restoring passivity to the meeting and contentment to the members' minds. Many of them were old enough to recall that memorable match—and even those who weren't knew all about it. Reminiscence flowed. So did argument—that other form of cricket-lovers' bliss.

"I tell you he's wrong" said one elderly man emphatically as they all drifted their way back to January offices and firesides. "Yorkshire won by five wickets. The Australians batted first and got about 100. Yorkshire were behind on the first innings but when the Australians went in again Hirst and Jackson skittled 'em out for 23. And Yorkshire were left to make 50 odd to win and did it with five wickets to spare. By God I remember it as clearly as if it were yesterday."

It is perhaps to add that little extra clarity to their vision that members turn up so keenly for the annual meeting. And, of course, for the pleasure of commiserating with each other that neither cricket nor cricketers are what they were."

Of course this uncharitable—nay misanthropic—attitude to the performances of first class cricketers was not confined to Yorkshire supporters at this time—nor I am sure, is it today. I went one bright May afternoon in 1952 to the famous Lancashire township of Nelson to see how the world-renowned Australian fast bowler Ray Lindwall was faring in his first season as the club's professional at a record fee of £1,300. Nelson were playing a club called Lowerhouse and Lindwall was in devastating form, taking eight wickets for 51—six clean bowled and two leg before.

I wrote in the Yorkshire Post as follows:

"At one time he had seven for 21—and if it had not been for a couple of dropped catches he would probably have taken all ten and given his side a decisive victory. For when stumps were drawn at seven o'clock, Lowerhouse had mustered only 122 for eight in reply to Nelson's total of 183 for six declared.

But were the 5,000 Nelson supporters wild with enthusiasm over Lindwall's performance? Not at all. They are paying him a lot of money and they expect him to earn it. And to earn £1,300 in the opinion of some of them you have to be more than a great fast bowler. You have to be a superman.

"Aye, it's about time he did summat" said a dour little man in a cloth cap as I applauded another Lindwall wicket. "He's done nowt up to now, tha knows. Six for 14 at Todmorden last week were his best."

Another supporter—an old man with a white moustache and a white silk muffler—leaned forward on his walking stick. "Not fast enough" he said decisively. "That's his trouble. Not half as fast as Connie."

He began to reminisce about Leary Constantine—he was Nelson's professional from 1929 to 1937—and was describing one of his remarkable feats with the ball when the next Lowerhouse batsman reached the crease. He broke off as he took his guard and we watched in silence as Lindwall walked back 25 paces towards the sight screen. The first ball was in the wicket-keeper's gloves before the batsman made his stroke. The second sent his off stump cartwheeling towards deep third man.

There was a roar from part of the crowd but my two companions remained silent. "Good ball that Fred," said the little man at last, a sudden burst of generosity getting the better of him. "Don't think he ever saw it."

The man in the muffler considered the point. "Aye," he said slowly, "not bad, not bad. But nowt like Connie, tha knows. He did more ner knock wickets out o' t'ground, did Connie. He smashed 'em i' two, Albert. Smashed em i' two."

The fifth ball of Lindwall's over accidentally hit the bat—and the new batsman was so surprised about it that he almost dropped it out of his hands. He made no stroke at the sixth for it was off the wicket and fell harmlessly into the wicket-keeper's hands. The man in the muffler shook his head. "He's tiring Albert" he said decisively, "tiring. They tell me he's been wi' a masseur in Burnley all week."

Besides being hard to please, the Nelson crowd is also aggressive. "What's thi bat for?" they shout when the ball thuds sickeningly on a batsman's ribs. "Tha's flayed on him" they cry when a batsman ducks at a bouncer. "Give him a bucket" they yell when a fieldsman drops a difficult catch.

Their approach to cricket is well illustrated by their favourite spectacle. It is not a classic drive through the covers or a text book late cut through the slips. It is not even a towering six out of the ground. The thing they like to see most of all is their opponents' wickets flying—and the further they fly the better they like it.

"That's why nearly all our professionals have been fast bowlers" Mr. J. Powis, the club chairman, told me. "We started in 1919 with Pat Morfee of Kent and then we had E. A. McDonald of Australia. Constantine came from the West Indies in 1929 and he was undoubtedly the most popular player there has ever been in the league. In the nine seasons he was with us we won the championship seven times."

The rules of Lancashire league cricket laid down that each of the 14 teams competing must have one professional but one only. Every team endeavoured to get a first class player not simply to improve their chances for the championship but to attract a high membership and good gates. This season, for instance, Nelson had 1,800 members paying annual subscriptions varying from 10s. to £3 3s. and at 1s. 3d. admission gate money on Saturday amounted to £220. Without the attraction of Lindwall these receipts would be nothing like so high.

Although the importation of star players may swell the treasurer's coffers and enable money to be spent on the ground it tends to turn the teams into one man bands. The only batsman who played Lindwall with any confidence on Saturday was R. E. Marshall, the former West Indian player who is now professional for Lowerhouse. He scored 60 and took four of the six Nelson wickets which fell. And no doubt the Lowerhouse supporters were far from being satisfied with that.

Lindwall himself is a quiet, modest man and when I spoke to him in the dressing room he was concerned about his comparative failure with the bat—his 26 on Saturday equalled his highest score of the season.

I asked him whether he would be playing for Australia in the test matches over here next year but he replied cautiously "I've got to be picked first."

On Saturday's performance he need have no fears on that score. Nelson supporters showed they are taking to him by contributing £22 to a collection to mark his bowling feat. And if he is good enough for Nelson he is certainly good enough for Australia."

Usually my search for cricket stories for the Yorkshire Post was confined to the summer months but in 1949 I went to the first Boxing Day cricket match organised by the Northern section of the Cricket Society and its highly enterprising secretary Mr. Ron Yeomans, later to become a prominent member of the Yorkshire committee. Mr. Yeomans was a journalistic colleague of mine on our sister paper, the Yorkshire Evening Post, and saw the publicity value in such an unorthodox event. The match, played at Collingham near Wetherby, drew quite a crowd and was so successful that it became an annual event. I wrote of that first match as follows:

> The Boxing Day cricket match on a matting wicket at Collingham between the Northern section of the Cricket Society led by Maurice Leyland and a village team caused surprise to the non-cricket enthusiasts who left their yule logs to see it.
>
> Mostly the wives of enthusiasts, they had gone to see a freak—a cricket match in the heart of winter. They cherished secret hopes of seeing icicles hang from the wickets, batsmen retire frost-bitten and a heavy snow plough used between the innings. Instead they saw a perfectly normal match and in conditions a good deal more pleasant than those provided at many a summer fixture.
>
> The sun gleamed on the players' flannels, the bowlers took their sweaters off and not even the umpires looked cold. But the non-cricket enthusiasts were only a small proportion of the 200 odd spectators. Most of them were the men one sees patrolling in front of the new stand at lunch time at Headingley. The sort of people who would gladly travel to the North Pole on Boxing Day to see a cricket match.
>
> They enjoyed themselves immensely. They leaned learnedly on the fence or drank coffee in the pavilion and wondered why no-one had thought of a Boxing Day cricket match before. To them it was a breath of summer, an intimation of paradise, a challenge to the muddied oafs who reign so supreme from September to May.
>
> There were all the ingredients of a test match. A flurry of photographers made the captains toss five times and the opening batsmen walk out twice and an army of schoolboys searched so intensively for autographs that they scarcely saw a ball bowled. They unearthed Herbert Sutcliffe having a quiet lunch in a car on the boundary and no doubt made him wish he'd stayed by the fire at home.
>
> As for the game itself the Cricket Society won easily. They batted first and scored 73 for seven in the 90 minutes allotted. Johnny Lawrence, the Somerset bowler, was top scorer with a sparkling 37. Leyland, to everybody's disappointment, was bowled for one and Arthur Wood and Billy Sutcliffe, the other stars in the team, did little better. Stars on these occasions rarely do.
>
> Collingham, against the devastating attack of Sutcliffe, Lawrence and Leyland, could only amass a modest 18 in reply and the match finished fully half an hour before the celebratory dinner at the Old Star Inn down the road was ready. Arthur Wood filled in time with a few wicket-keeping stories, however, and a jolly time was had by all.

But perhaps the most delightful non-first class cricket match I wrote up in the Yorkshire Post was that at Hovingham Hall, near Malton, in 1955 between Sir William Worsley's eleven and I Zingari, one of the oldest cricket clubs in England. The cricket match, played on one of the most perfect days I ever remember, had Len Hutton as the home team captain and contained a number of celebrities but it was really quite incidental to the main proceedings of the afternoon, which took the form of a garden fête and included entertainment by the Scarborough Highland Pipe Band and Dancers in full ceremonial regalia, with scarlet tunics glinting in the sunshine and green kilts swinging. There was also a tug-of-war, a balloon race, a bowls competition, a treasure hunt, a coconut shy and other attractions, all going on simultaneously with the cricket in the shade of the yews and the elms surrounding the idyllic cricket ground in front of the old 18th century house.

The fête had been organised by Sir William in aid of the British Legion, and Hutton, the star attraction, did not let anyone down. He scored 77 sparkling runs to the accompaniment of the Malton White Star Band playing the Eton Boating Song and other familiar airs and took five wickets for 43. "But" I wrote in my article, "although very seriously conducted the cricket was incidental to the pleasures of the afternoon. It was essentially a country and not a county match, that is to say you watched it slumbrously in the shade of the trees, listening to the strains of the band, and retired to the bar or the soft drinks counter at regular intervals. Clergymen strolled by in straw boaters and ladies of quality sat in deck chairs with parasols. Countrymen wiped ruddy faces with ruddy handkerchiefs and inserted stubby fingers inbetween collars and necks. Children frolicked in the long grass over the boundary edges and pleaded for more and yet more ice cream."

It must have been memories of this idyllic country cricket match at Hovingham Hall—my article on which brought me a kindly note of appreciation from Sir William Worsley—that inspired my first lyrical article on cricket written for the Yorkshire Post on the opening of the cricket season of 1957: "The cricket season opens this weekend" said the BBC announcer on Saturday "and we are now taking you over to Lords for a commentary by Rex Alston on the match between the MCC and Yorkshire." What magic the words conjured up—what beautiful vistas they unfolded! The curtains of winter were drawn back and summer stood revealed in all its glory. The sun shines out of a cloudless sky and we doze with our hats over our noses watching the run stealers flicker to and fro. The world and all its worries are forgotten and eternity is captured in an hour."

How this catastrophic opening paragraph got past the sub-editors I don't know, but I put my feet back on the floor in the second paragraph by saying that most of us had a shrewd suspicion that the dream and the reality did not often coincide—that we would spend more time with our raincoats over our noses watching the run stealers flicker into the pavilion.

> "I am never quite sure whether county cricket or village cricket provides the true glories. As far as aesthetic appeal is concerned, of course, the county matches stand supreme. The late cut which makes you hold your breath in wonder, the leg glance which induces an ecstasy of wild delight, are essentially attributes of the first class game.
>
> So too are the dignity and pomp. The pitch in village cricket is inspected from the pavilion door—if it has a door. The game begins with a "Come on lads, let's get cracking."
>
> In county cricket on the other hand decorum is all important. Fingers have to be prodded in the turf and gloomy glances exchanged with groundsmen. Further inspections have to be ordered in half an hour.
>
> But if county cricket is the game for artistry, village cricket is the game for character and charm. It is on the fields where square leg lies invisible down the banking and mid off picks daisies that the multi-coloured fabric of cricket is woven. The county pattern is all of a piece.
>
> It is only on the village fields, for instance, that women come into their cricketing inheritance. County cricket is essentially a man's game. Women may watch it but they never in any sense belong to it.
>
> In village cricket on the other hand women are as much a part of the scene as the pads and the gloves. Without their flowered frocks and stacks of sandwiches—

and their eternal talk about babies—no village game would be complete.

And yet for all the charm and character it still retains, is village cricket quite what it was? I hardly think so. There is too much apeing of the professionals these days—too much sartorial splendour. Demon bowlers no longer wear braces and swashbuckling batsmen no longer lack collars. Everyone is immaculate—and dull.

The aristocratic tradition has also disappeared. The village squire no longer exists to play—and if he did he would have no privileges. He would be given out leg before by his gardener without a qualm.

And what has happened to the clergymen—so essential a part of the village scene? You rarely see them nowadays—and if you do they no longer wear panama hats and stand under the shade of elms. Can it be that cricket and religion are not so closely akin?

It is a disturbing thought and not one to pursue at the beginning of the season. It has been said after all that we invented cricket in the first place to give ourselves an idea of eternity. It is not an idea we should lightly abandon.

9 THE 1950's—SEEDS OF REVOLUTION

Looking back at the cricket I watched in the 1950's it seems almost as distant as the cricket of my apprenticeship years in the 1930's. The cricket revolution which was to change the shape of the game almost out of recognition in the 1960's and 1970's had scarcely begun at the end of the 1950's but in retrospect one can see that its seeds were very effectively sown. The 1950's were the decade in which county cricket as it had been played successfully since the days of W. G. Grace, C. B. Fry and K. S. Ranjitsinhji finally lost its way. It gradually ceased to be a crowd-drawing attraction and it became apparent to discerning cricket spectators probably more clearly than to the players and administrators that something needed to be done if it was not to die of exhaustion and old age.

Too much county cricket was deadly dull. It lacked drama, colour, character and life. It was a bore. Too often even the dedicated supporter would come home from a day's cricket with the feeling that his time could have been much better spent. It was like watching indifferent TV—having sat down in front of the set and switched it on one could not draw up the resolution to get up and switch it off but watched it apathetically and without taking it all in. The undedicated went further. They did switch it off. The cricket audience steadily drifted away. Even the most compelling of county fixtures—such as the Roses matches in the north and the big Lord's fixtures in the south—failed to draw the crowds in any volume and the days of closing the gates at Headingley and Old Trafford on any occasion other than a test match were clearly gone forever. Upwards of 10,000 was considered a very good gate at a county game.

It is probably not fair to blame the players exclusively for this because other factors contributed. The greater pace and variety of modern life and the more diversive and sophisticated tastes of the post-war generation provided cricket with many new competitors as a recreation medium and, although the meteorologists often disputed it, the summers of the pre-war era certainly seemed in retrospect to be far kinder than the consistent soakers of the 1950's.

There was also the increasing commercialisation of sport which in cricket expressed itself in an elevation of the status of test cricket vis-à-vis county cricket because it paid much better. And also there were the actions of cricket's administrators who sought to solve the problem of falling attendances with the wrong remedies. There was great emphasis on the provision of "sporting" pitches which sought to give the bowlers more assistance and facilitate the achievement of more results in county matches in place of the all too frequent draws. But a side effect of this was that batting became more difficult and the batting stars who had always been the biggest crowd-pullers virtually ceased to exist.

So far as I can recall, the only batting stars produced in the 1950's were Peter May and Colin Cowdrey, with Tom Graveney and Ted Dexter arguably in that category.

Of star bowlers and all-rounders there were plenty—Bedser, Laker, Lock, Trueman, Statham, Tyson, Wardle, Appleyard, Bailey, Close and Illingworth, to mention the most prominent. Another factor limiting the development of star batsmen was, of course, the change in the lbw rule which made a batsman more vulnerable to off spin and in-swing bowling.

But the players were ultimately responsible for the decline in the cricket audience. They somehow lacked the zest of the pre-war and immediate post-war players. Both batsmen and bowlers seemed to have a defensive, negative approach to the game. The batsmen's primary purpose no longer seemed to be to score runs but to avoid losing their wickets. The bowlers' aims seemed not so much to take wickets but to prevent runs being scored off them. There was far too much defensive batting and negative bowling down the leg side and not enough attacking stroke play and attacking bowling on the off or on the wicket. Both batsmen and bowlers seemed to be completely unaware, or at any rate oblivious of the fact that crowds came to cricket matches to be entertained—and that if they were not entertained they went home as dissatisfied customers. There were far too many dissatisfied customers in the 1950's. Players may have succeeded in producing good averages for themselves but as public entertainers they failed dismally to satisfy their public and so stand condemned. It is they who were basically responsible for the introduction of the desperate remedies of the 1960's which so many of the real cricket-watching public and so many of the players bitterly regret.

This is not to say that the 1950's were utterly devoid of good dramatic cricket or of talented and colourful cricketers. If Yorkshire were the dominant force in county cricket in the 1940's and their leading batsman, Hutton, was the dominant player, then Surrey were the dominant county in the 1950's and Surrey's Peter May was the leading player. Surrey assumed Yorkshire's mantle and gave it added lustre by winning the championship seven years in succession from 1952 to 1958 inclusive. Yorkshire, however, were only demoted to second place in four years and took over the crown again from Surrey in 1959.

Peter May I remember as a modest, self-effacing, perpetually boyish character who first made his impact at Headingley in 1951 when I saw him score a most brilliant 138 against South Africa in his first test match appearance. It was soon self-evident that May would succeed Hutton as England's captain when Hutton relinquished that position and he led the side in three series against Australia in 1956, 1958/59 and 1961.

Although he was higher in the social scale than Hutton, having been educated at Charterhouse and playing his cricket as an amateur, May was curiously akin to Hutton in some ways and his career followed a very similar course, finishing at the even earlier age of 33 due to ill-health and nervous strain. He crowded 66 test appearances into his 10-year career as an England player (41 of them as captain). He was a pupil and great admirer of Hutton's and like him was a classic stylist. Both men were quiet, reserved and shy in manner and both were accused of being withdrawn and not being "one of the boys." There was a ridiculous charge against May that he had neglected his team in Australia on the disastrous 1958/59 tour, in which England lost four out of the five tests, because of the presence during part of the tour of his fiancée. May scored 27,592 runs in his cricket career with an average of 51. He scored 85 centuries and had a test average of 56.

Although May was the backbone of Surrey's batting in all the seven seasons in which they won the county championship in the 1950's and was very ably supported by such

Bob Appleyard, who retired prematurely due to ill health, was one of Yorkshire's most successful bowlers, taking 657 wickets in nine seasons at an average of 15.40.

people as Eric Bedser, Fletcher, Clark, Constable and later Edrich, Barrington and Stewart, it is probably true to say that the principal reason for Surrey's pre-eminence was the bowling of Bedser, Loader, Lock and Laker and the inspired, dynamic captaincy of Stuart Surridge, the Brian Sellers of his day.

Some of the less charitable commentators have also claimed that one of the major participants in Surrey's long run of success was the Oval groundsman, Bert Lock, whose pitches, they allege, were specially prepared to suit Surrey's bowling attack. No less a cricket authority than Brian Close is one of them. In his autobiography he tells of a conversation his brother Peter, a member of the Metropolitan Police Force, had with Bert Lock about the Oval wicket in which Lock told him that towards the end of the 1950's there was a little fluttering in the Surrey dovecotes which left him (Lock) furious. "All right" he said "they think they are good enough to win matches on their own. Let them try!" Comments Brian Close: "Ask yourself—how many times have Surrey won the championship since that point? And reflect if you will that for nearly 20 years the Oval square has been getting slower and slower until it is now (1978) one of the worst feather-beds in the world." He adds charitably "this is not to say for one second that in the 1950's Surrey were not a fine side, but contrast the help they got from their home pitches with what Yorkshire got on theirs."

How true this charge is I am not qualified to judge. The preparation of pitches and the assessments of their qualities are one of the esoteric mysteries of cricket which baffle most spectators. Players of long experience talk and write of wicket preparation being one of the most determining factors of the game and there is no question that it is very important. Perhaps some celebrated groundsman will sometime write a book on the dark art of concocting a binding agent out of animal blood and dung—a type of pitch which I gather the experts recognise more by smell than sight!

The aim of groundsmen in the 1930's was to make pitches fast and true and there was competition between groundsmen on this principle. When England's score at the famous Oval test match in 1938 reached 730 for five wickets, the Oval groundsman is said to have regarded his prowess in breaking the Lord's record of 729 for six in the 1930 match as of equal significance to Hutton's breaking of Bradman's record for the highest innings in a test match of 334! But while it is no doubt true that the preparation of placid wickets devoid of grass was responsible to some extent for the high scoring in the 1930's I cannot believe that it explains the relative superiority of the batsmen of those days, just as I cannot believe that Bert Lock's wickets at the Oval in the 1950's explain Surrey's long succession of championship victories.

Surrey's number one bowler, if test records are any criterion, was Jim Laker who took 193 test wickets with an average of 21.24, compared with Bedser's 236 wickets at 24.89 and Lock's 174 at 25.58. Laker, of course, was Yorkshire's biggest mistake. He was a native of Shipley, Bradford, and how he escaped the Yorkshire net I don't know. It was probably due to the war, for Laker was 17 when hostilities began in 1939 and presumably matured as a bowler during the time county cricket was suspended. His services would probably have turned the balance in favour of Yorkshire in several of those seven seasons of Surrey's triumph.

My outstanding memory of Laker is of a test trial match I saw in which he played at his native Park Avenue ground in Bradford in 1950. He had a remarkable analysis of eight wickets for two runs. Park Avenue has always had the reputation of being a "sporting" wicket when the turf is soft and the sun is shining but on this occasion, in the expert off spinning fingers of Laker, it was not so much sporting as completely unplayable. Laker's most remarkable performance, of course, was his unique feat in taking 19 wickets for 90 runs in the Old Trafford test against the Australians in 1956. No-one was more capable of exploiting a sticky wicket.

Today Laker is known to millions as one of the BBC's TV cricket commentators and is generally regarded as leading the field in this activity—probably because he is a typical laconic Yorkshireman who never talks for the sake of it and, when he does, never uses half a dozen words when two or three will do. In this respect he is the exact opposite of that brilliant wordsmith, John Arlott, and the irrepressible and highly entertaining Brian Johnston who lead the radio commentating field. Laker greatly upset the cricketing establishment towards the end of the 1950's with the publication of his outspoken book "Over To Me" and this resulted in his honorary membership of the MCC and Surrey being suspended. This affair was subsequently resolved by an apology and retraction of the offending statements.

The man who took the one Australian wicket which Laker did not take in the test match against the Australians at Old Trafford in 1956 was G.A.R. (Tony) Lock whom I chiefly remember as a left arm bowler with a very suspect action and little hair, who bowled faster than any other left arm spinner I have known. Like most people I thought he threw his faster ones and it was not surprising that he was prominent in the 1950's throwing controversy which shattered the dovecotes throughout the cricketing world—particularly in Australia and the West Indies.

Alec Bedser, who might qualify as the cricket doyen of the present day, I remember as one of the nicest of men about whom I don't think any cricketer has a wrong word to say. He took 236 wickets for England—a total only exceeded by Fred Trueman's 307—and was a keystone of England's attack in the early 1950's.

Although Surrey's contribution to English cricket in the 1950's can thus be seen as very important Yorkshire's was not insignificant. Len Hutton captained England in 23 test matches in the first half of the decade (in which period we recovered the Ashes in the 1953 series in England and retained them in the 1954/55 tour of Australia) and half a dozen other Yorkshiremen had regular places in the England team at one time or another—Wardle, Appleyard, Watson, Illingworth, Close and, the greatest of them all, Trueman. Several others—Don Wilson, Don Brennan and Ernie Leadbeater—made sporadic appearances for England too.

These were all great players but they did not succeed in producing a great Yorkshire side in the 1950's. And this despite the fact that they had the support of quite a number of other talented players who came very near to being selected for England—Halliday, Lester, Keighley, J. V. Wilson, Padgett, Stott, Taylor and J. G. Binks, who, after Don Brennan, was the wicket-keeper in this decade. Yorkshire's performance in the championship was not at all bad in the 1950's compared with what it was to become in the 1970's—once top, four times second, twice third, once seventh, once eleventh and once twelfth—but Yorkshire supporters all felt that with the talent available they should have done much better. And no doubt they would have done if the team had not been a house divided against itself.

Many people, including some of the players, have borne witness to the fact that the Yorkshire dressing room in the 1950's was not a happy place. Indeed it was a pit of discord and discontent. Fred Trueman, in his frank, fascinating autobiography, "Ball of Fire", is characteristically the most outspoken of these witnesses but, as is not always the case with Trueman's charges, there is no shortage of backing for what he has to say. And what he has to say is that the team was split from top to bottom with rival cliques, the senior players like Hutton and Yardley going their way and the youngsters such as Lowson, Close and himself staying "out in the cold." "There was terrible jealousy between the groups" he writes. "The younger players quickly learned never to approach the seniors for help."

Yardley, who was captain from 1948 to 1955, must accept a big share of the responsibility for this atmosphere of dissension and some people feel that he held on to the captaincy too long. It would certainly have been appropriate if he had handed over the leadership to Hutton when Hutton was made captain of England. As I have said before, Yardley was the best amateur captain Yorkshire ever had but, as Trueman among other members of his team has said, he was not the strong man that Yorkshire needed at the helm—he was "too nice a chap" and let forceful characters like Wardle and Appleyard get away with far too much. Trueman, who was no friend of Hutton's, says how galling it must have been for the captain of England to take orders from Yardley and although I imagine, knowing Hutton, that it did not worry him as much as it would have worried Freddie it was a very odd arrangement to say the least. There are some who think this was a big factor in Hutton's decision to retire at the early age of 39. If Trueman is to be believed, Yardley did not want Hutton to succeed him and did not announce his own retirement until just after Hutton had announced his.

The splits in the Yorkshire fabric were not repaired when Billy Sutcliffe, son of Herbert, took over the captaincy in 1958. Trueman has this to say about Sutcliffe: "What happened to him was really a disgrace to Yorkshire cricket. He was a very likable man and a superb bat—quite good enough to have walked into the England team had he been playing today. I fell out with the Yorkshire crowd during Billy's captaincy. They were on to him all the time, shouting insults like 'You'll never be as good as your father.' In many ways I'm glad my own son does not look as though he is going to be a cricketer because it must be hell to follow a famous father. Billy also failed to master Johnny Wardle and eventually a group of players got a petition together demanding his resignation. I refused to have anything to do with it, but Billy decided to pack it in after that. It must have broken his heart."

The running battle with Wardle was the main talking point amongst Yorkshire spectators in 1958 after the recovery from the surprise of Ron Burnet's appointment as captain in place of Sutcliffe. Burnet, an amateur, was the captain of the second team and would have been the first to admit that he was not up to county standards. Indeed he had very little experience of senior cricket. But he was a natural leader and a man of considerable courage—as he needed to be to carry out his brief to re-unite the divided Yorkshire team. The first result of his appointment was to deepen the division in the Yorkshire dressing room and Wardle was probably the most resentful because he had ambitions to become Yorkshire's first professional captain himself. The relationship between him and the new amateur captain was strained, to put it mildly.

It seemed odd to the spectators that Wardle should be the centre of the storm because on the face of it he was the most happy-go-lucky member of the team—extremely popular with the crowd and liked as much for his apparently cheerful personality as for his clowning in the field—never excessive like Trueman's sometimes was—and his ability to hit sixes in profusion. But those who knew Wardle realised that he had a quick temper, a difficult, unyielding nature and a somewhat exaggerated idea of his own importance—a fatal defect for a cricketer as for most other people.

The crunch came while Yorkshire were playing Lancashire at Old Trafford. Wardle had written a series of articles for the Daily Mail about the Yorkshire team and the new captain was one of a number of people subjected to strong criticism. Burnet's reaction was, after consulting the committee, to sack Wardle on the spot and he never played for Yorkshire again. He also forfeited his place in the England side which had been selected for the forthcoming tour of Australia. It was a tragic end at the early age of 35 to a career of considerable achievement. Wardle had taken 102 wickets for England at an average of 20.39 and for Yorkshire 1,537 wickets at 17.67. Wardle tended to be underestimated by Yorkshire supporters because of the eminence of his two great predecessors as the county's chief slow left arm bowler—Hedley Verity and Wilfred Rhodes—but Wardle was to prove to have been a far better bowler of his type than any of his successors right up to the present day.

Burnet did a wonderful job for Yorkshire not only in welding the team together again but actually taking them to victory in the championship in his second and final season, 1959. He recreated the team spirit which had been lost under Yardley and not recovered under Sutcliffe, and laid the foundations of the much more successful 1960's.

If it had been that other stormy petrel of the 1950's Yorkshire team, Freddie Trueman, who had been sacked instead of Johnny Wardle it would have caused much less surprise to Yorkshire supporters, although doubtlessly even more disappointment. Trueman was renowned all over the world for his unruliness and for being a "difficult" player to handle and the stories about his behaviour and escapades in England, Australia and the West Indies will be told as long as cricket is played. But one of the surprising aspects of Trueman's many-sided character was that he could often get on with forceful people like himself who liked to lay down the law far better than he could hit it off with the more reticent and diffident types. He got on very well, for instance, with R. W. V. Robins on an MCC tour of the West Indies whereas the mild-mannered, much more diplomatic Colin Cowdrey could not get on with Robins at all.

By one of God's mercies for which all Yorkshire supporters must be thankful, Trueman got on very well with Burnet and he tells in his book how he reacted in his first match under the new captain—how Burnet "ordered" Close to open the batting and when he objected told him he would go in first or go back home. "Close climbed down and I thought to myself that Ronnie had not made a bad start at all" writes Trueman. "Later Bob Appleyard wanted to go on bowling after Burnet had told him to take his sweater but Burnet was not impressed. 'Put your sweater on and do as you're told' was his reply as he walked away leaving Appleyard nonplussed.

"It was then," writes Trueman, "that I thought Burnet would do for me and I supported him right from the start, although I knew we would have to do a bit of carrying."

Trueman was undoubtedly one of the greatest fast bowlers cricket has ever seen and equally one of the greatest of cricket characters. He made a dramatic entry into test cricket in the 1952 match against the Indians at Headingley in which, as I have already recalled, India opened their second innings with 0 for 4 on the scoreboard, Trueman taking 3 wickets. Always the showman, he revelled in maintaining the image he had created for himself as the blunt, tough, belligerent, uncompromising Yorkshireman who called a spade a bloody shovel and cared not a four letter word for authority of any description.

He rushed in like a bulldozer where angels feared to tread, particularly in the corridors of power in the pavilion at Lord's—and must have made himself more disliked among the cricketing establishment than any other player in history. He was a walking compendium of all the characteristics that southerners love to hate about Yorkshiremen. He was, they claimed, loud-mouthed, brash and uncouth, conceited, self-opinionated and unbearably arrogant, he had primitive manners and no sense of social decorum, he was crude, boring and emotionally uncontrolled and immature. But, and it is a very big but, he was a wonderful fast bowler!

Just how wonderful, only Fred Trueman fully appreciated—for he was never reticent about his qualities. The only man who has ever floored Trueman in discussion was Richard Hutton, Leonard's son, and himself a distinguished Yorkshire cricketer, who once asked him gravely "Would you describe yourself as a modest man, Freddie?" But many other good judges have assessed him very highly and one of his proudest possessions is a letter from Herbert Sutcliffe written to him when he had taken 250 test wickets. It said: "I am amazed at the way you have always kept going despite bowling so fast. In figures alone this must prove that you are the greatest bowler the world has ever seen." That, says Trueman in his book, will do for him.

In view of the fact that he was so strongly disliked at Lord's and that if he had been a good boy he would have no doubt played in at least 20 more test matches than the 67 in which he actually appeared, his feat in being the first English bowler ever to take over 300 wickets in test matches is prodigious by any reckoning. It is a record which will not last because test matches are nowadays played with such frequency, but it is one of the greatest records ever. One has only to compare it with the figures of other bowlers to see that. Wilfred Rhodes in his long career played in only nine fewer tests than Trueman and took a total of 127 wickets. Larwood took 78, Bowes 68, Farnes 60. Trueman's nearest competitors are Underwood 265, Statham 252, Bedser 236, Snow 202 and Laker 193.

Trueman's autobiography "Ball of Fire" does something to explain the contradictions of his character, but not much. He makes it clear that his ferocity on the field—his burning hatred of all batsmen—was to a great extent simulated to foster his public image. The ferocious scowls and glares, usually made with hands firmly on hips, were largely contrived and in fact he was the chummiest of men, with a penchant for visiting his opponents' dressing rooms, sometimes to excess.

But there was nothing simulated about his hatred of the cricketing establishment and some of its occupants—in particular 'Gubby' Allen, whom he has never forgiven for humiliating him in public by taking him down to the nets at Headingley the day before a test match and, in front of a crowd of people, asking him to pitch the ball on a handkerchief he had put on the pitch.

Trueman says the kind of person dominating cricket throughout most of his career came from a wealthy family, played cricket for his university and then a county without ever proving much. "The game was full of people like this, relics from the Victorian era. Some of them had won England caps as amateurs in the '30's who from what I hear wouldn't have made the Yorkshire second team if they had been professionals.

They looked down on the man who made his living from the game . . ."

He is very scathing about the occupants of the long room at Lord's. "In a phrase," he writes in one telling sentence, "I suppose I was determined to bloody well show them all. And the more the MCC put me down the harder I tried. Some of these characters from the long room never missed an opportunity to belittle me and tell me that I was not so quick or so good as the men of their day, which, in some cases, was shortly after underarm bowling went out of fashion."

It is clear to the reader, if not to the writer, that this great bowler went right through his career with an outsize chip on his shoulder and if perhaps he had recognised this and made allowances for it, his path might not have been strewn with quite so much disaster. But, unfortunately, he regarded any compromise with his fixed opinion on the establishment as unforgivable weakness. He boasts that the only man he would ever call "Sir" was the Duke of Edinburgh and when the Duke of Norfolk, the MCC's weird choice of manager for the 1962/63 tour of Australia, and normally the politest of men (whom Trueman himself describes as "a real gentleman") so far forgot himself as to call out in Melbourne "Trueman, come here!" he did not ignore the summons as would have been the diplomatic way to express his feelings but proceeded to give the Duke a lecture to the effect that he had a dog at home he spoke to like that, and he did not care if he was the premier earl of England or not—he must address him properly. "He took it very well indeed" is Fred's patronising comment.

Trueman, of course, was endowed with as much tact as a steam-roller and many of the stories told about him, most of them no doubt apochryphal, are attributable to this defect in his character.

Thus he got himself into trouble on this same Australian tour when the local papers and television programmes to his mind seemed to be showing more interest in whether the Duke of Norfolk's horses were running, whether David Shepherd was preaching and what Ted Dexter's wife (who was a model) was wearing than in the cricket being played. "I became extremely fed up with all this, reasoning that we had come to Australia to play cricket, so I was frank when a newspaper asked me what I thought about the tour to date. I told them I was a bit confused, not knowing whether we were supposed to be playing under Jockey Club rules, for Ted Dexter Enterprises or engaged on a missionary hunt. The paper printed it rather prominently and I was in trouble with the management again."

Is it any wonder that someone invented a story about him sitting at the top table during a dinner given in honour of the Indian tourists in 1952 at which he nudged a high-ranking Indian diplomat in the ribs and said "Hey, Gunga Din, pass t'salt!" Trueman's comment on this is that the story has one fatal flaw. The establishment would never have seated England's most junior cap in such an exalted position!

Also apochryphal no doubt is the story of the dinner given by a local sheikh in Aden en route for Australia. One of the hosts pointed out the sheikh to Trueman and told him he had 196 wives. "Has he?" was the alleged reply. "Does he know that if he gets another four he can have a new ball?"

On the same tour he agreed that he said to David Shepherd, now Bishop of Liverpool, who had just dropped a catch off his bowling: "Kid yourself it's Sunday, Rev., and keep your hands together."

Surprisingly enough the story about Raman Subba Row missing a catch off Trueman

Left: Johnny Wardle, another England player who left Yorkshire prematurely. Below: Ray Illingworth, currently the Yorkshire team manager, shakes hands with the Queen after leaving the county to captain Leicestershire and subsequently England.

in the slips and letting the ball go for four runs in a test match at Trinidad, Trueman also acknowledged as true. As Subba Row passed Trueman at the end of the over he apologised and said "Sorry, Fred, didn't get a touch." Replied Trueman "Yes I noticed. What about the four runs?" "I'm sorry about that, too," said Subba Row. "It might have been better if I'd kept my legs together." Replied Trueman: "It's a pity your mother didn't!" Trueman says that as much as anything led to £50 being subtracted from his good conduct bonus.

One of the best known stories, also based in the West Indies, is about Trueman calling an umpire a "cheating black bastard" and hastily adding "and there's no colour prejudice about that—if you weren't black I'd call you a cheating white bastard." This would seem to be founded on fact but greatly exaggerated. What happened, according to Trueman, is that one of the umpires in a test at Georgetown complained to the English captain, Hutton, that he had been called a black bastard. Hutton gave Trueman a stern reprimand in the dressing room in front of all the other players and Trueman was so outraged that he asked the team manager if he could go home at once. The next morning he met the umpire at the top of the pavilion steps and asked him why he had told Len he had called him a black bastard. His reply was that he had not—he had said it was one of the Yorkshiremen on the field but he knew it wasn't him.

Having the reputation of being the enfant terrible on every tour he ever went on certainly made life very difficult for Freddie. He was frequently blamed for crimes he did not commit. This was the case during his first disastrous tour of the West Indies under Hutton's leadership in 1953/54. Freddie was gauche and raw and admitted later that it would probably have been better for his long-term future if he had not been selected. He was constantly in trouble—sometimes deservedly and sometimes not.

At Barbados the wife of a dignitary was not amused by some ostensibly flirtatious remarks of his. An English county lady complained to Hutton that she had been jostled in the lift by two of the MCC team whom she identified as Trueman and Lock. The captain summoned the offenders to meet her in the hotel lounge next morning and make their apologies. They duly proferred them and the good lady soundly dressed them down. "I thought you took that very well" said Hutton afterwards. "So did I" said Trueman, "considering it weren't us."

At home there was a complaint to the Yorkshire committee about Trueman's bad language and disgusting behaviour at an hotel in Bristol during the Yorkshire match with Gloucester. But he was able to prove to the committee when summoned before them that at the time he was not with the team in Bristol at all because he was playing in a test match at Lord's.

The manageress of a Worksop hotel wrote to the committee saying that Trueman would be barred from entering the premises again because of his disgraceful behaviour. He had never stayed at the hotel in his life. "You can be sure if ever my team mates got mixed up in a spot of bother then always I would be blamed for it, even if I was 200 miles away."

But if his reputation as a boor was not always deserved there is no doubt that his truculence and lack of sensitivity made him at times an embarrassment and problem for all the captains he played under—particularly, perhaps, his Yorkshire team mate Len Hutton. Hutton is emphatically not a vindictive man but he never forgave Trueman for his behaviour on that first West Indian tour and despite him taking 134 wickets that season for under 16 runs apiece he was not selected for the Australian tour of 1953/54 and never played for England again under Hutton's captaincy.

And Brian Close makes many harsh criticisms of Trueman as a team mate in his autobiography. Close's career with Yorkshire started the same day as Trueman's when, along with Frank Lowson, they were given a trial in a match against Cambridge University in 1949. Close admits that he and Trueman always had a love–hate relationship, respecting each other's professional abilities but not always respecting each other's judgements or integrity.

Close says of Trueman "Fred was always a truly great player but sadly he was not always a great colleague."

Indeed he charges Trueman with trying to replace him as Yorkshire captain in 1968 in a story which for sinister intrigue has all the ingredients of an espionage melodrama. The story concerns one of Yorkshire's most devoted supporters, Mrs. Betty O'Neill, a South Yorkshire woman who ran a business in Cornwall and who every season sent a £5 note to the ground where Yorkshire were opening their season's programme for the team to have a drink on her—it was possible to do this on £5 in those days.

But owing to the vagaries of the Post Office, the letter in 1968 arrived at the ground after the team had left and went the rounds for some weeks before it was finally delivered at Close's home address on June 19th, the day on which he was to attend a meeting of the cricket committee at Headingley. Close says that two days previously he had received a telephone call from Crawford White, the cricket writer, who, to his complete astonishment, told him that there was a rumour that he was in a "bit of bother" with the committee. Close had no knowledge of this and said so. Crawford White commented that forewarned was forearmed and that if he left Yorkshire, Leicestershire would like him.

So, knowing something was in the wind, Close went to the Yorkshire cricket committee meeting and the chairman, Brian Sellers, told him what it was. "It seemed", writes Close, "that I had 'misappropriated funds intended for the team' and that sounded a serious charge and for a moment I couldn't understand what the man was talking about. Then Mrs. O'Neill's cheque was mentioned. I had it in my pocket . . . and threw it onto the table, the envelope black with re-addressings and postmarks. The chairman read it and said 'Oh, that's that then.' No apology. Just brusque acceptance. What he had said to me was horribly, totally false but there was more to come. The committee had been told that I was absorbed in horse racing to the detriment of the team's cricket; and one further charge was that the senior players were not satisfied with my captaincy."

That, he says, was news to him, but on reflection he bagan to suspect that Trueman was the committee's informant. As acting captain in Close's absence—and he had just missed six matches because of injury—Trueman was the only man in the team in touch with the committee. Close said as much to the meeting but one member of the committee, Ronnie Burnet, very quickly said "It hasn't come from Fred." Comments Close: "He said it just a bit too quickly. I was sure I was right. And the meeting finished in no time at all after that. Brian Sellers told me 'You are the captain. You'd better go and find what the trouble is all about.'

"I went up to the dressing room and caught Fred's eye and threw Mrs. O'Neill's note and cheque onto the table telling him 'Fred that's that cheque I've spent.' No comment. At close of play I went for a drink with the lads and sure enough my two most senior players, Ray Illingworth and Jimmy Binks, echoed my thoughts: the stirring must have come from Fred. I saw Fred and told him 'If you want my job so badly you can have it.'"

Trueman makes no reference to this alleged incident in his autobiography but he does reveal how much he would have liked to be captain of Yorkshire. And he recalls how very nearly he succeeded in this ambition at the very time that Close was being called before the cricket committee. Trueman describes how, after making the decision to retire at the end of the 1968 season ("I had seen Yorkshire deal cruelly with older players, discarding them like so much rubbish regardless of the loyalty they had shown over the years") he went to see Sir William Worsley because he considered the president of the club should be the first to know and Sir William was one man in cricket administration he respected completely. ("In fact I thought him the only real gentleman in the game, apart from the Duke of Norfolk.")

He told Sir William of his decision and tendered his resignation but to his great surprise Sir William refused to accept it and delivered what Trueman describes as a bombshell. He said "We are to hold a meeting next week and you will probably be offered the captaincy of Yorkshire."

Adds Trueman: "When I had recovered my powers of speech I told Sir William that if someone had only hinted about the possibility I would have been delighted to play on for another two or three years, but it was too late." Trueman had announced his retirement in the newspaper he wrote for regularly, the Sunday People. At Sir William's behest he rang the paper to try and stop the announcement but it was too late. The early editions were already coming off the press. "So by a couple of hours I missed being captain of Yorkshire. I will regret it for the rest of my life," he comments.

Later that night Trueman visited Brian Sellers at his home, told him of his resignation and had a couple of drinks with him. Sellers said, according to Trueman, that perhaps he had helped the committee out of a difficult situation. "He didn't elaborate but I did wonder whether they were going to sack Brian Close from the captaincy and give him the chance of either playing under me or leaving."

In view of the fate that was to befall Brian Close two years later, on November 25th, 1970, this Trueman episode is a clear indication of the almost incredible duplicity of the anti-Close faction on the Yorkshire committee. Whether Trueman contributed to this duplicity I have no way of knowing, but Close's story about the cricket committee meeting has never been denied to my knowledge.

In spite of his many defects, Trueman also had some virtues. He was always a great trier and could be extremely loyal and unselfish if treated the right way. And in his personal relationships he could be kind and generous. In middle age he has matured into a man of considerable intelligence and perspicacity. He is one of the most entertaining and perceptive of radio commentators on cricket and has developed a geniality which completely belies his earlier brashness and belligerence. He was named sports personality of the year in the 1979 Society of Authors awards for his part in bringing cricket to life on radio, during the test match broadcasts.

The doyen of radio commentators, John Arlott, has summed him up in his brilliant biography "Fred: Portrait of a Fast Bowler." He talks of him as having four distinct personalities—the basic Fred Trueman; Fred Trueman the fast bowler; Fred Trueman the man; and Fred Trueman the public image. These four identities, says Arlott, are often contradictory. "He can be uproarious but also—though not often—silent, moody; he can be generous—and mean; he could bowl his heart out—or turn it in; he can be harsh—or gentle; he can be genuinely witty—and horribly crude; almost hysterically funny—and a complete bore; he can be intuitively understanding—and chillingly embarrassing; he can be arrogant—and as uncertain of himself as a schoolboy; he is pulled this way and that by his doubts and his emotions; he wants desperately to be liked and he is at bottom, lonely. Least of all is it generally understood that in the urge to succeed in the craft in which he excelled he lived constantly on the sharpest edge of his nerves."

It was a proud day for all Yorkshiremen when Trueman took his 300th test wicket at the Oval against the Australians in August, 1964, and I was glad I was there to see it. He describes how he put himself on to bowl to make sure of getting the last three wickets he needed before the Australians were all out. "Just before lunch on the Saturday I saw Ted Dexter standing at the wicket looking a bit vacant, ball in hand. I asked him what he was going to do and he said he was thinking of putting Peter Parfitt on to bowl. I said "No you're not", took the ball from him and put myself on. There was time for one over before lunch and with the fifth ball I knocked back the middle stump of Ian Redpath. With the sixth and last I had Graham MacKenzie caught at slip."

Trueman describes the tension during lunchtime, which I recall very clearly, and how people flooded into the Oval after the news was spread by radio and television that he was on the hat trick for his 300th test wicket. He didn't get the hat trick but he soon got his 300th wicket. It was a wonderful climax to a wonderful career.

10 THE 1960's—DRASTIC CHANGES

The 1960's were a dismal decade. They represented the first phase of the revolution in first class cricket which has now been in progress for over 20 years. The '60's saw a continuing sharp decline in attendances at county matches which fell by something like 75 per cent in comparison with 1950. County membership figures also showed severe reductions and there were few counties which were free from financial difficulties. Cricket was clearly in decline.

The 1960's also saw the end of the historic distinction between amateurs and players and the last Gentlemen v. Players match was played in 1963. And four years later came the formation of the Cricketers' Association which, although not affiliated to the Trades Union Congress, was in effect a players' trade union.

Most significant of all, the 1960's brought the introduction of one day limited overs cricket with the launching of the Gillette Cup 60 overs a side competition in 1963. This was to be followed in the 1970's by the establishment of the John Player League of 40 overs Sunday afternoon cricket and the 55 overs Benson and Hedges Cup competition.

There were correspondingly fundamental changes in cricket's administration and the historic Marylebone Cricket Club (MCC) ceased to be the parliament of cricket and reverted to being what its title had always fallaciously suggested it was—a body of minor and local governance chiefly related to the laws of cricket. Its powers were taken by the International Cricket Conference and, in England, the Cricket Council and the Test and County Cricket Board. Finally the 1960's introduced the era of commercial sponsorship which in the pursuit of solvency has virtually handed over the financial control of first class cricket to the television authorities, a process culminating in the Packer revolution. Cricket finances in the late 1970's came to depend on commercial sponsorship by firms interested chiefly in obtaining television publicity for themselves as much as the game of cricket depended earlier on the provision of a bat and ball and a set of wickets. There was little shelter from the barrage of television-seeking advertisements and all the principal cricket grounds of the world rapidly became plastered with these obnoxious notices to an increasingly obscene degree. You could not see a ball bowled at any of them without a placarded reminder that Guinness was Good For You or Bile Beans would lubricate your digestive tracts.

It is easy to decry all this indecent exposure and the blatant commercialism behind it but it is not easy to suggest how cricket could have survived without it in a world dominated so completely by mercenary motivation and individual self-aggrandisement. Cricketers and cricket administrators are human and in an age in which commercial exploitation is the principal pre-requisite for survival who can blame them for resorting to such tactics? It is the way of the world. But one is forced to ask what W. G. Grace would have thought about it. In my purely personal sphere I ask myself what my cricketing guide and mentor, my father, would have thought about it, because cricket has changed as much since he died in 1962, as it changed in the lifetime of the famous W.G. I am quite sure my father would be horrified if he saw how his beloved Headingley had been defaced and disfigured, even to the extent of hanging dozens of advertisements all round the front of the players' pavilion, like so much commercial washing on the line.

In view of all this it is hardly surprising that I look back on my cricket watching in the 1960's with less enthusiasm than that with which I look back on earlier decades. Possibly the commercialisation of cricket was not the only thing that was wrong. The 1960's brought drastic changes in my own personal sphere, prominent among them being my removal from Yorkshire to London. No longer could I chase off on Saturdays and if business permitted (and it usually did) on weekdays as well to matches at Headingley, Park Avenue, Bramall Lane, Harrogate, Scarborough and Huddersfield. The only county cricket grounds within reasonable travelling distance of my home in St. Albans were Lord's and the Oval and although I "repaired to the matches of the Southron folk" when I became severely cricket starved Middlesex and Surrey were poor substitutes for my own Yorkshire. The cricket was just as good—sometimes better—but the partisanship was lacking. And I soon found it is an essential constituent of cricket-watching pleasure.

My identification with the team and its players was not nearly as strong as it once had been—even when I was watching Yorkshire I could not shiver with apprehension when Boycott went through the nineties in the way I had done with Sutcliffe and Hutton—but there was plainly something seriously lacking when I didn't really care who won and who lost and who scored centuries and who was out for ducks. It was not the same. I got this essential ingredient at the test matches, of course, and I went to many of them at both the London grounds. But the 1960's were not a very exhilarating decade for England. England had lost the Ashes in Australia in 1958/59 under May and did not win them back again until the 1970/71 tour under Illingworth. We did not do much better against the West Indies, losing the 1963 and 1966 series, and we lost the rubber against South Africa in 1965—sadly the last, before politics and racial prejudice put an end to cricket with that tragic country.

Few of the test matches I saw in this drab decade stand out very clearly in my memory. I recall a century by Sobers in the Headingley test against the West Indies in 1963 (I went up "home" for that), a century by Graham Pollock at Trent Bridge for the South Africans in 1965, which I reckoned the finest innings I had seen since the war—the fluency of Pollock was breathtaking—and a remarkable last wicket partnership of 128 between Higgs and Snow for England in the final test against the West Indies at the Oval in 1966. The only outstanding bowling performance I can remember was Trueman's, taking his 300th wicket in test cricket at the Oval in 1964 to which I have already referred.

May and Graveney continued to dominate the England batting in the early 1960's but Ted Dexter was a new force to be reckoned with and he captained England in two series against Australia in 1962/63 and 1964. Dexter was a delightful batsman to watch, with a fluency and style and devil-may-care attitude very reminiscent to me of Denis Compton. He played cricket primarily as a game—which was the last thing it seemed to be in the dour hands of other leading batsmen of the period such as M. J. K. Smith, John Edrich and, most laborious of all, Geoffrey Boycott, whose long test career began in 1964.

The 1960's were also a decade of distasteful incidents which disfigured the reputation of cricket throughout the world. The most publicised were the Graveney affair, the

D'Oliveira affair and the Close affair—the latter being two-pronged inasmuch as it involved the sacking of Brian Close first as captain of England and second as captain of Yorkshire. All these incidents had an element of tragedy about them but all were also symptomatic of the ailing state into which first class cricket had declined. The word cricket could no longer be legitimately used as a synonym for honesty, decency and fair play.

The Graveney affair opened the decade with a bad odour by excluding the most graceful and stylish of England batsmen from county and test cricket for the whole of the 1961 season. This was due to the fact that the MCC would not agree to him being given a special registration with Worcestershire following his departure from Gloucestershire in a blaze of unseemly publicity during the previous winter, when he had been sacked as the Gloucester professional captain and replaced by an amateur and old Etonian, Tom Pugh.

I was not in any sort of contact with cricket in Gloucestershire so I cannot write with any knowledge of this affair but I have read Graveney's own account of it in his book called "Tom Graveney on Cricket" and he makes no bones about attributing his dismissal to "the age old reason that they (Gloucestershire) wanted an amateur in charge." Whatever the rights and wrongs of this affair it did, as Graveney admitted, nobody any good—"Gloucestershire, the game of cricket or me. If it proved anything it is that loyalty counts both ways—that a county can expect it from the players and the players have a right to it from the county too."

The D'Oliveira affair was what E. W. Swanton called "a melancholy saga with world-wide implications and repercussions." It resulted in the MCC calling off their tour to South Africa in the winter of 1968/69 and later the last minute cancellation of the South African tour of England at the request of the British Government in May, 1970.

There was a widespread conflict of views on the many different aspects of this affair but about two things most people agreed—the bearing and conduct of Basil D'Oliveira himself throughout the whole of his ordeal was exemplary and the intrusion of politics into cricket was deplorable.

The "melancholy saga" began when the selectors of the England team to tour South Africa, comprising the president of the MCC, A. E. R. Gilligan, the treasurer, G. O. Allen, and Messrs. Insole, Bedser, Kenyon, May, Cowdrey and Ames, omitted to pick the Worcester all-rounder D'Oliveira who, besides being a perfect gentleman, also happened to have been born in Cape Town of Cape-coloured parents.

There had been considerable speculation on whether the selectors would pick D'Oliveira in view of his racial origins and the question of whether or not he would be acceptable in South Africa and naturally the anti-apartheid brigade seized on his non-selection as a blatant case of racial prejudice. Actually there were perfectly sound cricketing reasons for not selecting him because he had had a poor season for Worcester following an undistinguished tour of the West Indies, but he had greatly strengthened the case for his inclusion in the South African party by his performance in the final test against the Australians at the Oval in the summer just over (the only test for which he had made the grade). He had scored a magnificent 158. And the team for South Africa was selected immediately the match was over!

If the MCC had stuck to their guns all would probably have been well. The carefully orchestrated outcry over D'Oliveira's exclusion would have died down and the tour would have gone ahead but with an ineptitude which staggered belief the selectors made confusion worse confounded by a subsequent announcement that as one of the chosen party, Tom Cartwright, had withdrawn for health reasons, D'Oliveira had been selected to take his place. This news, not surprisingly, was received with disbelief in South Africa and the Prime Minister, Mr. Vorster, declared that the MCC had bowed to pressure and that the South Africans were not prepared to accept a man thrust upon them by the anti-apartheid movement.

Great efforts were made to salvage something from the wreckage, culminating in a trip to London by two members of the South African cricket board, but finally the MCC had to announce that since their side was not acceptable the tour would be cancelled.

The imbroglio caused a special meeting of the MCC to be held at Lord's and amid stormy exchanges the committee were accused of mishandling the issue. Thanks to a postal vote the committee won the day.

But the echoes of the D'Oliveira affair were far-reaching and were the spur to the anti-apartheid movement to resort to all manner of unscrupulous tactics to prevent the return visit of the South Africans in 1970—a visit which the great majority of English cricketers and supporters favoured. The proposed tour became the issue of an all-out war between the two parties (although only one side resorted to violence) and county cricket grounds had to be protected by barbed wire from the assaults of the anti-apartheid thugs masquerading as ardent idealists. The Prime Minister, Harold Wilson, described the tour as "a big mistake" and the decision to carry on with it in face of the violent opposition "very ill-judged." The Cricket Council was urged to cancel it by Members of Parliament, the United Nations Association, the British Council of Churches and the TUC. A number of African countries threatened to withdraw from the Commonwealth Games and less than three weeks before the tour was due to start there was an emergency debate in the House of Commons.

A few days later the president of the MCC was summoned to the Home Office by the Home Secretary, James Callaghan, and requested to cancel the tour "on the grounds of broad public policy." The cricket authorities had now no alternative but to comply. It was no longer a cricketing matter. It had become a major political issue. And cricket with South Africa in either country has been non-existent ever since. I have no time at all for apartheid and have seen it in disgusting operation in South Africa. But the hypocrisy of the anti-apartheid movement which raises no objections to sporting contests with much more tyrannical regimes in other parts of Africa, not to mention Russia, is enough to make one sick.

The best that can be said of the Close affair is that it was very much a cricketing matter and remained so throughout. Brian Close was a controversial character by nature and dissension followed him like an albatross throughout the whole 28 stormy years of his career with Yorkshire, Somerset and England. He talks himself in his frank autobiography "I Don't Bruise Easily" of a jinx "lurking around" which popped up with disastrous consequences on "every big occasion in which I have been involved."

Some people might describe it as a chip on the shoulder for the truth about the tragedy of Close is that most of his misfortunes were self-inflicted. This was certainly the case with his dismissal as England's captain in 1963 and was to some extent the case with his sacking from the Yorkshire captaincy in 1970, although along with a great many other Yorkshire members I always felt that the Yorkshire committee must bear the main responsibility for this piece of idiocy which was probably the greatest mistake the Yorkshire

Four captains of Yorkshire who all played for England: top left N. W. D. Yardley (1948–55); top right D. B. Close (1963–70); bottom left G. Boycott (1971–78); bottom right J. H. Hampshire (1979–80).

County Cricket Club have ever made, and one from which they have shown little sign of recovery over the past decade. Yorkshire's cricketing fortunes have stayed in the doldrums ever since the evil day when Close was called to Headingley and given 10 minutes by A. B. Sellers, the chairman of the cricket committee, to choose whether to resign or be sacked. Although he is too much of a Yorkshireman to relish the downfall of his former county team, Close would not be human if he did not derive a certain grim satisfaction from the way things have turned out.

Close made his debut for Yorkshire, aged 18, along with Freddie Trueman and Frank Lowson in a match against Cambridge University in 1949 and made an immediate impact by doing the double in his first season and, by playing in a test against New Zealand, becoming the youngest man ever to play for England. The following season he became, at 19, the youngest player ever to be selected to tour Australia and as such was introduced to the controversial atmosphere which he was to live in for the rest of his career.

The critics who said he was not prepared for a tour of Australia—that he was being made to run before he had become an accomplished walker—were proved right and the Australian experiment was an unmitigated disaster. He writes a chapter on it in his book under the doleful heading "A Tour of Misery" and no-one, least of all Close, can measure the side-effects it had on his future, or how much it contributed to the fact that, great cricketer though he was, he never attained the heights for which at 19 he seemed to be inevitably destined.

That he had some character defects is obvious from his own account of this first Australian tour. "The MCC party," he writes, "included giants who were more or less names on cigarette cards to me—Denis Compton, Cyril Washbrook, Doug Wright, Freddie Brown and of course Len Hutton, had all been master cricketers before the war. I badly needed someone to advise me. I was desperately anxious for one of these great players to take me under his wing, to talk cricket to me, to tell me what a tour involved, to discuss the position and what it was like to play against the greatest of all test opposition. From the beginning to the end of the tour none of the senior players offered me one single word of advice about anything." He goes on to write "Freddie Brown, Len Hutton, Cyril Washbrook, Reg Simpson, Denis Compton—you made my life hell. And I had so admired and respected you all when I set out."

One wonders whether this is a denunciation of these great players or of himself. One can believe that Compton or Washbrook or Wright or Brown or Simpson or Hutton could have refused to give him a kind word without any reason but not that all of them should have failed to do so. Caesar's remark is surely applicable "The fault, dear Brutus, lies not in our stars but in ourselves."

One of the most remarkable facts about Close's test career is that it spanned a longer period—27 years from 1949 to 1976—than that of any player in history other than Wilfred Rhodes, whose career spanned 30 years. Close was dropped and recalled with almost clockwork regularity over these 27 years and although this was sometimes due to his temperament it was more often due to his irregular form, both as a batsman and as a bowler.

On his day he was undoubtedly one of the best players in the game—a dazzling, stylish, aggressive left-handed batsman who was a complete joy to watch and an effective right arm bowler who could open the innings as a fast swing bowler and be brought on later in the innings as an off-spinner. He was also a brilliant fielder near the wicket and certainly one of the most courageous players the game has ever produced.

The knocks he received in his suicidal position at the shortest of short legs would have put most people in a wheelchair. The story is told of one fearful blow on the forehead from which the ball rebounded so far that it was caught by Philip Sharp in the slips. Someone said later to Close that if it had been any harder it would have killed him. "Not at all" replied Close. "It would have rebounded and been caught at cover point."

But unfortunately—and again it is difficult to assess how much of this was due to temperament—his "day" did not come all that frequently and although he was a very successful captain of England, unbeaten in any of the seven tests when he occupied that position, his performance rating in international cricket is not brilliant. He played in 22 tests, scoring 887 runs for an average of 25.34 and took 18 wickets at an average of 29.55. His record for Yorkshire was much the same. He scored 22,650 runs, average 31.94, and took 967 wickets, average 24.29. A good all-round performance but not the spectacular performance his early years predicted.

Close had all the raw materials for producing cricketing genius but somehow lacked the ability to put them together in the right way. Someone once said that genius consists of an infinite capacity for taking pains and perhaps it was that which Close lacked. He was a magnificent starter but a poor finisher. I have seen him many a time come in and bat superbly for the first hour and then, just as he appeared all set for a magnificent century, he would be out to a careless shot which batsmen of his calibre should never make.

Close himself writes of his habit of being dismissed most unexpectedly but he attributes this as usual to his jinx. He recalls a test stand with Colin Cowdrey of 51. "I scored 34 of them while Colin was missed three times. Colin went on to get a hundred; I went out to an absolutely brilliant catch off what was not really a chance."

He confesses, too, that he did not make as many runs as he would have liked to make and that one of the things he most regretted was his failure to score a test century. "I have been got out when I most desperately wanted to stay in. And this has, over the years, been invariably attributed to my being a 'big head', 'playing irresponsibly,' or just plain 'chucking my wicket away.' I say—no I insist—that it has been none of these; but I'm hanged if I can put my finger on what it was. Let me give you a few examples of why I believe some kind of bad luck has always dogged me . . ."

The greatest piece of destruction wrought by his jinx was his displacement as captain of England in 1967 following the famous Edgbaston incident in Yorkshire's match against Warwickshire, in which Close was blamed for allegedly wasting time during Warwickshire's second innings and so preventing the home side from gaining victory. Warwickshire needed eight to win with four wickets standing when the match ended. Close was summoned to an enquiry at Lord's and the verdict was "We came to the unanimous decision that the Yorkshire team used delaying tactics during Warwickshire's second innings and that these tactics constituted unfair play and were against the best interests of the game. Furthermore the committee hold the captain, Brian Close, entirely responsible for these tactics and they have therefore severely censured him and this decision will be conveyed to the Yorkshire County Cricket Club."

Close puts forward a vigorous defence for his actions at Edgbaston in his autobiography and explains his decision to lead the Yorkshire team off the field at the critical juncture as follows: "A little later it started drizzling again. This not only handicapped the bowlers but also the fielders who were sliding around. I made an appeal which the umpires rejected and as we took our places again it started to throw it down so we all raced off the field. Evidently whilst we were in the dressing room and the umpires had not quite got off, the rain suddenly stopped. As soon as this was pointed out we returned to the field with the last ten minutes to go."

Close no doubt defended himself just as vigorously before the enquiry and in his book says "I say quite firmly and unequivocally, ten years later, that if I had that time over again, I would do exactly what I did against Warwickshire at Edgbaston in August 1967. I would say exactly what I said at the time. I would refrain from saying what on all sides I was urged to say, i.e. I am sorry. I am not sorry for any single aspect of my captaincy in that game. I started it by trying to win and I ended it by trying to prevent the other side winning. That is the way I have played cricket all my life and as far as I am concerned it is the only way to play the game. And what made it all so damned illogical was that game against Warwickshire had nothing whatever to do with the England team, or how I skippered it. Probably the whole secret lay in something I had been told a month before by a newspaper man and it may perhaps indicate the sort of influence these chaps can have when you know the sort of information they acquire. He had said to me 'For God's sake, Brian, keep your nose clean because they are just waiting at Lord's for a chance to prevent you leading the side in the West Indies.' Good comforting stuff for an England captain."

But most other observers believe that it was because he would not apologise that he was replaced by Colin Cowdrey as English captain for the forthcoming West Indies tour and that he deprived himself by his attitude of fulfilling his great ambition to lead an English team on an overseas tour. I am reluctant to condemn the stubborness of my Yorkshire compatriots in resisting pressure to give in, but fighting for a principle is one thing and sheer cussedness is another and if Close had been big enough to recognise that he was in the wrong on this occasion, he would have saved himself and his many admirers—among whom I would like to be counted—a great deal of distress. What really convinced me he was in the wrong was not my own judgement because I was not present, but the judgement of two very distinguished Yorkshire critics who I am sure would have supported Close if there had been any justification for his conduct. They were J. M. Kilburn of the Yorkshire Post and Bill Bowes of the Yorkshire Evening Post.

Close's dismissal as captain of Yorkshire on November 25th 1970 was a very different story. This is still to my mind the most disgraceful incident in the history of Yorkshire county cricket and all those who were in any way responsible for it—and that obviously includes a large majority of the committee—should still bow their heads in shame every time Close's name is mentioned in their presence. Close was treated abominably and the manner in which he was sacked by Brian Sellers eclipsed in one tragic episode the greatness of the ex-Yorkshire skipper in the eyes of thousands of members of the club.

About the virtues of the decision to sack Close as captain I have many reservations because he had an excellent record and is now in retrospect widely rated as one of the best captains the game has ever produced. But I recognise the fact that he must have been a very difficult fellow to deal with in view of his excessive supply of Yorkshire obstinacy and his completely uncompromising nature.

He took over the Yorkshire captaincy from J. V. Wilson in 1963 and in the eight seasons he held that position, Yorkshire won the championship four times and were in

Back row: G. Cope, G. Boycott, N. Smith, C. Old, R. Hutton, J. Hampshire, B. Leadbeater, J. Woodford.
Front row: D. Wilson, P. Sharpe, B. Close, D. Padgett, T. Nicholson.

The Yorkshire team in Close's last year as captain, 1970. Since his departure no award has been won by Yorkshire.

the top five three times. Only in one season did Yorkshire do badly—in 1969 when they fell to twelfth.

Compare this with the team's performance in the eight seasons under Boycott's captaincy and the excellence of Close is clearly indicated, although I know any captain is dependent to a very large extent on his team and that Close had a much better side than Boycott. But I cannot believe that if Close had captained Yorkshire from 1970 to 1978 they would have fared anything like so disastrously as they did under Boycott. Their positions in the championship were as follows: 1971, 13th; 1972 10th; 1973 14th; 1974 11th; 1975 2nd; 1976 8th; 1977 12th and 1978 4th. The 1970's, it goes without saying, have been the most disastrous decade in Yorkshire's history.

But Close's qualities as captain are not really the point at issue in this connection. It was not Close's sacking which aroused the fierce reaction among the county membership but the manner in which it was carried out. Close described what happened in his book and nobody has ever denied that this was substantially true.

He writes under the heading "The Worst Day of My Life" and tells how, after a season in which Yorkshire had risen from 12th to 4th place in the championship, he was telephoned by John Nash, the Yorkshire secretary, and asked to report at Headingley the following day. He had heard nothing about what was in the wind and thought it was a routine meeting.

To his surprise he found on arrival that there was no committee in session and just Mr. Nash sitting across the table from where he was asked to sit, and Brian Sellers sitting at the end of the table. He says the circumstances as much as the atmosphere made him just a bit apprehensive but nothing in the world could have prepared him for what was about to hit him.

Brian Sellers looked along the table and said "Well, Brian, you've had a good innings".

"As soon as he said that" writes Close, "I knew something very funny was going to happen, but I still wasn't prepared for the next bit. The committee had had a meeting, said the chairman, and they had decided that my services were no longer required and that I had to make a decision whether to resign or be sacked."

The shock was petrifying and Close tells how he felt the bottom had dropped out of his world. He asked "How long have I got to decide because I'd like to have a word with my wife?"

"You've got ten minutes" replied Brian Sellers. "Before you leave this office we want to know. We have prepared two statements for a public announcement and whatever you decide will decide which statement is issued." Mr. Nash added that the county were going to issue their statement at two o'clock and it was then some time between half past ten and eleven.

Close realised that if he resisted he would be plunged into yet another controversy and he shrank from the thought of it. He had had enough. He asked for the two statements to be read over to him and—still not thinking very clearly—decided that resignation was the lesser of two evils. In any case ten minutes did not give him much opportunity for calm reflection. So he said he would resign.

"At once the tension went out of the atmosphere in that room. Well, it went out of John Nash and Brian Sellers anyway. Vaguely I realised I had taken the pressure off them but I hadn't taken it off myself. All I wanted to do was to get out of that room, away from Headingley, and talk to Vivienne (his wife). I drove away with my mind still in a whirl. I wanted to cry. As I drove along Kirkstall Road my vision misted up so much I had to stop. And then I was sick, there at the side of the road."

His wife was out when he arrived home, but when she was told what had happened she said "Don't you realise that by resigning you've done all their dirty work for them?" "It was then that I began to realise just how it would look to all that loyal band of Yorkshire supporters who had just supported my benefit. I had taken their money and just walked out on them."

He telephoned some of his friends and they said Vivienne was right. So he rang up Mr. Nash and told him he had changed his mind and decided not to resign but be sacked. Mr. Nash "stammered and stuttered" and said they had already issued the prepared statement that he had resigned. It was 12.45. Close said that he had been told the statement was not to go out before 2 pm and that Mr. Nash had better 'phone the newspapers and amend it and that was that.

The announcement naturally created a cricket sensation and most of the 11,000 Yorkshire members were outraged. An action group was formed to challenge the committee's action and at the annual meeting of the club in Leeds Town Hall on January 30th, 1971, open warfare broke out and a vote of no confidence in the committee was passed by 570 votes to 507. It was not officially a vote of no confidence because the chairman ruled such a motion out of order, pointing out to the accompaniment of much derision that for such a motion to be put the club rules required that a fortnight's notice should be given. A vote was actually taken on the motion to support the annual report and accounts but its effect was just the same.

The only other annual meeting I had attended was the one I have referred to in an earlier chapter—a most decorous affair held in, of all places, the Leeds City Museum and attended by about 50 members. Every satisfaction was expressed with the way the affairs of the club were being conducted and genial votes of thanks to the president, secretary and other officials were passed with unanimous applause.

I reported my impressions of the Close meeting in my book "Nowt So Queer As Folk" as follows:

> "It had been expected that there would be a much larger attendance than usual at the 1971 meeting because of the Close controversy and for that reason the main hall in the town hall had been booked. But no-one expected over a thousand members to turn up and even less did anyone expect the report and accounts to be thrown out.
>
> The mood of the majority of the members was angry to say the least, and although the committee under a skilled chairman deputising for the president, Sir William Worsley, did their very best to smooth things over, a showdown was insisted upon and the committee were defeated.
>
> Brian Sellers gave the reasons why the committee had dismissed Close—his opposition to Sunday cricket and his behaviour off the field were quoted, as well as his refusal to carry out the committee's wishes in team selection and in the 'blooding' of new players—but Sellers' speech, although delivered with his usual pugnacity, did not give much satisfaction. Most people agreed with the leader of the action group formed by the rebels, Mr. Jack Mewies, a Skipton solicitor. He said that what the action group complained about, and what he himself was deeply ashamed of, was not so much the dismissal of Close as the manner of his dismissal. To loud

here-here's and applause he went on to say 'It is disgraceful that he should have been given 15 minutes in which to decide whether to resign or be sacked (it was actually 10 minutes). I think this committee is not fit to govern a club like Yorkshire and I move a vote of censure and no confidence in the committee.'

Not even Close's best friends would say that he was an easy man to get on with and he said himself, apropos these events, that he was no angel. There had clearly been incidents in which he was culpable. One was a match with Warwickshire at Edgbaston when Yorkshire were accused of time wasting on the field far beyond the bounds of tactical justification. Close was severely censured for his conduct after a formal investigation by the advisory county committee.

Another incident was at Old Trafford when Close was accused of swearing at the president of the Lancashire committee—he did not deny this in an interview on television but merely said that 'Something had happened' after the game when in the heat of the moment he had spoken to a man who had made some comment to him. But he insisted he did not know the man was the president of Lancashire and said that when he had discovered this he had written a letter of apology to him.

These incidents were no doubt regrettable but in the view of most Yorkshire members did not add up to an adequate reason for the dismissal of an exceptionally talented captain. The action group held a meeting on February 14th and decided unanimously to demand a special general meeting at which they would propose a vote of no confidence in the committee and call for their resignation.

But it never came to that. The committee made concessions to the action group by effecting various changes in the rules of the club and Sellers resigned as chairman of the cricket committee. And that was about all. The fire of the action group seemed to fizzle out and the administration of the club went on much as before.

The loss of Close had, however, disastrous repercussions on the team's performance and the committee's report for the first season without him, 1971, began as follows: 'It is with regret that your committee has to report that the season 1971 was without doubt the worst in the history of the club, both from a playing and a financial viewpoint.' The team had dropped from fourth in the championship in Close's last season to 13th under the new captain, Boycott—the lowest on record since the turn of the century."

This was not the first time—nor indeed was it to be the last—on which the Yorkshire committee split the membership down the middle. There had been a number of other disastrous decisions in the 1950's and 1960's which had exacerbated if not always caused unrest and dissension in the dressing room and in the members' enclosure and had led to talented players leaving the club before their time. The committee's reactionary attitude towards the appointment of a professional as captain was thought by some to be chiefly responsible for Len Hutton quitting at the age of 39. Had he been invited to be captain of Yorkshire in succession to Yardley he would, I think, have accepted the job and been able to use his tremendous skill and experience to the club's advantage for another four years at least. But although he had been a highly successful captain of England, Hutton was never invited to captain Yorkshire. Yet in 1960—only five years after Hutton's retirement—the committee had to swallow their outdated principles and pride, and appoint a professional as captain who could not hold a candle to Hutton as either leader or player. And he, J. V. Wilson, was 39 at the time.

The committee was also directly responsible for losing the club the services of a third England captain, Ray Illingworth, who moved to Leicestershire in 1969 because the Yorkshire club refused to give him a contract. He captained Leicester most successfully for 10 years, and during that time twice won the Ashes against Australia and led Leicestershire to their first county championship victory ever.

Other England players who left Yorkshire earlier than they should have done because of discontent of one sort or another were Willie Watson (who also had a successful subsequent career with Leicestershire), Frank Lowson and Ken Taylor. And one captain, Billy Sutcliffe, resigned after two seasons and a captain presumptive, Geoffrey Keighley, withdrew before he was appointed. Nor must the sacking of Hedley Verity's successor, Johnny Wardle in 1958 aged only 35, be forgotten. There were probably good reasons for the latter decision because Wardle was a rebel and a disruptive influence, but no good reasons have been advanced for any of the others.

The insuperable conclusion is that Yorkshire survived in the 1950's and 1960's as a successful cricket team in spite of the committee rather than thanks to the committee. The remarkable thing is that in view of this antediluvian administration, Yorkshire were able to win the championship seven times in these two decades. Who can doubt that with administrators geared to their own era instead of that of A. B. Sellers and company, they would have done a great deal better?

Brian Close may conceivably have had the Yorkshire committee primarily in mind when he wrote: "Post-war cricket was run for a long time by administrators who stuck rigidly to pre-war mental attitudes. Professionals were treated almost as serfs and were expected to regard themselves as fortunate, even privileged, to be in the game at all."

Close and other players have dismissed the Yorkshire committee as a crowd of bunglers and ignoramuses and perhaps the denunciation has been overdone. Close, for instance, writes gleefully elsewhere of a Yorkshire committee member who sat in the pavilion at Chesterfield in a match against Derbyshire watching Dougie Padgett of Yorkshire score 142 and remarked "Taylor's playing well today, don't you think?" Ken Taylor was not even in the team! Knowing the Yorkshire committee as I do—and one member of the period was a close friend of mine—I have no hesitation in saying that this story is probably apochryphal. But I wouldn't be sure . . .!

11 THE 1970's—THE PACKER MADNESS

The 1970's represented the second decade of revolution in cricket, culminating in the Kerry Packer catastrophe, which has already done much to destroy the game as I have known it and threatens to replace it with another game which still may retain the title cricket, but will bear little more resemblance to the cricket I have watched for the past 50 years, than a baseball game in America. For Kerry Packer has no more intention of preserving my sort of cricket than British Railways have of reintroducing Stephenson's Rocket.

The metaphor is not far-fetched, because Packer looks upon my sort of cricket in precisely the same way as British Rail regards the Rocket—as an interesting museum exhibit. Packer sees cricket as a game which has stood still since W. G. Grace, while the world around it has evolved and changed out of all recognition. And his intention is to bring it, screaming in protest if necessary, into the modern age. He wants to exploit its commercial potential to the last halfpenny by introducing every sort of gimmick he and his cohorts can conceive. As Alec Bedser, manager of the 1979/80 England touring team, commented when he was plunged into these absurdities on arrival in Australia, "I don't know what the hell it's all coming to. We'll be playing with balls with bells on next." And he wasn't joking at all.

What Packer and his band of cricket pirates fail to realise is that it is precisely because cricket as we know it in England has changed so little since W. G. Grace that it retains its charm and attraction. Transform it in the way they are doing in Australia and its charm and attraction will vanish and with it all the thousands of spectators who love it so much. There will be nothing left for them to cherish. New crowds may be drawn to this bastardised form of cricket—we see them already at the Sunday League matches, swilling down their ale, shouting obscenities and occasionally getting arrested for disorderly conduct—but they will not be cricket supporters as I have known them over the past 50 years, any more than the game they will be watching will be cricket.

Can nothing be done to prevent the total destruction of traditional cricket? Can cricket lovers and the authorities who represent them fight off the attacks of this aboriginal monster and preserve the white pads and cream flannels, the red ball and the yellow wickets, the leg glances and the late cuts, the slow flighted googlies and the fast outswingers, the lunch interval and the tea interval, the score-cards and the tea urns, the covers and the sight-screens, the dreamy introspection between ten past two and quarter past four—these and all the rest of the essential ingredients of cricket as I have always known it. I hope so. It will need time and skill and effort but it can be done.

It must be admitted that in many ways the cricket authorities have played into the hands of the enemy in the 1970's. It will be said that they had no alternative method of financing cricket, but it was they who threw the floodgates of commercialism wide open by introducing sponsorship on a large scale. And it was they who, by supporting a system which consistently underpaid first class cricketers, made it possible for Kerry Packer to recruit 51 of the world's leading players to the ranks of his World Series set-up and so disrupt the whole organisation of international cricket. Had the International Cricket Conference, the Cricket Council and the Test and County Cricket Board been more forward-looking and less rooted in the past, the Packer crisis might never have arisen. But it is easy to be wise after the event.

Some critics of the authorities argue that the rot was started by the introduction of one-day cricket in the form of the Gillette Cup in 1963, followed by the John Player League in 1969 and the Benson and Hedges Cup in 1972. First class cricket, they contend, is not by its nature compatible with the one-day or half day variety, which has always been the exclusive preserve of club cricket, and its introduction has been self-defeating—it has reduced the essential high quality of first class cricket and adulterated it into an appropriate medium for the crude commercialism which in the end could destroy first class cricket as it has always been played.

I don't support this argument entirely. There is no doubt that part-day cricket and the present plethora of competitive events, both in the test and county spheres, have exerted much extra pressure on the players and made the training and development of talent much more difficult. The technique and mental approach required for limited overs cricket is quite different from that needed in three day cricket and the constant switching from one to the other must leave the players mentally and physically exhausted at the end of the season. As for the up and coming players, the lack of stability in their training environment must affect their development adversely.

It is not surprising, therefore, that there has been a notable decline in the quality of cricket and cricketers in the last 10 or 20 years. When I look back on the 1970's I can recall very few great players who were groomed in that decade. Viv Richards, Gordon Greenidge, Andy Roberts and Joel Garner who were all born in 1951 or 1952 are four West Indians who definitely come into that category, but Ian Botham, David Gower and Graham Gooch are the only outstanding English cricketers I can think of and they are as yet largely unproved. As for the rest of the current England team not one of them, excluding Botham and Boycott, would have been considered for a test team in the 1930's. Is the reason for this that one day cricket and its slap-happy style just does not produce Huttons, Comptons, Cowdreys, Mays, Stathams, Truemans, Lakers and Locks? And even less so Hobbses, Sutcliffes, Larwoods and Wilfred Rhodeses?

But despite its dangerous side-effects, I do not cry out for the abolition of limited overs cricket. Provided the limits are not too tight, this brand of cricket can be very entertaining. It is certainly not the same as three day cricket and the purists will continue to deplore the hit-and-miss techniques employed by the batsmen and the wholly negative tactics of many of the bowlers, whose only object seems to be to stop the batsmen scoring rather than to take wickets. These approaches are most employed in the John Player Sunday League which is confined to 40 overs. Forty overs, I believe, are too few for any first class fixture and usually produce what is little more than a blind-swiping match.

The Benson and Hedges matches over 55 overs, and the Gillette matches over 60 overs, do, however, provide scope for a reasonably satisfactory display of first-class cricket as it should be played and although the accent is still perforce too much on negative fast-medium paced bowling and impatient, undisciplined batting these matches do often provide real nail-biting excitement which three-day cricket produces so rarely. This sort

Cricket's whiz-kid, Kerry Packer, with Tony Greig, former England captain (top) and Yorkshire County Cricket Club's new president, Norman Yardley, talking to former wicket-keeper, Don Brennan, a member of the small committee appointed to inquire into what is wrong with Yorkshire cricket.

of cricket rightly draws the crowds and keeps the turnstiles turning and so helps to pay for the traditional cricket over three and five days. It is a necessary evil and I am all in favour of it—provided it is not played to excess.

Of course even five-day test cricket has suffered under the lash of commercialism, principally by over-exposure. On a quick calculation which I will not guarantee to be accurate, there were something like 200 test matches played in England, Australia, New Zealand, Pakistan, India and the West Indies in the 1960's compared with 80 in the 1920's—there were no doubt even more in the 1970's for which I have no complete record. Twenty tests a year or more are far too many and are debasing the whole concept of international cricket. Many of these so-called test matches are contested by very inferior sides which would never have got anywhere near a test match in the 1930's and the fact that all performances in them go solemnly into the record books, to be subsequently compared with the run and wickets aggregates and averages of players such as Hobbs and Rhodes, whose figures were compiled in incomparably more testing circumstances, make complete nonsense of the exercise.

If commercialism is the main factor behind most of the regrettable developments in the 1970's it does not serve as a reason for the disastrous decade experienced by Yorkshire, who never won the championship or even any of the one day competitions. In 1971, 1972, 1973 and 1974 they were never higher than 10th in the championship and after a brief rally in 1975 (second) and 1976 (eighth) sank back to 12th in 1977. Kent put in the best performance of the decade, winning the championship twice and sharing it with Middlesex once.

It is ironic that the captain of Yorkshire during all but two years of the decade was probably the best batsman in the world for most of those years—Geoffrey Boycott. But although he was a very unsuccessful captain he should not be made a scapegoat for Yorkshire's consistent failure. This was more a case of no-one (except Boycott himself!) fulfilling his batting or bowling promise. On paper Yorkshire had quite a good team in 1971 when Boycott took over the captaincy. There were Hampshire, Sharpe, Lumb, Leadbeater, Padgett—all capable batsmen—Richard Hutton (son of Leonard), a talented all-rounder, and there were Old, Nicholson, Cope and Don Wilson—all experienced bowlers. With Bairstow keeping wicket this was a team worthy of a much higher place than 13th in the championship. And with Cooper, Carrick, Robinson, Bore, Woodford and Johnson as colts the future seemed reasonably assured. But such optimism was not justified by events. The players performed indifferently and not one of the colts had by the end of the decade scaled the heights expected.

In 1980 the same situation existed—competent capped players (Hampshire, Lumb, Carrick, Stevenson, Bairstow, Cope and Old) promising youngsters (Athey, Sharp, Love, Sidebottom) but none except Old and Bairstow so far achieving traditional Yorkshire class—that is to say good enough to play for England. Perhaps this is a further example of the dangerous side-effects of one day cricket.

Boycott's failings as a captain were apparent for all to see. He is a great batsman by any standards although in my experience I must say he is the dullest great batsman to watch I have ever seen. He has a faultless defence and tremendous powers of patience and concentration but whether by choice or otherwise his stroke play is remarkably restricted and gets more so as he gets older. He has none of the artistry and style of Hutton, none of the hooking power of Sutcliffe, none of the vigorous and aggressive driving of Leyland. He is a prodigious run-getter but his performances have always struck me as looking more effective in the scorebook than they do on the field, where they seem to consist chiefly of prods and pushes.

But as a captain Boycott has always left much to be desired. He has plenty of cricket intelligence and a shrewd grasp of strategy and tactics but he has not the personality that good captaincy demands. He is broody and introspective and not a good mixer. Above all Boycott is a supreme egotist. He has a fierce sense of dedication to his own success as a batsman and this inevitably deprives him of some of the necessary qualities of leadership and the capability of inspiring team spirit which are the essential prerequisites of a successful captain.

The Yorkshire committee should have known this when they appointed him. It took them eight years to find out and when it at last came to the crunch they handled the matter of his replacement with just the same lack of tact and diplomacy as they had employed in sacking Brian Close eight years earlier. They revealed themselves to be just as adept at doing the right thing in the wrong way as before they had succeeded in doing the wrong thing in the wrong way. I have written about the cruel way they treated Close. They went one better with Boycott and sacked him a day or two after the death of his mother, with whom he lived as a bachelor in the South Yorkshire mining village of Fitzwilliam. The deposed captain of Yorkshire was duly photographed by the newspapers walking behind her coffin at her funeral.

Various excuses were eventually put forward for this supreme piece of insensitivity, but what they amounted to was that it was not the committee's fault that Boycott's mother had chosen an unfortunate time to die. Boycott was incensed by the committee's decision and as his many ardent champions rose in outraged indignation it was clear that the committee once again had an internecine battle on their hands.

I would not say the committee would have entirely avoided this outcry if they had used more finesse because Boycott's supporters were very vocal and blind to his defects. There was clearly only one way in which he could have been relieved of the captaincy without opposition and that was to have persuaded him to resign the captaincy. It could have been put to him that this was in the best interests of Yorkshire cricket, to which he is devoted. This was obviously the way the matter should have been approached but I doubt very much whether such tactics were even considered. Boycott was treated like Close as a servant of the club—in the old autocratic manner that should have been abandoned 30 years ago.

Whether Boycott could have been persuaded to resign amicably is doubtful because it takes a very big man to see his own faults in a sufficiently clear light to prompt such action. But if such a tactic had been tried and failed the committee would have been on far stronger ground when they were forced to defend their action at an extraordinary general meeting of members convened at the insistence of the Boycott supporters.

The meeting was held in the Royal Hall, Harrogate, in December 1978 (Leeds Town Hall was under repair and unsafe to use) and was attended by the largest number of members in the club's history. I went along to the meeting, like many other members I am sure, with very ambivalent feelings. On the issue of Boycott's captaincy I fully agreed with the committee that it was time for a change and consequently voted against the resolution put forward by the Boycott supporters "that Geoffrey Boycott be re-appointed captain and be invited to serve as such for the 1979 season."

There was a vigorous debate on Boycott's virtues and failings and while most of the younger members were in favour of the resolution the older heads were against it and, including the proxies, it was heavily defeated by 4,826 votes to 2,602.

On the resolution proposed by the committee "that this meeting has confidence in the committee of the club as now constituted"—the result was much closer and the proxies were instrumental in carrying this resolution by 4,442 votes to 3,607. I found it very difficult to vote on this one and finally plumped for the committee because in this instance I supported their action. But I was far from having "confidence in the committee of the club as now constituted". The wording of this resolution was tantamount to a confidence trick. If the committee had been completely honest and straightforward the resolution would have specified that one was supporting the committee in this particular issue and not in general terms. I am quite sure a great many of the members who voted for the committee's resolution did so with great reluctance.

A rather futile third resolution was put to the meeting expressing no confidence in the members of the cricket sub-committee and recommended their resignation en bloc from the general committee. This seemed superfluous—it was the general committee who were ultimately responsible, not the sub-committee they appointed to look after the day-to-day matters, and the resolution was defeated by 4,216 votes to 3,346.

The asinine comment of the committee on this meeting in their report to members for the year read as follows: "Following the massive legal costs of 1977 for the Packer case it was doubly disappointing that we should have to spend in excess of £11,000 in connection with the special general meeting. How much nicer it would have been if these sums of money could have been spent on improvements on our Yorkshire grounds." The £11,000 could have been so spent if the Boycott matter had been handled by the committee less maladroitly!

There was a reasonably happy ending to all this trauma. The committee pocketed their pride by offering the recalcitrant Boycott a two-year contract to remain as a player and Boycott pocketed his pride by accepting this at the last moment—after he had denounced his employers without mercy on the Parkinson show on television and in numerous press interviews.

Altogether it was not a happy augury for the "new era" which the committee promised would open in 1979 with the "bold and universally acclaimed decision" to appoint Raymond Illingworth cricket manager with sole charge of team selection in co-operation with the captain, John Hampshire." Yorkshire started quite well in the rain-ruined summer of 1979 but could not sustain their performance and finished the season seventh in the championship table and once again without a trophy of any description.

Boycott (trust him!) was perverse enough to finish way ahead of anyone else at the top of the national first class averages with a total of 1,538 runs and the remarkable average of 102.53, but he and his opening partner, Lumb, who averaged 44, and wicket-keeper David Bairstow who was selected for Australia, were the only players to distinguish themselves. Hampshire had a poor opening season as captain with the bat, averaging only 30, and the young hopefuls, Love, Sharp and Athey, finished up with averages little over 20, all failing to fulfil their promise. Yorkshire's bowling was even worse and only Chris Old, with a total of 42 wickets for an average of 22.33, came in the first 50 bowlers in the national averages. There was clearly much for Illingworth and Hampshire to do if Yorkshire's tattered reputation were to be restored in the 1980s.

As I write—after the end of the 1981 season—that reputation, I greatly regret to say, has gone from bad to worse. Yorkshire have still not got near to winning the championship or any of the other awards and after being 7th in the table in 1979 and 6th in 1980 were 6th again in 1981. John Hampshire lasted only two years as captain and, having been replaced by Old for the 1981 season, sought and obtained a transfer to Derbyshire at the end of that season. He headed the Yorkshire batting averages in his last season and his departure will leave Yorkshire weaker than ever.

What is even more depressing is that Yorkshire cricket has been plunged into a new round of bitter controversy by an unedifying public battle between Illingworth and Boycott who are clearly at daggers drawn and are about as likely to bring unity to the Yorkshire camp as pigs are to fly. Boycott says it is all Illingworth's fault because he has been spiteful and not put him in the team when he should have done and Illingworth says it's all Boycott's fault because he's only interested in Boycott and not in the team at all. No doubt there are faults on both sides and when the battle reached the Yorkshire committee room amid great media publicity the committee very sensibly decided not to take sides publicly and urged both contestants to work together for the good of all.

This is very unlikely to happen and it looks at the moment that one of them or both of them will have to go. Whatever happens there is likely to be an outcry and the Reform Group of Yorkshire members, which was formed by Boycott fans during the previous captaincy crisis, has already poured petrol on the fire with some enthusiasm by denigrating Illingworth's performance as manager and demanding his immediate dismissal. The committee responded to this provocation by releasing for publication the result of a poll among the Yorkshire players which showed that they almost unanimously backed Illingworth and would prefer not to have Boycott in the team at all.

This prize example of maladroitness was typical of the committee's actions in recent years and was greeted with incredulity by many members. For whatever Boycott's sins he had surely not deserved such scurvy treatment as this. The players discredited themselves by their arrogance in taking such a poll but that the committee should seemingly approve this procedure can hardly be described as anything but reprehensible.

As the Sunday Telegraph commented in a leader "The latest turn in the Boycott affair—players being polled on the suitability of England's most experienced batsman as captain or even as a member of the side—shows a state of affairs more suited to the gutter than the gulley. For all his record breaking virtuosity Boycott is clearly not the easiest of team mates but he surely deserved better than this. Perhaps there was some sort of a case for Yorkshire's captain (Old) carrying out a private poll. There was certainly no case for the club to promulgate its findings. It is high time the Yorkshire club acted on an old Yorkshire adage—nowt said, soonest mended."

So, once again, Yorkshire County Cricket Club members are bitterly divided. Many would say the Boycott–Illingworth feud was quite predictable when Illingworth was appointed manager, but if Illingworth had proved capable of inspiring the team in a way which Boycott had failed to do, all might have been well. This Illingworth has singularly failed to do in three years and has clearly put his head on the chopping block.

Illingworth may have his failings—he is said to be a bit of a barrack room lawyer—but he is really no more responsible for Yorkshire's failings than Boycott was before him. The truth which the Yorkshire committee and members must eventually grasp is that Yorkshire are just not a good enough side to win any trophies and have not been for the past 13 years. There are probably two main reasons for this. One is that the colts have failed to achieve their potential over all that period and the other is that Yorkshire are competing with all the other counties on grossly unequal terms. While other teams include star players from India, Pakistan, New Zealand, Australia, South Africa and the West Indies, Yorkshire restrict themselves to players born within the county boundaries.

This is very laudable and all Yorkshire supporters would be sorry to see the system changed. But changed it must be if Yorkshire are ever to get to the top again. The ban on imported players is limiting and impracticable and some would say xenophobic and out-dated. As long as they cling to this policy they are likely to remain a second rate team. So often it is the imported stars who make the difference between a winning and a losing team. This was well illustrated at Headingley last season when Lancashire trounced Yorkshire almost entirely due to Clive Lloyd and Mike Holding.

In a desperate attempt to ward off another prolonged affray, probably culminating in yet another expensive extraordinary meeting, the Yorkshire committee have now appointed a small sub-committee to conduct a full inquiry into what is wrong with Yorkshire cricket. Yet everyone except the comittee know very well what is wrong with Yorkshire cricket—they don't win the championship any more and the committee seem powerless to do anything about it! Perhaps the sub-committee should start its inquiry by investigating the inadequacies of its parent. To quote the Sunday Telegraph leader again: "Not so long ago Yorkshire county cricket was revered for its excellence; to-day it is in peril of being reviled for its mediocrity, bickering and intrigue."

That is a sad comment on the present state of affairs and a sad conclusion to my half-century of Yorkshire cricket.

12 MY LAST TEST MATCH

I began this book with the first test match I ever attended—against Australia at Headingley in 1930—and I will finish it with the last test match I have seen to date, that against Australia at Headingley in 1981.

In these 51 years some aspects of cricket have changed a great deal and others have changed very little. One of the ways in which cricket has not changed at all, and which has been very well illustrated at recent test matches at Headingley, is the authorities' Olympian disregard for the people on whom cricket depends more than anyone else, the television moguls included. I refer to the spectators. It is they who seem to come last and matter least in the cricket administrators' scale of values.

The Headingley test matches in 1978, 1979 and 1980 were all wash-outs. In 1979 there were under three hours' play on the first day, no play at all on the second and third days, four hours' play on the fourth day and it doesn't matter how much play there was on the fifth day because no-one was interested any more. Like many thousands of others I paid a good deal of money for reserved seats for these matches and it was money thrown away.

Now I fully appreciate that the cricket authorities cannot be held responsible for the appalling English weather, which makes cricket the most unsuitable game for playing in this country that has ever been invented. I also realise that the finances of cricket in all probability would not permit the reimbursement of cricket spectators who get nothing for their money but a great deal of frustration and the risk of pneumonia—although I cannot see why spectators who pay at the gate and are deprived of a day's play by the weather should not be given tickets of admission for the following day.

This in fact was done at Headingley in 1979. Spectators who could produce their tickets for the previous washed out days were admitted free on the final day, Tuesday. This was a laudable gesture although it was not much use because interest in the match had by Tuesday vanished and in any case few people would have been in a position to produce the necessary evidence of having paid for admission the previous day as they had no foreknowledge of this offer, which was made over the loudspeakers on the Monday.

No, what I am getting at is not that the cricket authorities should take over the risks of the weather from the spectators by returning their money when play is abandoned—that would be too much to ask. What I believe spectators have a right to demand is that every effort should be made to provide as much play as possible when conditions are suitable. This was very clearly not the case at Headingley in 1979— or, indeed, has it been the case at most other grounds in the country in any season since 1930. For 50 years to my knowledge the spectator has been deprived of cricket to which he was legally and morally entitled and his legitimate complaints have been treated with a cynical indifference amounting to contempt.

As far as one can see practically no attempt has been made to invoke modern science and technology in the task of drying cricket fields quickly after rain and the technique employed at most grounds has changed scarcely at all over the last 50 years. At some of the county grounds they are way back in the last century and it is not very long ago since at Park Avenue, Bradford, for instance, they didn't possess a motor roller and the ground staff had to trundle on the field with a fearsome-looking roller which looked as if it had come straight from Hambledon.

This antediluvian attitude reached its apotheosis of absurdity at Headingley in 1979 when, following the wash-out of the 1978 test, it was announced, with a great blowing of trumpets, that a new, advanced method of protecting not only the pitch and the bowler's run up but *the whole playing area* against the weather was to be employed for the first time, should the necessity arise. The necessity arose all right—shortly after lunch on the first day—and the new invention was proudly produced as though it had been specially designed by the combined brain power of Newton and Einstein. Alas, it was not some miraculous new chemical process but merely a very large sheet of cellophane which was solemnly laid over the playing area by a squad of groundsmen working with military precision for about 20 minutes. Indeed it only needed the president of the Yorkshire committee to come out and inspect them on horseback to complete the inspiring spectacle!

It continued to rain all Thursday and most of Friday and few people even thought about cricket. But Saturday was a lovely day, fine from the start with glorious sunshine in the afternoon. Thousands turned up at Headingley but what happened? Nothing. Not a single ball was bowled and the waiting spectators were so furious that if it had not been for the fact that most of them were stolid, sensible Yorkshiremen they would probably have burned the pavilion down in protest, and they would have had every excuse.

Knowing the reluctance to play after rain I decided to keep in touch with events at Headingley by radio and drove over to Harrogate in the afternoon sunshine after the news came that play for the day had been abandoned at 2.25 pm. On the way to Harrogate we passed three or four village cricket matches in progress and the failure to start at Headingley became more and more incredible. Had the new cellophane covers disintegrated and turned the pitch into a quagmire or what?

The Sunday papers explained the mystery next day—and ventilated the anger and frustration of the thousands who had waited vainly at the ground and the other thousands who had stayed at home. It was not the fault of the covers. The wicket and the run ups, indeed the whole of the playing area, were bone dry. But in the out-field there had been a persistent damp patch and play had been abandoned for that reason.

It was rather like a coronation being cancelled because the king had a slight headache and the cricket writers did not spare the authorities in their wrath. No less an authority than Denis Compton wrote in the Sunday Express that he "cringed with embarrassment as the patient, paying spectators—who, remember, did not have any money returned—shouted their protests."

"In fact," Compton went on, "the entire Old Trafford wicket in the 1956 test, when Jim Laker took his record 19 wickets against the Australians, was wetter than Headingley yesterday. The sun was shining warmly at the time and the damp patch was being mowed at five o'clock. Groundsman Keith Boyce said 'My staff could easily have dried this area to allow play today.'"

As far as one could determine the major responsibility for this appalling episode fell on the umpires. But it could just as easily have been the Cricket Council, the Test and

County Cricket Board, the MCC, the Yorkshire committee, the Leeds Cricket and Athletic Club (the owners of Headingley cricket ground), the groundsmen, the players or even the Transport and General Workers' Union, if the man who drives the motor roller is a member.

Spectators really do feel that there is a sort of conspiracy on the part of first class cricket officials to restrict the actual playing of cricket to an absolute minimum. Disgraceful episodes like this one tend to encourage such an attitude. So do the flagrant absurdities of the "further inspections of the wicket" charade which buoy up hopes but in the end result are often as tormenting as the Spanish inquisition.

So is the enthusiasm with which the players and umpires race from the field into the pavilion at the slightest sign of raindrops. So is the obvious reluctance of umpires and players to come back on to the field again once they've got off it. So are the crazy contradictions of the "bad light" regulations which in practice frequently seem to take the players off the field when the light is clearly better than it was half an hour previously. And keeps them off when it is better than it has been all day! Light meters are now used by some umpires but cricket's technological obscurantism is such that they clearly regard them as modern gadgets to be used with suspicion, like motor rollers and easily movable sight-screens.

These failings of first class cricket do not produce satisfied customers and must have contributed to the marked decline in support for three day county cricket in my cricketing life-time. The days of large crowds at Roses fixtures are over. Another respect in which spectators are badly treated is that of covered accommodation and general amenities such as bars, restaurants and toilet facilities. At grounds like Lord's, the Oval and Old Trafford they are, I suppose, adequate but at Headingley, and even more so at Yorkshire's other grounds, they are a disgrace. The main bar in the members' enclosure at Headingley is in an airless, concrete dungeon beneath the main stand, quite out of sight of the play and more reminiscent of a coal mine than a cricket ground, while the subterranean toilet facilities make the cruder types of French urinals seem as modern as the Ritz. As for Park Avenue, to my mind the best ground for watching cricket in the country, the seats on the pavilion have become so warped and bent by the climatic ravages of the last 100 years or so (they look as if they had been installed by the Romans) that they no longer fit the contours of any human posterior, male, female or hermaphrodite. Whatever the cricket is like, a day at Park Avenue is an agonising physical experience.

These, then, are the trappings of cricket which have not changed in the 50 years I have been attending county cricket matches. What of cricket itself? I know that to all grey beards like me few aspects of life today seem as attractive as they were 50 years ago. It is an inalienable habit of human beings to be nostalgic about the past. Nevertheless I am sure that cricket in the 1980s is not nearly as good as it was in the 1930s. The talent of the players is not comparable. Can anyone seriously argue that the quality of the two teams competing in my first test match between England and Australia in 1930 is in any way equal to the two teams representing these two countries in 1981? The England team in 1930 was: Hobbs, Sutcliffe, Hammond, Duleepsinjhi, Leyland, Geary, Duckworth, Chapman, Tate, Larwood and Tyldesley (R.). The England team in the last test in 1981 was Gooch, Boycott, Brearley, Gower, Gatting, Willey, Botham, Taylor, Dilley, Old and Willis. How many of this team would have obtained places in the 1930 test? Certainly not more than two—Boycott and Botham would be selected in place of Duleepsinjhi and Geary.

And how many of the Australian team in the 1981 test—Dyson, Wood, Chappell, Hughes, Yallop, Border, Marsh, Bright, Lawson, Lillee and Alderman—would have been chosen in preference to Woodfull, Ponsford, Bradman, Fairfax, McCabe, Richardson, a'Beckett, Oldfield, Grimmett, Wall and Hornibrook? No more than two again, Lillee and Alderman probably being preferred to a'Beckett and Hornibrook. And it is safe to say that there was no season in the 1970s when more than three modern players would have been substituted for contemporary players in the 1930s.

Another way in which cricket has changed is in the viciousness of the modern game. There was a great cricket crisis in the 1930s over so called body-line or leg theory bowling in Australia by Larwood, Voce and others. This was an unpleasant intrusion of intimidation into the peaceful cricketing scene, deplored by many, in England as well as in Australia. But as I remember body-line bowling, its intimidatory aspect was very muted compared with modern fast bowling, which is not so much body-line as head-line.

I don't blame modern batsmen for wearing these monstrous helmets as defence against bouncers from bowlers such as Holding and Garner at all because they make little secret of the fact that they are aiming at causing batsmen physical injury. Indeed far from being ashamed of such tactics they seem to glory in them. Freddie Trueman always professed to hate batsman and he bowled his share of bouncers. So, going further back, did Bill Bowes. But never in the past was there the unveiled threat to life and limb which modern fast bowling contains. It may please the new denizens of the cricket ground terraces, who have grown up in the contemporary atmosphere of violence, and they may derive some sadistic satisfaction from seeing a batsman knocked unconscious. But to the cricket lovers I grew up with, such attitudes in the bowlers and in the spectators are anathema and bouncers which are aimed at the head should be banned from the game without any shadow of doubt.

The third way in which cricket has changed in my experience is in its complete commercialisation (to which I have already referred) and its division into two distinct branches—the traditional cricket and the one-day limited overs game. These two developments are linked because they have evolved, so to speak, in tandem. The commercialisation of cricket and its domination by sponsorship and television grew apace with the extension of the one-day game. This was logical because the one-day game—or instant cricket as some people call it—is much more geared to the demands of the sponsors and the television audiences they require than traditional cricket.

One day cricket, let's face it, is knock-about stuff which is much more likely to appeal to the masses than the leg glances of Len Hutton or the late cuts of Denis Compton. As I see it the longer the commercialisation and the one-day game with which it is linked are clearly "the growth sector" of cricket this is the type of cricket which is going to increase and this can only be at the expense of the traditional game. Soon with the commercially-minded players geared overwhelmingly to the commercialised game the talent and training necessary for traditional cricket will disappear and we shall be left with one day cricket only. As I have said I am not totally opposed to one day cricket as it can provide excellent entertainment but if it replaces the traditional game it will be a great tragedy.

What are the prospects of preserving the all-important balance between the two games, of ensuring that we don't get too much of the one and too little of the other? This is the task of cricket administrators and it is a grave responsibility. The omens are not good.

Park Avenue, Bradford, as it was before the football stand was pulled down.

The vital need is for cricket to preserve its independence and not be swept along with the band-waggon of the commercialists. In Australia this already seems to have happened. The unholy alliance between the Australian Cricket Board and Kerry Packer and his cronies seems to have put the commercialists firmly in control and they are hard at work converting cricket from a serious game into what cricket lovers consider to be a complete farce—cricket with pretty coloured pads and wickets, black sightscreens, aluminium bats, spaceman-like suits and helmets, floodlights and white balls. The sensitivities of these cricketing cretins are obviously non-existent and one wonders with mounting apprehension what they will do next to "popularise" the game.

The obvious next move is to bring sex into it and I'm waiting for bunny girls to sell the scorecards and topless girls in bikini briefs (or less) parading round the field during the lunch and tea intervals competing for the "bust girl of the match," the champion to be selected by the captain of the winning team. It would be quite a rational development in the lurid nightmare into which instant cricket is developing.

But as I watched my last test match at Headingley it was not of Kerry Packer and his lunatic kinsmen that I was thinking. I was thinking of the day at Headingley 51 years earlier when as a boy of nine I saw a rather more distinguished Australian than Kerry Packer score 309 runs in a day. I little realised that Bradman's brilliance was to be matched by a superb innings by Ian Botham who had recently been relieved of the England captaincy. Botham came in to bat in England's second innings when the score stood at 135 for 7, they having followed on 227 runs behind the Australian first innings total of 401. With noble assistance from Dilley and Old he took the total to 356 and when the last wicket fell his own score was 149 not out. Thanks chiefly to Willis, who took 8 for 43, Australia were skittled out for 111, England winning a remarkable victory by 18 runs. It was undoubtedly one of the best tests in cricketing history and did much to restore one's ebbing faith in five day cricket as an exciting entertainment. When England repeated this achievement at Edgbaston the restoration of faith was complete.

As I watched Botham hit the ball all over the field at Headingley it was almost like seeing a reincarnation of Bradman and I wondered what the effect would be on my companion, 13-year-old Nicholas.

"You won't see an innings like this again in a hurry, Nicholas," I said, as Botham reached his century with another boundary, recalling what Mr. Fox had said to me about Bradman's innings in 1930.

"He's a great player, Botham," he replied omnisciently. "But Don Bradman scored over 300 in a day here you know."

"Yes" I said, "I saw him. It was my first test match."

"Did you?" he said, adding, as though I was referring to the Battle of Hastings, "that was ever so long ago."

"Yes," I said, "it was 51 years ago to be precise. But I remember it as if it were yesterday . . ."

As I recalled the excitement of that day I wondered what Nicholas might be telling his companion about Botham's brilliant innings at Headingley during a test match 51 years hence—in the year 2032—or whether cricket would by then be a thing of the past, having been replaced as England's national game by Packerball, a combination of cricket and baseball played, as Alec Bedser had predicted, with a ball with bells on. For the sake of Nicholas and the legion of cricket lovers yet unborn, I sincerely hope this will not prove to be the case.